The Only
GUITAR
BOOK
You'll Ever Need

From Tuning Your Instrument and Learning
Chords to Reading Music and Writing Songs,
Everything You Need to Play Like the Best

Includes Expert Advice from
Marc Schonbrun and Ernie Jackson

Adams Media
New York   London   Toronto   Sydney   New Delhi

Aadamsmedia

Adams Media
An Imprint of Simon & Schuster, Inc.
100 Technology Center Drive
Stoughton, MA 02072

For information about special discounts for bulk purchases, please contact Simon & Schuster Special Sales at 1-866-506-1949 or business@simonandschuster.com.

The Simon & Schuster Speakers Bureau can bring authors to your live event. For more information or to book an event contact the Simon & Schuster Speakers Bureau at 1-866-248-3049 or visit our website at www.simonspeakers.com.

Interior line art by Ernie Jackson. Photos by Evan Copp. Model: Anthony Babino.

Manufactured in the United States of America

14 2021

ISBN 978-1-4405-7405-4
ISBN 978-1-4405-7406-1 (ebook)

Contains material adapted from the following title(s) published by Adams Media, an Imprint of Simon & Schuster, Inc.: *The Everything® Guitar Chords Book* by Marc Schonbrun, copyright © 2006 by Simon & Schuster, Inc., ISBN 978-1-59337-529-4; *The Everything® Guitar Book, 2nd Edition* by Ernie Jackson, copyright © 2007, 2002 by Simon & Schuster, Inc., ISBN 978-1-59869-250-1; *The Everything® Guide to Digital Home Recording* by Marc Schonbrun, copyright © 2009 by Simon & Schuster, Inc., ISBN 978-1-60550-164-2; *The Everything® Guitar Scales Book with CD* by Marc Schonbrun, copyright © 2009 by Simon & Schuster, Inc., ISBN 978-1-59869-574-8; *The Everything® Music Theory Book with CD, 2nd Edition* by Marc Schonbrun, copyright © 2011, 2007 by Simon & Schuster, Inc., ISBN 978-1-4405-1182-0; *The Everything® Rock and Blues Guitar Book* by Marc Schonbrun, copyright © 2003 by Simon & Schuster, Inc., ISBN 978-1-58062-883-9; and *The Everything® Songwriting Book* by C.J. Watson, copyright © 2003 by Simon & Schuster, Inc., ISBN 978-1-58062-956-0.

Contents

For Guitar Lovers

Welcome to *The Only Guitar Book You'll Ever Need*! You are embarking on quite a journey, so plug in and hold on. Guitar playing is a vast and open-ended topic. The goal here is to equip students with the material required to advance toward their full potential.

There is no single "right" way to play guitar. In fact, it's the diversity of performers that keeps such a wide audience interested. This book will show you all the important techniques and concepts that make the guitar what it is.

This book is designed for anyone with an interest in the guitar, whether you've just picked it up or have been playing for a while. The chapters in this book are organized in a logical order, but you should feel free to skip around. Whether you've played for twenty years or twenty minutes, there is something here for you.

This book covers all aspects of guitar from the most basic techniques to more complex chords. At first, new concepts and sounds may seem foreign, even unsettling. In time, these will become familiar. You'll be able to see your own progress by revisiting old material. Melodies that are a challenge when you begin will seem easy after a few months of practice using this book as a guide.

Throughout this book, musical examples help to illustrate ideas that are discussed in the chapters. All the examples use standard notation and tablature. If you can't read music yet, don't worry. That's covered here too.

The focus of this book is application, not theory. Each chapter consists of new material followed by extensive discussion on where to use the new ideas and concepts. You'll be able to hone your skills and find your own sound with the skills you learn from this book. Let's get started!

PART 1

The Basics

The Origin of the Guitar

There are many theories on the origin of the guitar. In fact, the ancient pictures, drawings, and paintings of many cultures suggest a guitar, though these are actually stringed instruments of varying types. For example, Babylonian excavations in Central Asia unearthed cave carvings dating back to 1900 B.C. that show musicians playing together. The carvings feature stringed instruments resembling guitars as well as techniques like strumming and plucking of the strings. Similar stringed instruments like the okongo or cora are still used in parts of Africa to this day.

EARLY GUITARS

Early Egyptian drawings show stringed instruments that resemble very complex lyres and harps. Ancient Rome was heavily influenced by Egyptian culture, and as a result there were many versions of these two instruments in early Western cultures. Around A.D. 400, for instance, the Romans brought their tanbur, also known as the chitara, to Spain.

Varying types of stringed instruments developed in the pre-Christian Babylonian, Egyptian, and Hittite cultures of the Middle East as well as in Roman Italy, Greece, and Turkey in the Near East. All these instruments had certain aspects in common. Each had some sort of sound box and a long neck. Cords or strings were stretched down the neck and over the sound box. Players used one hand to strum (perhaps with a plectrum, or pick, of some sort) and the other to stop the strings at various points along the neck; as a result, they could sound a wide variety of notes, both singly and together.

Musical Notes

The Greeks had a stringed instrument called the *kithera*. Though the spelling is close to the word *chitara*, it is not a direct ancestor of the modern-day guitar. The kithera is closer to a lyre or harp.

Medieval Europe

In the early Middle Ages, as the Moors passed through Egypt on their way to conquer North Africa and Spain, they brought the ud, a direct antecedent of the guitar, to Western Europe. The Moorish influence in Spain prepared the groundwork for the development of the guitar in Europe. By the thirteenth century, references to and pictures of guitar-like instruments begin to appear in historic documents from all over Europe.

The Four-Course Guitar

It is possible that makers of the Roman-style chitara and the Arabic ud influenced one another. By A.D. 1200, the four-string guitar had evolved into two types: the guitarra morisca (Moorish guitar), which had a rounded pear-shaped back, a wide fingerboard, and several sound holes somewhat like a lute; and the guitarra latina (Latin guitar), which resembled a small version of the modern guitar, with one sound hole and a narrower neck. On either of these instruments, each pair of strings was called a course.

In 1487, a musical theorist named Johannes Tinctoris described an instrument he called the guiterra or the ghiterna, whose sides were "tortoise-shaped." Guitar historians today believe that what Tinctoris actually saw was a round-back lute. In Italy, these instruments were known as the viola da mano and chitarra.

Musical Notes

The guitar has many forebears and cousins—the lute, the Middle Eastern ud, the Indian sitar, the banjo, the koto of Japan, the bouzouki of Greece, the vihuela, the yue-chin, chirar, balalaika, rehab, kayakeum, santir, ombi, vambi, nanga, samisen . . . and on and on.

The Six-Course Guitar

While the guiterra was small and had four courses, the Italian chitarra was larger, with six courses. Both had thongs or cords tied at various places along the neck to make frets or squared-off divisions of the neck. These two instruments became the favorites of wandering troubadours or minstrels. These virtual one-man bands had to master a variety of instruments, including pipes, whistles, and flutes, plus perform songs, tell stories, and provide any other form of entertainment that would earn them money and keep them from facing the displeasure of aggravated patrons.

Here's how an eleventh-century Swiss poet named Amarcius described a minstrel's performance: "When the citharist

Musical Notes

Minstrels did not use the "guitars" to accompany their stories but to play small instrumental interludes between verses or tales or to sing folksongs.

appears, after arranging for his fee, and proceeds to remove his instrument from its cover of oxhide, the people assemble from far and near, fix their eyes upon him and listen with soft murmurs as he strikes the strings with his fingers stretched far apart, strings which he himself has fashioned from sheep gut, and which he plays now tenderly, now with harsh booming sounds."

The Lute

The lute held court as the major stringed instrument for a long while, but it had a number of drawbacks. First of all, there was no standard lute, so some were large and some smaller. Some had eight strings, while others had twelve or even more. They were difficult to balance and play, and forget about keeping one in tune!

Soon after the reign of King Henry VIII, around 1550, the guitar became one of England's more popular stringed instruments. But for some time to come, rival camps of lutenists and guitarists would lose no opportunity to badmouth each others' instrument and musicianship. In 1556 in France, for example, it was reported that while the pear-shaped lute had been a popular instrument, people were playing the guitar even more.

Musical Notes

A keen musician himself (and rumored to be the composer of "Greensleeves"), King Henry VIII had more than twenty guitars among his collection of musical instruments in Hampton Court Palace.

COMPOSITIONS FOR THE GUITAR

The earliest known music for the guitar was written for a Spanish form of the instrument known as the vihuela. "El Maestro," by the Spaniard Luis Milan, was published in 1535 for the use and enjoyment of Spanish courtiers and aristocracy. Seven books of music survive, written in tablature. This early form of music is a sort of diagram showing each string of the guitar and indicating where it should be stopped along the neck. Above the diagrams are notes indicating time values, or how long each note should be sounded. The diagrams show pieces of varying degrees of difficulty, including a series of regal dances known as pavanes.

Ten years later, Alonso Mudarra published a music book called *Tres Libros de Musica en Cifras para Vihuela*. This book contains several sophisticated, sometimes even dissonant, pieces that include a recurrent bass line that gives the music a syncopated, energetic feel.

By the early seventeenth century, there were a number of books and primers on playing the guitar, particularly in France, where the instrument had become popular.

Adaptations of lute music and arrangements of dances and fantasias encouraged the use of the guitar as a member of an ensemble or as an accompaniment to songs.

The music of this period was not played with the same rigid structure as classical music is today. There was room for improvisation, particularly when it came to variations of melodic phrasing and ornamentation. Advanced players, as always, could perform florid single-note passages and counterpoint and figured bass runs. Generally, however, the fashion for most guitar players of time was to play rather basic music, mainly strummed chord patterns.

By 1600, the five-course guitar had replaced the earlier four-course and six-course guitars. The tuning also became more standardized, predominantly ADGBE. The Italian guitarist Giovanni Paolo Foscarini wrote some sophisticated new pieces for the instrument in the 1630s, while a fellow countryman, Francesco Corbetta, became one of the foremost guitar virtuosos. Corbetta traveled widely throughout Europe, popularizing the instrument.

MANY MUSICAL MODIFICATIONS

By the end of the Baroque period, two significant changes had occurred. The guitar's five courses were replaced by six single strings, and they were tuned in the modern style of EADGBE.

Many changes were taking place musically by this time. The modern piano made its first appearance, and the guitar began to fade from popularity. It was soon considered a more frivolous instrument of seduction and amour. A German diarist wrote, "The flat guitar with its strum we shall happily leave to the garlic-eating Spaniards."

Romance, lasciviousness, and the guitar have been fairly consistent partners for

Musical Notes

Early guitars had gut strings in courses or pairs, with a variety of tunings. A four-course guitar had ten frets and was often tuned to either FCEA, GCEA, or CFAD. The top three stings were tuned in unison, while the bass string (either F or G) was tuned in octaves, or eight notes apart.

Musical Notes

In 1799, Fernando Ferrandiere published a method book for the six-string guitar called *The Art of the Spanish Guitar*. In that same year, Don Federico Moretti wrote the first standardized book on the six-string guitar, *The Principles of Playing the Guitar with Six Strings*. Guitar scholars believe both method books were derived from an earlier publication by guitarist Antonio Ballesteros, titled *Obra para Guitarra del sexto orden*.

a while, not just in the modern age of heavy-metal rockers. For example, Ronsard, a famous fifteenth-century French poet, wrote:

It is the ideal instrument
For ladies of great learning,
Lascivious ladies also play
To advertise their yearning.

Gaspar Sanz, guitarist to the viceroy of Aragon, Spain, was as much a philosopher as a musician. His comments about the instrument and its players stand as well today as they did when he wrote the introduction to his method book on the guitar in the late seventeenth century: "[The guitar's] faults . . . lie in whoever plays it, and not in the guitar itself, for I have seen some people accomplish things on one string for which others would need the range of an organ. Everyone must make of it what he can, good or bad."

The Napoleonic war, at the turn of the nineteenth century, was responsible for making the guitar popular again. The war, which raged throughout Europe, reintroduced Europeans to the guitar-based music of Spain. This period led to the work of such composers and performers as Fernando Sor, Mauro Guilliani, Matteo Carcassi, and Fernando Carulli.

The first modern concerto for guitar and orchestra, "Concerto No. 1 in A Major," was composed and performed by the Italian virtuoso Mauro Guilliani. Among other things, it uses the right-hand thumb for bass notes and features a strong orchestral structure, with variations on a theme, a slow second movement, and finally a lively third movement.

Musical Notes

Dionisio Aguado (1784–1849), a Spanish classical guitarist and composer, invented the tripodison, a guitar accessory used to hold the guitar instead of letting it rest on the right leg. This minimized the damping effect of the guitarist's body on the guitar's back and sides.

THE CLASSICAL GUITAR

Two people are responsible for the classical guitar as it is known today. The first was the brilliant guitar-maker Antonio Torres. Torres revolutionized the process of the building of a guitar, making a careful study of how it made its sound, where the sound came from, and how he could improve it. The other was the Spanish virtuoso Francisco Tarrega.

The Torres guitar, developed between the 1850s and the 1890s, had more volume than previous designs. It included a larger, deeper body and an aesthetically pleasing shape that is familiar today. Torres was the first maker to use "fan" bracing underneath the top. He once built a guitar with a spruce top and papier-mâché back and sides to prove his theory that it was the top that produced most of the volume.

Tarrega adopted the newly designed instrument and composed and arranged hundreds of pieces for it. Ironically, Tarrega did not perform much in public. He was, however, an influential teacher, with a close circle of students and friends who acted almost like disciples in the world outside Tarrega's home and studio.

And then, at the dawn of the twentieth century, there arrived a young, self-taught musician named Andrés Segovia. Before Segovia, people believed it was not possible for a solo guitarist to perform effectively to a large audience in a concert hall. Since Segovia, the world has become filled with guitarists in concert. In 1924, he made his debuts in London and Paris. He performed, transcribed, taught, and discovered a tremendous amount of music for the guitar. He also encouraged many composers to write for the instrument. He managed to reawaken the public interest in the music of J.S. Bach, and he arranged many Bach pieces for the guitar, which he also performed and recorded.

Of Segovia's many gifts to the world, perhaps his most lasting was to make the guitar the popular instrument of the twentieth century. He also standardized the way guitar fingering is notated on scores (by showing the string number written within a circle over a series of notes that could be played elsewhere on the instrument), and settled the debate among classical guitarists about nails versus fingertips (by popularizing the use of plucking the strings with the nails of the right hand). By traveling and performing throughout the world, Segovia brought respect and recognition to the instrument and left behind a vast body of work and pupils who have gone on to become maestros in their own right.

FLAMENCO

There are many different styles of playing, and while the guitar was gaining legitimacy in concert halls, a parallel evolution was taking place in the bars and cafés of nineteenth-century Spain. Flamenco has three aspects: singing, dancing, and guitar playing. It grew from the melding of Arab, Christian, Jewish, and Spanish folk music and the Middle Eastern influence of seven centuries of Moorish and Arabic occupation, particularly in Andalusia, in the north of Spain, where a large population of gypsies lived.

The Heartbeat of Spain

It was the Andalusian gypsies who turned flamenco into the heartbeat of Spain, although its roots are probably in Roman-occupied Spain. The composers Kodaly and Bartok discovered in their research into folk tunes that beautiful folksongs have a way of ending up as "beggars' songs." In the same way, the outcasts of Spain—the gypsies—

adopted and preserved the musical traditions of the Moorish Arabs who had once ruled the land.

What remained, and became idiosyncratically gypsy, were the traditions of whip-cracking dance rhythms, and the troubadour's ability to improvise, composing verses about anything and everything at the drop of a hat. In the underground jargon of eighteenth-century Andalusia, someone flamenco was a dazzler, a "dude with attitude." And the music came to be popularized by performers considered by many to be the haughtiest and most flamboyant of the gypsies.

Spain is a dancing country, and the simplest nineteenth-century village dance orchestra might consist of a guitar and a tambourine, with dancers wielding castanets. By the 1850s and beyond, it was also a country at war with itself. But whether royalist or revolutionary, the tradition was never to shoot a man with a guitar—at least until he was given a chance to play, anyway.

Flamenco on the Move

The rhythmic and melodic early forms called seguidilla and rasgueado developed new and exciting forms in the café cantantes, bars with areas for performers. Gradually, guitar players developed short instrumental melodic interludes with variations called falsetas.

What had for centuries been campfire entertainment suddenly found itself on a stage attracting the attention and applause of Europe's leading writers, poets, painters, and musicians—including Chopin, Liszt, George Sand, Alexandre Dumas, Edouard Manet, and Jules Verne—who discovered the joys and inexpensive excitement of Spain on their "grand vacations."

Ramon Montoya is considered the father of modern flamenco guitar. He was influenced by Patino, Paco Lucena, and Javier Molina. Before his passing in 1949, Ramon Montoya pioneered the recording of the style and developed its traditions and techniques. In doing so, he enriched the music's vocabulary and established himself as one of the first flamenco virtuosos of the twentieth century.

His real contribution, however, was to be the first person to break free of the role of accompanist and become established as a solo instrumentalist. When he performed in concert in Paris in 1936, he met with great acclaim.

Musical Notes

The flamenco guitar sounds different from the classical guitar because instead of rosewood, cypress wood is used for the back and sides. The use of the capo (a clamp that goes around the neck and shortens the string length) also affects the tone, giving the strings a more treble sound.

It has been said that as flamenco has moved from the cafés to the nightclubs, the players have become more circus-like in the manner in which they play the guitar— wearing gloves, putting the instrument behind their heads, anything to attract and hold an audience's attention. Nevertheless, the twentieth century has produced some stunning players, such as Sabicas, Carlos Montoya, Nino Ricardo, Paco de Lucia, and Paco Pena.

THE ELECTRIC GUITAR

In combination, the European troubadour traditions of folk music and the spiritual music of African slaves evolved into a guitar- and banjo-based music that first became ragtime and then morphed into jazz. The guitar's role was problematic, though, because it never seemed loud enough to cut through all the other instruments of the group. That was one reason for the banjo's popularity. It might not be as sophisticated a musical instrument as the guitar, but in an ensemble situation it held its own against a blaring cornet, braying trombone, squawking clarinet, and the thumping of a drummer and the crash of his cymbals.

> ### Musical Notes
>
> George Breed, a U.S. naval officer, received a patent in 1890 for "an apparatus for producing musical sounds by electricity." His patent diagram resembles a very early figure-eight shaped instrument with six strings activated by electricity and magnetism.

In 1907, Lee DeForest invented the triode. A triode is a vacuum tube capable of (are you ready?) amplifying weak electrical signals. This component provides an output strong enough to be fed into a loudspeaker. This invention would soon lend itself to the circuitry found in radios and old phonographs.

More Volume

The search for more volume led Lloyd Loar, an engineer at the Gibson guitar company, to play around with electrified guitars and amplifiers. In 1924, his experiments with magnetic coils led to the development of a basic pickup, which was, in effect, a giant magnet shaped like a horseshoe that acted as a microphone for each of the strings of the guitar. The signal was then fed through a speaker with a volume control and a tone control. It was all very rudimentary stuff. Gibson didn't get the idea, though, and Loar left and formed the Vivitone Company, which produced commercial guitar pickups during the 1930s.

The First Commercial Electric Guitar

The real breakthrough came in 1931, when Paul Barth and George Beauchamp joined forces with Adolph Rickenbacker to form the Ro-Pat-In Company (later renamed the Electro String Company). They then produced the first commercially available electric guitar, the A22 and A25 cast-aluminum lap-steel guitar, known as the "frying pan" because of its shape.

Strictly speaking, the "frying pan" wasn't really an electric version of a traditional guitar; rather, it was more of a lap-steel or Hawaiian guitar. However, in 1932 Ro-Pat-In produced the "Electro," which was an archtop, or F-hole, steel-string guitar fitted with a horseshoe magnet. Gibson finally caught on and adapted their L-50 archtop model into the now famous ES-150 electric model, which first appeared in 1936.

The musician who was to make the electric guitar a household word, Charlie Christian, was not actually the first electric guitar player. That role fell to Eddie Durham, who played a resonator guitar in Bennie Moten's jazz group from 1929 and recorded the first electric guitar solo, "Hittin' the Bottle," in 1935, with Jimmie Lunceford's band. He then made some historic recordings in New York City in 1937 and 1938 with the Kansas City Six, a spin-off group of musicians from Count Basie's Big Band that featured Lester Young on clarinet as well as saxophone. For the first time, the guitar was easily a match in volume and single-note improvisation for Young's saxophone and clarinet as well as the trumpet of Buck Clayton.

There was one fundamental problem with the electric guitar, though—it kept feeding back. The amplified sound from the speaker would cause the body of the guitar to vibrate until a howl started that could only be stopped by turning the volume off. Guitarists found they were continually adjusting their volume levels to stop their instruments from feeding back. The answer was to create an instrument that didn't vibrate in sympathy with its amplified sound.

The Solid-Bodied Guitar

There's no definitive agreement about who produced the first solid-bodied guitar. Guitarist Les Paul created a "Log" guitar, using a Gibson neck on a flat piece of wood. He went to Gibson to get it into production, but Gibson, once again, was not impressed and turned him down.

At the same time, country guitarist Merle Travis was working with engineer Paul Bigsby, and they produced about a dozen solid-body guitar prototypes. However, the man who made the first commercially available solid-body guitar was Leo Fender, the owner of an electrical repair shop. In 1946 he founded the Fender Electrical Instrument Company to produce Hawaiian guitars and amplifiers. Encouraged by an employee, George Fullerton, Fender designed and eventually marketed a line of solid-body guitars called the Fender Broadcaster in 1950. The Gretsch drum company manufactured drums called Broadcaster, however, and told Fender he couldn't use that name. So Fender changed the name of his guitar to the Telecaster. The rest is history.

The solid-bodied electric guitar paved the way for the popularization of urban blues and an R & B boom in the 1950s, with such great musicians as Howlin' Wolf, Muddy Waters, B.B. King, and so forth. These musicians in turn influenced a generation of young rock-and-roll players in the 1960s in England, including Eric Clapton, Jeff Beck, Robert Fripp, and Jimmy Page.

AND BEYOND . . .

Perhaps the most revolutionary advance of the last thirty years has been the development of MIDI, or musical instrument digital interface, a computer protocol that allows computers, synthesizers, and other equipment to talk to each other. While electronic music has been primarily a computer- and keyboard-oriented process, the guitar synthesizer is coming into its own. In the past it has had some problems with delay and tracking (which deals with how quickly, in effect, you can play one note after the other), but that seems to be disappearing with each new generation of equipment.

An example of the new guitar is the SynthAxe, developed in England in 1984. This guitar synthesizer is played via an innovative fretboard touch system. The neck acts as a MIDI controller, allowing the player to produce a full range of synthesized and sampled sounds.

Other guitarists have experimented with adding extra strings to the existing six, ranging from seven to forty-two or more. But one thing seems constant: All of the players of the experimental guitars end up going back to the traditional, simple six-string guitar, regardless of what else they play.

Where the guitar goes from here is anyone's guess, but one thing is certain. Somewhere in the background of just about any music you like, you're likely to hear the twang and strum of a simple six-string guitar.

History of the Guitar at a Glance

1700 B.C.	Rumor has it that Hermes, the Greek messenger of the gods, invents the seven-string lyre, the forerunner of the guitar. Meanwhile, at about the same time in Egypt, pictures of a guitar-like instrument are being painted on the walls of tombs.
500 B.C.	The kithara develops from the lyre.
1265	Juan Gil of Zamora mentions the early guitar in Ars Musica.
1283–1350	The guitarra latina and guitarra moresca are mentioned multiple times in the poems of the Archpriest of Hita.
1306	A "gitarer" is played at the Feast of Westminster in England.
1381	Three Englishmen are sent to prison for making a disturbance with "giternes."

1404	Der mynnen regein, by Eberhard Von Cersne, makes reference to a quinterne.
1487	Johannes Tinctoris describes the guitarra as an instrument invented by the Catalans.
1535	"El Maestro," by Luis Milan, is published, and contains the earliest known vihuela music, including courtly dances known as pavanes.
1551–1555	Nine books of tablature are published by Adrian Le Roy. These include the first pieces for five-course guitar. The addition of the fifth course is attributed to Vicente Espinel.
1552	Guillaume Morlaye's book of songs and dances for the guyterne is published in Paris.
1674	The Guitarre Royal, by Francesco Corbetta, is published. Dedicated to Louis XIV of France, it increases the guitar's popularity.
1770–1800	The instrument's five courses (doubled strings) are replaced by single strings, and a sixth string is added to the guitar.
1800–1850	Fernando Sor, Mauro Guilliani, Matteo Carcassi, Ferndinando Carulli, and Dioniso Aguado all perform, teach, write, and publish their compositions. The guitar begins to enjoy wide popularity.
1833	Christian Frederick Martin arrives in New York City and founds the Martin guitar-manufacturing company.
1850–1892	Guitar maker Antonio Torres develops the larger, more resonant instrument known today as the guitar.
1902	The Gibson Mandolin-Guitar Manufacturing Company is founded in Kalamazoo, Michigan, and quickly becomes one of the most famous guitar manufacturers in the world.
1916	Segovia performs at Ateneo, the most important concert hall in Madrid. Previously, it was thought that the guitar did not have the volume for this type of venue.
1931	The Electro String Company is founded, and the A22 and A25 cast-aluminum lap-steel guitars, known as "frying pans" because of their shape, become the first commercially produced electric guitars.
1950	The Fender Solid Body Telecaster first appears.
1960	The guitar is finally accepted as a serious musical instrument for study at the Royal College of Music in London.
1960s	Jimi Hendrix falls off stage by mistake and breaks his guitar trying to throw it back on stage. It becomes part of his stage act and starts a trend.
1969	The Alembic Company is founded by Ron and Susan Wickersham.
1974	The "Chapman Stick" is finalized by Emmett Chapman.
1982	The Roland Guitar Synthesizer becomes commercially available.

2

Tuning, Care, and Maintenance of Your Guitar

Though the basic anatomy of the guitar is simple—a nylon or steel string is attached at high tension and is plucked to produce a variety of pitches—the instrument needs constant care to be played at its prime efficiency. This chapter introduces you to the standard components of the electric and acoustic guitar as well as the most common maintenance techniques, such as selecting and changing strings, tuning your guitar, and performing basic repairs.

GUITAR ANATOMY AND DESIGN

Guitars come in a variety of shapes, sizes, and types, but there are certain things they all have in common. A guitar has three basic parts: a body, a neck, and the headstock (also referred to as a tuning head). You can learn how to maintain your instrument by understanding the various components better.

Body

There are basically two types of guitar bodies: hollow body and solid body. The hollow body of an acoustic guitar (shown in Figure 2-1) is what produces the instrument's sound. The body of the acoustic guitar is composed of the top, sides, and back. The top, or "face," of the instrument lies just below the strings. The sound hole is the round hole in the center of the top, from which the sound of the instrument emanates. The sides are the narrow pieces between the front and the back, which is the large surface parallel to the top. Generally, the back and sides of the instrument are made out of the same kind of wood, while on the majority of instruments the top is a finer, thinner piece of wood (or laminate, in the case of less expensive guitars). The top is the part of the guitar that most defines the overall sound of the guitar.

Some acoustic guitars have a piece of plastic called a pick guard glued to the top just below the sound hole. Just as the name implies, the pick guard is designed to protect the top of the instrument from damage you might inflict with your pick.

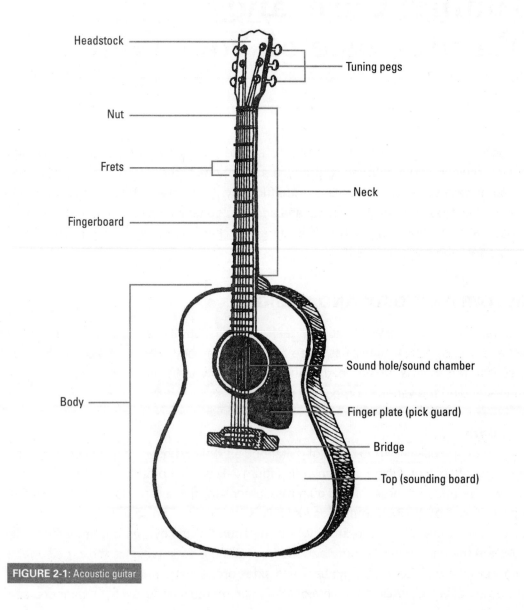

Headstock

Tuning pegs

Nut

Frets

Neck

Fingerboard

Sound hole/sound chamber

Finger plate (pick guard)

Body

Bridge

Top (sounding board)

FIGURE 2-1: Acoustic guitar

In a purely electric guitar (shown in Figure 2-2), the body is made of a solid piece of wood to avoid feedback, the screeching that results from resonance when the sound of a guitar is amplified. Below are some commonly used woods in electric guitars:

- **Maple:** Curly, flamed, and bird's-eye are various types of maple wood used in guitars. This is a bright-sounding wood.
- **Mahogany:** This hardwood provides a warmer, rounder tone than maple. It is usually found in Gibson Les Paul guitars.

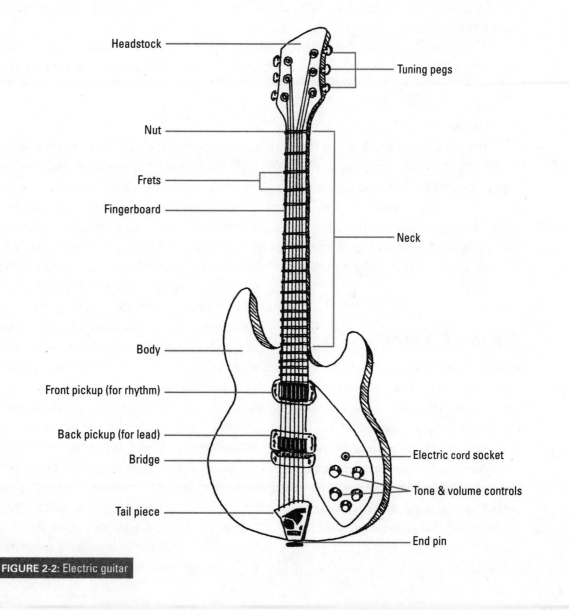

FIGURE 2-2: Electric guitar

- **Alder:** This wood is most commonly found in guitars with an overall sonic balance. It is usually favored by players with a broad range of playing styles.
- **Swamp ash:** This is a lightweight American wood with a bright and distinct tone.

A solid-body electric also houses the electronic pickups (which convert the motion of the strings into an electronic signal that can be sent through an amplifier of some kind), and volume and tone controls (which vary the loudness and bass and treble frequencies of the signal). There is also a socket called an output jack, into which you insert a special plug or jack. The other end of the jack goes into a corresponding socket in an amplifier.

In addition, the body has a bridge, made from either wood or metal, which anchors the strings. There are also strap pins or posts, which you can use to attach a shoulder strap.

Neck

The neck is usually fixed to the body with bolts or glue, though it might also be formed along with the body in one piece. It often has a metal truss rod running through it to strengthen it and help adjust for any slight warping or twisting. The neck is faced with a flat piece of wood (usually mahogany or ebony) called the fingerboard or fretboard. The fingerboard is divided into sections called frets. These sections are marked off by pieces of wire set into the wood, called fretwire. By stopping a string in between the fretwires—that is, "in the middle of the fret"—you determine the different pitches or notes you can make on each string. The strings run from the bridge, along the neck, and across the nut—a piece of wood, plastic, or metal at the top of the neck with slight grooves for each of the six strings—to the tuning pegs.

The neck of a guitar also provides a primary "tonal color" for the sound of the instrument. Different types of wood give the guitar a distinctive sound. Maple, which is a hard wood, produces a bright clear sound. Mahogany, which is softer than maple, produces a warmer sound. Another component of the guitar neck is the different types of neck joints. Most guitars have

Musical Notes

How does an acoustic guitar work? When a guitar string is plucked, it produces vibration. This vibration is transmitted through the bridge into the body of the instrument, causing the inside of the body to resonate, which in turn causes the front and the back of the body to vibrate. Compressed waves of sound are then created inside the body and projected out of the soundhole.

a bolt-on neck. Screws connect the neck to the body—usually in a Fender Stratocaster or Telecaster. A neck-through design means that the neck continues all the way from the headstock to the strap pin at the bottom of the instrument. In this design, the body is actually made up of small wings that are glued to both sides of the neck. A set-in neck glues the neck and body together. This design is usually found in Gibson Les Paul guitars.

Headstock

The headstock holds the tuning pegs (also called tuning machines, machine heads, or tuning gears) that the strings are attached to. In a six-string guitar there are six tuning pegs. Each tuning peg has a knob you can turn with your fingers. The knob tightens or loosens the string tension and thus put each string into "tune." A headstock that is flat (Figure 2-3) or tilts back (Figure 2-4) determines the effect on tone. Flat headstocks are the continuation of the guitar neck. Tilt-back headstocks are broken up into two types: integral and spliced. Integral tilt-back headstock design uses one large piece of continuous wood. A spliced headstock consists of a separate piece of wood glued on to the end of the neck.

Headstocks may have their tuning arranged with three tuning pegs on each side (like a Gibson Les Paul), or with six in-line pegs (like a Fender Stratocaster).

FIGURE 2-3: Flat headstock

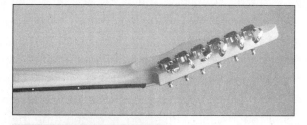

FIGURE 2-4: Tilt-back headstock

NAMES OF THE STRINGS

Every fret on every string of the guitar produces a note, and every note has a name, which is represented by a letter. The names of each of the notes on your instrument are important; you'll need to know where to find them in order to read music or to communicate with other musicians. Going from the sixth string (thickest) to the first string (thinnest), the strings are named E, A, D, G, B, and E. The sixth string and the first string are the same note, two octaves apart.

Because you're going to need to know the names of your strings for so many reasons, take the time to learn them now. To help you memorize them, try this little phrase: "Every Adult Dog Growls, Barks, and Eats."

Try playing each of the strings in order while saying the names out loud as an exercise. Then test yourself by pointing to a string at random and saying the name of that string as quickly as possible.

TUNING YOUR GUITAR

Before you play your guitar you'll have to get it in tune. Most beginners are a little confused by this process when they start, but it becomes second nature pretty fast, and it's essential to sounding good on guitar.

The best way to tune your guitar is to use a "chromatic tuner," which is an electronic device that listens to the pitch of each string, tells you what note it is, and then advises you with a visual display whether you need to tune the string higher or lower to get it in perfect tune.

If you aren't using a chromatic tuner, you'll need a "reference pitch" from another source. This could come from another guitar or a piano, in which case an E would be a good pitch to tune to, since you can tune your bottom and top strings right off. Or it could come from a "tuning fork," which is a piece of metal shaped like a wishbone—you strike the double end against your hand to make it vibrate, and then touch the single end against the body of your guitar or against your ear to hear the note.

If you use a tuning fork, the note it produces will probably be an A (also marked 440 on the fork, which is the number of "cycles per second" of that note), so you would use it to tune your fifth string, and then tune the rest of your guitar around that string.

Assuming you've got your sixth string in tune, let's move on to learning how to tune the rest of the strings. If you play the fifth fret of your sixth (E) string, the resulting note will be an A, which is the pitch your fifth string is supposed to be. If you play the fifth fret of your fifth (A) string, the resulting note will be D, which is the pitch your fourth string is supposed to be. The only time this pattern changes is when you tune the second (B) string to the third (G) string—in that case you play the fourth fret of the G string to hear the B you need to tune the second string. Give it a try!

Here are some steps to tune your guitar:

1. Make sure your sixth string is in tune.
2. Play the sixth string, fifth fret (A), then tune your open fifth string (A) until they sound the same.
3. Play the fifth string, fifth fret (D), then tune your open fourth string (D) until they sound the same.
4. Play the fourth string, fifth fret (G), then tune your open third string (G) until they sound the same.
5. Play the third string, fourth fret (B), then tune your open second string (B) until they sound the same.
6. Play the second string, fifth fret (E), then tune your open first string (E) until they sound the same. Then double-check your first string against your sixth string—they should be the same.

Musical Notes

How often should you tune your guitar? You should tune your guitar every single time you pick it up. Guitars (particularly cheaper ones) tend to go out of tune quickly. Make sure it's in tune when you begin to play it, and check the tuning frequently while you're practicing, as the act of playing the guitar can cause it to go out of tune.

STRING ESSENTIALS

Strings don't last forever. In fact, depending on how much you play and practice and on whether you live in a hot climate or not, you might have to change your strings as often as once a week. In general, however, once every eight to twelve weeks is about average. If a string breaks, it's probably time to change the whole set rather than to just replace the one that broke. Strings lose their stretch and vibrancy over time because of salt from sweaty fingers and rust. You can also find a variety of problems with bridges and nuts and so forth, which we'll get into later on.

You can extend the life of your strings by cleaning them after each session. To get rid of the grunge under the string, some players "snap" each string by pulling it back slightly, as if the string were on a bow, and then snapping it back to the fingerboard.

Strings come in a variety of gauges, or thicknesses. The thicknesses are described in fractions of an inch. Choosing a gauge of string is very much a personal decision. In general, the lighter the string gauge, the easier it is to bend and hold down the strings for lead playing. The thicker the gauge, the better the volume, the longer the sustain, and the easier it is to keep the guitar in tune. A thicker gauge is also easier for rhythm playing.

Common Gauges

ULTRA-LIGHT	.008 (first string) to .038 (sixth string)
EXTRA-LIGHT	.009 (first string) to .046 (sixth string)
REGULAR	.010 (first string) to .050 (sixth string)
LIGHT	.011 (first string) to .052 (sixth string)
MEDIUM	.013 (first string) to .056 (sixth string)
HEAVY	.014 (first string) to .060 (sixth string)

Strings come in three different types: nylon, usually for Spanish or classical-style guitars; bronze, used for acoustic steel-strung instruments because they have little electrical quality; and steel strings, used for electric and acoustic instruments. You should never put steel or bronze strings on guitars that use nylon strings. This will ruin the instrument quickly because of the increased tension these strings put on the neck.

With the exception of the first and second strings (and sometimes also the third), which are plain metal, steel strings are made up of a thread or core of wire around which another piece of wire is tightly wound. There are three types of winding:

- **Flatwound:** Most commonly used on archtop guitars, these strings consist of a flat ribbon of steel wound around a core of wire. Flatwound strings don't squeak the way other strings can when you move your fingers along them, but they can produce a somewhat duller tone and are more likely to crack.
- **Roundwound:** Most electric steel strings are roundwound, in which a piece of steel is wound around a steel core. They have a brighter tone than flatwound strings, and often last longer, but they seem a little tougher to play at first.
- **Groundwound:** These are conventional roundwound strings that have been ground down to create a partially flat surface.

CHANGING STRINGS

Guitars are pretty rugged instruments. Changing strings regularly will improve the guitar's sound, help keep strings from breaking at the wrong moment, and help identify possible maintenance problems. (You may discover a rattling tuning peg or a gouged bridge or nut.) Old strings tend to sound dull and lifeless, and they become brittle with age. This makes them feel tougher to fret and harder to keep in tune.

Removing the Old Strings

An old wives' tale has it that replacing strings one at a time is better for the guitar because it maintains tension on the neck. Not true. Funny as it may sound, guitar necks have "memory," and guitars themselves are made of sterner stuff. However, replacing strings one at a time can be more convenient. (A string winder, as shown in Figure 2-5, makes the job of winding new strings easier.)

A potential problem with taking all the strings off at the same time is that on guitars with a movable bridge, the bridge will move. This isn't something you want to happen because resituating a bridge can be a pain. And if the bridge is not positioned properly, it can affect the tuning of the strings and the feel of the neck as you play. A good compromise is to replace the strings three at a time. Replace the bass strings first, putting them in rough tune with the old treble strings, and then replace the treble strings, putting them in tune with the new bass strings. Then you can adjust the tuning of all six new strings.

Musical Notes

It can be tedious to turn your tuning pegs while putting on new strings. Save yourself time by buying a string winder, which fits over the tuning peg and allows you to turn it far more quickly.

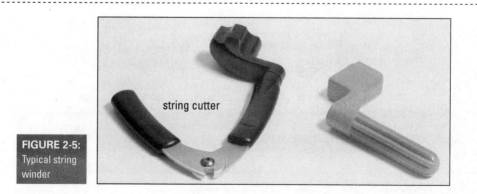

string cutter

FIGURE 2-5:
Typical string winder

You can unwind the strings by using the tuning peg to lessen the tension, or you can try a more radical approach and use wire cutters to snip the strings near the tuning peg. Once you have the old strings off the guitar, throw them away.

Guitar Bridges

The bridge is what holds the strings in place at the end of the guitar. There are various types on different guitars. Here are the most common:

- **Pin bridge:** Found on steel-string acoustics; pins anchor the strings at the end of the bridge
- **Fixed thread-under bridge:** Primarily found on classical guitars (shown in Figure 2-6)
- **Through-body bridge:** Found on Strat-style and Tele-style guitars; strings go in the back of the guitar, through the body, and up into a metal bridge
- **Tailpiece bridge:** Also known as a "stop" tailpiece; found on Les Paul–style guitars
- **Tremolo style bridge:** Some guitars have "whammy bars" that allow you to give the guitar a vibrato sound. The strings are attached to a metal block that pivots back and forth, making the strings vibrate when the whammy bar is moved.

It is important to know what kind of bridge your instrument has so you can properly change strings and keep your instrument in tune.

Classical Guitars

Classical guitars have fixed bridges, which allows you to replace the strings all at once if you like. Nylon strings aren't as springy as steel, and attaching the strings to the bridge can be tricky at first.

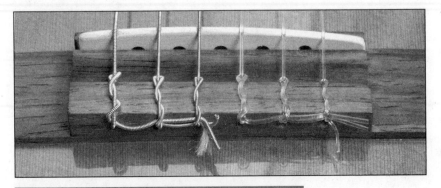

FIGURE 2-6: Nylon strings attached to a fixed thread-under bridge

Pass the string through the hole in the bridge, leaving about an inch and a half sticking out the back. Loop the short end back up, and wrap it behind the long end and then under itself. Pull it taut by tugging on the long end of the string. You may have to practice this a few times. Don't cut the string until everything is in place and in tune.

Thread the long end through the hole in the tuning peg at the head. (Figure 2-6 shows the order of the strings on the head.) Bring the end of the string over the roller (or capstan) in front of the hole and under itself. Make sure the string sits in the small groove on the nut. Then take up some of the slack of the string and tighten the tuning peg by winding the bass strings from right to left (counterclockwise), and treble strings from left to right (clockwise). As it picks up the slack of the string, the tuning peg will tighten and lock itself in place. While the string tightens, start tuning it and stretching it by pulling on it at various times. Once the guitar string is in place and in tune, snip away the excess string, leaving maybe a couple of inches at the tuning peg, and an inch or less at the bridge.

Steel-Strung Acoustic Guitars

Steel-strung acoustic and electric guitars have a moveable bridge, so when you change the strings you want to be careful not to dislodge it. It's a good idea to change the strings one at a time, or three at a time, but not all at the same time in order to keep the bridge anchored in its best position.

Acoustic guitars often have pin bridges that anchor the end of the string by popping the string into a hole and keeping it in place with a pin. First, loosen the string tension at the tuning peg. Then ease out the bridge pin.

Bridge pins can stick sometimes, so carefully use needle-nose pliers to ease the pin out of its hole. Some of the newer string winders have a notch by the end of their tuning-peg holder that is used specifically for this purpose. Be careful not to dig into the wood. Once the pin is out, you can remove the string.

Place the end of the new string that has a little brass ring into the bridge-pin hole. Then wedge the bridge pin back into the hole, locking the ring and the string in place. You'll notice that the pin has a slot. Make sure the slot faces forward, that is, toward the tuning pegs.

Now pass the string over the bridge post, making sure each string fits snugly into the groove on the bridge and on the nut. Thread the loose end through the hole in the tuning peg post. If you want, you can

Musical Notes

New strings need to be constantly checked and then "played in" before they settle into the correct tuning. When they're put on correctly, new strings will make your guitar sound brighter and make it easier to play.

kink the string a little to help keep it in place. Take up the slack on the string and then turn the tuning peg clockwise for the treble strings, and counterclockwise for the bass strings, tuning the string as the tension increases.

After all the strings are attached, retune the guitar carefully, bringing all the strings up to concert pitch. Be careful; you don't want to break a string. The best technique is to turn the tuning peg a couple of times, then check the tuning until you get the string in tune. When the string is in tune, clip the end off at the tuning peg, leaving about an inch of extra wire protruding.

Electric Guitars

With electric guitars, you attach the string to the bridge by passing one end through a hole and threading the string up to a brass ball, which keeps it in place.

Some guitars use what is called a locking nut system, such as a Floyd Rose tremolo unit (as shown in Figure 2-7). These can make strings difficult to change. The strings are clamped into place at the bridge saddle using a special Allen key. It's a good idea to use a piece of wood or a pack of playing cards to take up the tension when a string is changed; this stops the unit from rocking back and forth. On tremolo units, when one string is changed, the tension on all the strings changes.

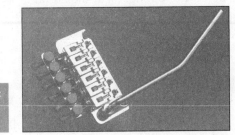

FIGURE 2-7:
Floyd Rose
tremolo unit

In order to use these bridges, you must snip off the ball end so that the string can be fitted into a small vise-like mechanism that holds the string in place. When all the strings are changed, you can remove the wood or playing cards supporting the bridge. Tune the strings as usual, using the tuning pegs. Then make the final adjustment on the bridge anchor using an Allen key. But be careful not to tighten the strings at the bridge too soon. If you overtighten a string, when you remove the block supporting the unit, the string may snap as the tension increases.

Remember, if you have a guitar with this kind of bridge, the spare strings need to have the ball ends removed. Get in the habit of carrying wire cutters around in your guitar case.

BASIC REPAIRS AND MAINTENANCE

The simplest thing to do to maintain your guitar is to keep it clean. Following is a list of basic, important guitar maintenance duties:

- Dust can gather anywhere on the instrument and cause problems. Use a soft cloth or feather duster, which can clean without the danger of scratching.
- Wipe down the guitar after every playing session and before you put the guitar back in its case—front, sides, back, fingerboard, and back of the neck as well.
- Clean each string. The natural oils from your fingers cause the strings to corrode, a process that over time can damage the strings' ability to sound good. These oils can seep into the fingerboard and eventually injure the wood of the instrument. Hold a cloth between your thumb and index fingers and run it along the length of each string.
- If the guitar has not been used for a while, first dust it and then rub down the wood with furniture polish or, better yet, guitar polish. (Some types of furniture polish contain abrasives that can damage the guitar's finish.) Never put polish directly onto the instrument; it can damage the finish. Put your cleaning solution onto a cloth first.
- Use a mild jeweler's or chrome polish for the metal parts, making certain first that it's not abrasive.
- Avoid keeping your guitar in a place that's subjected to direct sunlight for long periods of time or to drastic changes in temperature and humidity. This will help keep the guitar surface from cracking.
- Depending on the weight and your strength, try to carry your guitar in a hard case. If you're just going to a gig and back, then a good padded nylon gig bag will offer some protection, but not much. A leather gig bag, though much more expensive, is a better choice.

If you do accidentally chip the surface of your guitar, take the guitar to a professional guitar repairperson, who will easily fix the problem. If you decide to do it yourself, bear in mind that when you add or remove varnish, you can drastically change the wood's ability to vibrate and thus also alter the guitar's sound.

When traveling, keep your guitar inside the vehicle if you can. A guitar in the trunk or luggage compartment can be subjected to extremes of heat and cold. If you have to put your guitar in the trunk, try to put it as close to the passenger compartment as possible. If you're hit from behind, it will stand a better chance of surviving the accident.

ALTERATIONS AND SETTING UP THE GUITAR

Don't fiddle with the things described in this section until you're comfortable with the idea that you know what you're doing and why you're doing it. In most cases, if you're consistently unhappy with the way your instrument plays or sounds, you'll be better off taking your guitar to a repair professional, who may even be able to fix these things while you wait. Professional repair people often spend time watching the musician play and talking about what the guitarist thinks is right or wrong about the instrument before deciding the best way to set up the guitar. Remember, you're paying the expert to do an expert job.

Adjusting the Bridge

By adjusting the bridge, you can alter the action of your guitar. The action describes the height of the strings above the fingerboard. The higher the action, the more strength you need to use to fret a note. High action can be useful for rhythm playing, when you are principally playing chords all the time. Blues players who use slides often use a high action so the bottle-neck doesn't scrape against the frets.

The lower the action, the easier it is to fret the note. This can be useful for fast, single-note lead-guitar playing. Ideally, you want to set the action as low as you can without getting fret buzzing. This is really a trial-and-error process. (Bear in mind that the thickness or gauge of string you use can make a difference in playability as well.) Before you make any adjustments to the action, make sure you are using a new set of strings. Old strings can affect the action and intonation.

On most electric guitars, each string has an adjustable saddle on the bridge. Either the saddle has a screw that will adjust the whole bridge saddle at one go, or each string has an individual screw that can be raised or lowered. Sometimes it's necessary to adjust the whole bridge saddle by filing it down. This should not be done by anyone but a professional repairperson.

By changing the action, you are also affecting the intonation of the guitar. When you raise or lower the action, you alter the tension and distance between the bridge and the nut. This affects the way the strings play in tune. The distance between the nut and the twelfth fret must be identical to the distance between the twelfth fret and the bridge saddle. If it isn't, the guitar won't play in tune. The easiest way to test this is to play the string open, and then play the note or the harmonic at the twelfth fret. The notes played should be identical, though the fretted note or harmonic will be an octave higher. If the note at the twelfth fret is sharp, the string is too short and must be lengthened by moving the saddle back and away from the nut. If the note is flat, then move the saddle toward the nut.

Adjusting the Neck

Temperature changes, humidity, and age can cause guitars to swell and contract. This in turn can affect the setup of the guitar. For example, a slight bow in the neck can cause fret buzz or make it difficult to get a clean note at a particular fret or series of frets. You can sometimes adjust the neck by manipulating the truss rod. The truss rod runs down the center of the neck just under the fingerboard. Not all guitars have them (such as classical guitars), and even some that do won't allow you to adjust them. Usually you can see whether the truss rod can be adjusted because there is a plate at the headstock near the nut. Once removed, you will see a rod (or sometimes two) that has an adjustable screw or nut end. If you have a new guitar, it probably came with a truss rod wrench.

If your guitar bows out between the seventh and twelfth frets, you'll see a large gap between the strings and fretboard that makes playing the string at this point very hard. Tighten the truss rod, as you face it, by turning the nut clockwise a quarter turn. Give the instrument a few moments after each turn to settle into its new position.

If the frets buzz and the neck bows inward at the same place, you can loosen the truss rod by turning the nut counterclockwise a quarter turn at a time (as you face the guitar). Again allow the instrument to settle after each quarter-turn adjustment.

If you can't fix the problem within a few turns, stop. Overtightening or overloosening the truss rod can ruin a guitar and make it permanently unplayable.

Loose Connections

If you hear a rattle, try strumming the instrument and touching various potential culprits with your free hand until you touch the correct object and the rattling stops. For example, a rattle might come from a loose screw in a tuning peg or a loose nut on a jack socket. It's a good idea to gather a small toolkit of screwdrivers, pliers, wrenches, and such that will fit the various sizes of screws and nuts on your guitar.

Tuning Pegs

Tuning pegs, tuning machines, or machine heads (all different names for the same thing) are easily replaced if gears get worn or a part breaks off. If more than one tuning peg is giving you trouble, it's probably a good idea to replace the whole set.

The tuning pegs screw into the wood of the head, so take off the string, unscrew the tuning peg, take the peg to a guitar store, and try to get a matching peg. Then screw the new peg into place in the same position as before.

Strap Pins

These are little buttons that you use to attach a strap to the guitar. They usually have regular screw bodies that can sometimes work themselves loose. If tightening the pin with a screwdriver doesn't work, dab a little plastic wood or carpenter's glue on the end and put it back. If you still have trouble, go to a professional. If you have a more active playing style and find that the strap comes off more often than not while playing, you may want to consider using strap locks. These specially designed strap buttons will not come undone unless they are specifically released.

Electrical Problems

Dust and other grunge can affect the electrics of your guitar. If your volume or tone controls start to crackle when you turn them, or you're getting a weak or inconsistent signal, you may have dust or something else on the control. Turn the knobs vigorously back and forth to see if you can work out the dirt. If that doesn't work, try spraying the controls inside with aimed blasts from a can of air. If all else fails, go to a professional, who will give your controls a thorough cleaning.

The crackle can also indicate a loose wire in the jack plug. Take off the jack plate and look for the loose connection. If you spot it, use a soldering iron to reattach the wire to its appropriate lug. If you're uncomfortable doing this, take it to a professional.

Replacing a pickup is not that difficult. Often the pickups that came with your guitar aren't as good as ones you could buy to replace them. Make sure you get a pickup that's the same size and type as the one you're replacing so it fits into the existing holes drilled into the body.

Make sure you know which wire is supposed to be soldered to which connection. Then seat the pickup in the cavity left by the old pickup, and screw it into place. Again, don't attempt this if you don't feel confident you can do the job.

3

Basics of Physical Position

Before you begin playing the guitar, you must be comfortable holding the instrument. Though it may sound like a simple first step, it is an important one. Keep in mind that playing the guitar is a physical activity. If you have medical issues with your shoulders, back, neck, or lower abdomen, consult a physician who can guide you on a specific approach to learning the guitar. One of the most common reasons people put down the guitar for good is because of a physical limitation.

LEG, SHOULDER, AND NECK CONNECTION

It is a medical fact that sitting for a prolonged period of time in one position creates more stress in your back than when you are standing. This is because your bottom pushes tension up through your spine all the way up to your shoulders and neck. If you happen to work in an office and sit in a chair most of the day, you may have a habit of slouching forward or down in your chair. If you are accustomed to this posture, you may have a tendency to slouch over your guitar as you hold it. These postures will overstretch your spinal ligaments and cause the discs and other structures in the spine to strain. If you already have back or shoulder injuries, you may want to consult your doctor before beginning on your guitar career.

You will also need to think about the strength of your fingers, wrists, and hands. Some medical conditions, such as carpal tunnel syndrome or arthritis, may affect your ability to play the guitar. Check with your doctor or a professional guitar instructor to see if there are any known methods of playing around any injuries or conditions you may have. You never want to further injure yourself or aggravate your medical conditions. You can also ask around among your friends and relatives to see if anyone has a guitar you could practice holding to test your body's weaknesses before you invest any of your own money in an instrument.

Remember, it is important to have fun playing the guitar! Pain is not fun. So be sure you are comfortable and feeling good about playing guitar. This is an important first step.

SITTING WITH ACOUSTIC AND ELECTRIC GUITARS

Even before you sit with your guitar, you must have the proper chair. The best type of chair to sit on with a guitar is one without arms. This kind of chair will allow more freedom for unobstructed left-to-right movement. Ideally, this chair should be height adjustable with a cushioned seat. An adjustable piano bench will work as well. Make sure that the chair or bench is high enough so that you can bend your legs at a ninety-degree angle at the knees with your feet flat on the floor. Your back should be straight, with your shoulders relaxed. Your arms should be resting at your sides. Ask yourself, "Do I feel comfortable?" Hopefully, you do.

Next, with your left hand hanging naturally to the side of your body, slowly raise it to the guitar and lightly grab the neck by the top. Do your best not to lean forward with the guitar on your lap. (Figure 3-1 shows how to sit with an electric guitar; Figure 3-2 shows how to sit with an acoustic instrument.)

Playing guitar is a physical activity that requires muscle movement. Keep in mind that any overexertion creates tension. As tedious as it may sound, you really need to practice sitting with the guitar as well as playing it. Being comfortable is always important.

FIGURE 3-1: Sitting with an electric guitar

FIGURE 3-2: Sitting with an acoustic guitar

STANDING WITH GUITARS

The guitar should hang comfortably against your body, leaving both your arms free. If the strap is adjusted properly, the neck of the guitar should describe about a forty-five-degree angle when compared to the ground. The bridge should be about level with your waist and the head about level with your shoulder. Standing with an electric guitar (as shown in Figure 3-3) is vastly different from standing with an acoustic guitar (Figure 3-4) because of the different shapes and weights of the instruments. Electric guitars tend to be heavier because of their solid-body construction. Acoustic guitars can be cumbersome because of their depth.

FIGURE 3-3: Standing with an electric guitar

FIGURE 3-4: Standing with an acoustic guitar

Gravity is not your friend here. The deceiving thing about standing with a guitar is that the strap allows both hands to be independent, but the guitar is still hanging from your shoulders. While it may look like there is less stress on the back, that is not always the case. It looks really cool when you when you see those rock stars hanging their guitars down below their knees, but the future back pain is not worth the look. After you know what you're doing, you can adjust the instrument any way you want. But for now, as a beginner, don't make your life harder than it has to be. Playing with the guitar slung too low can really strain your hands, wrists, shoulders, and back.

Whether you are sitting or standing with your guitar, using a strap is always a good idea. Since there are many different guitar straps on market, the best thing to do is to take your instrument to the store and try some on. If you have neck or shoulder issues due to injury, again, please consult with a physician.

POSITION OF LEFT HAND ON THE NECK

To begin with, the best way to fret a note cleanly is to find the right amount of pressure it takes to use your fingertip to make a note sound clear. This is the key to developing a good left-hand technique. Pressing too hard will cause pain.

First, let the edge of the neck of the guitar rest in the palm of your left hand. You'll notice that your thumb and fingers automatically fall to either side of the neck. Now place the left-hand thumb in the middle of the back of the neck so that there is a nice space between the neck and your palm. You should be able to pivot your whole hand on the ball of your thumb without banging into the neck.

The best practice for thumb placement is to keep your thumb on the back of the neck so that it lies between your first and second fingers, as shown in Figure 3-5.

When you fret a note, use the tip or pad of your finger to press the string firmly to the fingerboard, as shown in Figure 3-6.

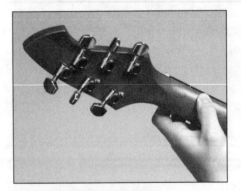

FIGURE 3-5: Thumb placement

FIGURE 3-6: Fretting a note

If you position your left hand on the neck so you can put your thumb immediately behind the place where you're pressing the string to the fretboard (as if you're trying to pinch your thumb and finger together through the neck, as shown in Figure 3-7), you'll get maximal pressure on the note, and it will sound clean.

Place the tip of your first finger on the first string at the first fret (as illustrated in Figure 3-8). Now pluck the string with your right-hand thumb.

FIGURE 3-7: Left-hand position

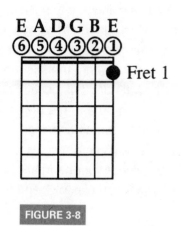

FIGURE 3-8

In the diagram, each vertical line represents a string. Each horizontal line represents a fretwire. The double line at the top represents the guitar nut. The black dot or number represents the finger you should use to stop that string at that fret—in this case, at the note F on the first string.

Press the string to the fretboard roughly in the middle of the fret (between the fretwires). If you press too close to a fretwire, the string may be muted; too far away and the string may buzz. To make sure you don't mute other strings, make a point of using your fingertips and keeping your fingers as close to perpendicular to the strings as possible by arching your wrist slightly (like a swan's neck). The classical guitar technique helps in this regard.

Though a lot of players allow their left-hand thumb come over the top of the neck, it's hard for beginners to do. Remember, the more your hand is cramped up like this, the harder it is to play the note well (that is, without any buzzing sound), and the more your muscles may ache.

As soon as your hand or fingers get sore or start to hurt, stop! It will take a little time to build up the strength in your fingers. Playing a little bit often is better than playing a lot in one go.

RIGHT-HAND POSITIONING

The right hand can be used fingerstyle, which means that each finger on the right hand is used to manipulate the strings. Alternately, you can hold a plectrum, or pick, in your right hand to strum various rhythms or pick out notes on the strings.

Fingerstyle

The basic fingerstyle position is to use the fingernails to pluck the strings. (Initially, you may use your fingertips as well.) The fingers are held vertical to the strings with a slight arch in the wrist. The thumb plays the three bass strings, while the first finger plucks the third string, the second finger the second string, and the third finger the first string. The little finger is usually not used.

For the moment, it's probably a good idea to practice strumming all six strings first with your thumb and then using a pick. The key is to place your fingertips on the pickguard (the piece of plastic or laminate placed under the strings on the body of the guitar) to anchor your hand and then to brush your thumb across all the strings. We'll discuss more complex pick and fingerpicking techniques later.

Holding a Pick

The size and thickness of guitar picks vary greatly to accommodate the different playing styles and strings. In the beginning, you'll want one that has a medium size and thickness. Buy yourself two or three and experiment.

Let the pick lie flat on your first finger, and then comfortably hold it in place with your thumb as shown in Figure 3-9. You can then use it to strum the string with up-and-down motions, as shown in Figure 3-10. The movement comes from your wrist, not your fingers.

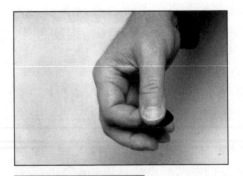
FIGURE 3-9: Holding a pick

FIGURE 3-10: Using the pick to strum

To get a feel of what to do, take your right hand and extend the fingers, thumb, and first finger, lightly touching at the tip. Now, with the fingertips still touching, shake your hand up and down at the wrist in a gentle, comfortable motion. This is the motion you want to use to strum the guitar strings.

HOW NOT TO HOLD A GUITAR

Now that you have mastered the basic positions, you'll have to choose the one that you feel most comfortable with. To avoid injury, remember to stick to proper positioning and not let your body get lazy and start to slump. Here are a few pointers on what not to do when positioning yourself for guitar play:

- When sitting, do not lean forward. This posture will only cause muscle pains after continuous playing.
- When standing, don't hold the guitar so low that you have to stoop low to play it. Keep it up near your chest between your neck and waist.
- Remember not to press harder on the neck than you need to produce a clear note.
- Don't hold the guitar behind your head. It looked cool on Jimi Hendrix, but it's not very practical in the end.
- Don't try to hold the guitar between your legs or on top of your head. Once again, it looks cool, but it's not very practical.

Strange guitar contortions may be intriguing in music videos, but they are not practical for good guitar playing and can actually cause injury to the inexperienced player. To get the most out of your guitar and optimize its sound quality, you'll need to respect the instrument (and your body) and hold it correctly.

4

The Basics of Reading Guitar Music and Tablature

Learning to play the guitar is unlike learning other instruments. For example, if you were a pianist, you would most likely have learned to play the instrument through years of private study that would have included a heavy focus on sight-reading—the ability to look at a written page of music and play it immediately. However, there's nothing wrong with taking a more informal approach to learning music. Plenty of famous musicians have never learned to read music. This chapter will help you understand the basics you'll need to read guitar music.

THE MUSICAL ALPHABET

Now it's time for you learn the musical alphabet. The musical alphabet consists of seven notes, which are named for the first letters of the alphabet: A-B-C-D-E-F-G. At the end of this sequence, the notes repeat themselves. When you reach A the second time around, you're playing the same note except that it's one octave (or eight notes) higher than the A you started with.

This difference depends on the "frequency" or number of beats per second (bps) at which a string vibrates. This frequency doubles every time you go up an octave. For example, the open A string on the guitar vibrates at a frequency of 110 bps. The A one octave higher, played by fretting the twelfth fret on the A string, vibrates at a frequency of 220 bps.

This note sequence can be started on any note you like (such as A-B-C-D-E-F-G-[A]; F-G-A-B-C-D-E-[F], and so on). No matter where you start, the sequence still repeats after seven notes. There are five more notes in the musical alphabet that are variations on the seven letters you are about to master.

BASIC ELEMENTS

There are two basic elements to reading and writing music: the name of the note and the length of time that note should last. Over time, these two elements were combined into one elegant system, called musical notation. A five-line "staff" developed, and the note's position and appearance on the staff told musicians how long to hold the note before playing the next one.

The first thing you need to do is understand where notes are written and where they are placed. Look at the music staff shown in Figure 4-1. The music staff is made up of five lines with four spaces.

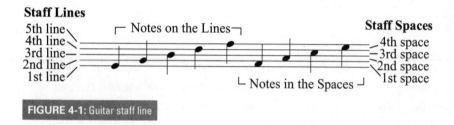

Staff Lines

5th line
4th line
3rd line
2nd line
1st line

┌─ Notes on the Lines ─┐

Staff Spaces

4th space
3rd space
2nd space
1st space

└ Notes in the Spaces ┘

FIGURE 4-1: Guitar staff line

The modern staff is split into two halves, each of which is called a clef. Each clef has a particular sign at the beginning to tell you which staff you are using. These clefs are called the *treble clef* and the *bass clef*. When piano players read music, they play the treble clef with their right hand and the bass clef with their left hand.

Treble clef:

Bass clef:

Notes that appear below or above the clefs appear on what are called ledger lines, or individual lines where each note is written. Ledger lines are lines that extend the range of notes when needed above or below the staff lines, as shown in Figure 4-2. Ledger lines can become difficult to read as the notes get higher. In this case, the symbol 8va . . . is used to show that certain notes should be played one octave higher than written.

Ledger Lines Above the Staff

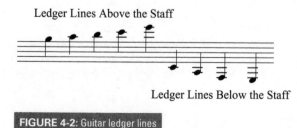

Ledger Lines Below the Staff

FIGURE 4-2: Guitar ledger lines

Look at Figure 4-3. Notice that in between the treble clef and the bass clef is one note on a ledger line. That note is called middle C because it falls in the middle of the two clefs. On the guitar, it is usually played on the third fret of the fifth string.

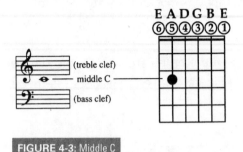

FIGURE 4-3: Middle C

Those of you who are quick off the mark may have figured out a little problem when it comes to playing certain notes on the guitar. You may have noticed that you can play the same note (as it appears on the treble clef) in different places on the guitar. E, on the top space, for example, can be played on the fifth fret of the second string or on the open first string. For the moment, you'll only need to worry about reading music in the first position—that is, around the first fret.

NOTE NAME IDENTIFICATION

You'll notice that even though you are learning about the musical alphabet, you don't necessarily have to start on the note A. Since you are learning about guitar here, look at music notation as it relates to the guitar. Figure 4-4 shows the names of the notes played at various frets.

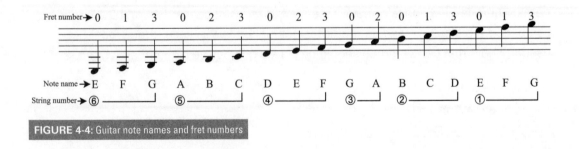

FIGURE 4-4: Guitar note names and fret numbers

GUITAR TABLATURE

Another way to write down music is to use tablature. Instead of showing the notes to be played, the way music notation does, tablature is designed for a particular instrument and shows you where to stop a particular string to play the desired note. A version of this kind of music notation was used by Renaissance and medieval lute players for years. You can show complex fingerings this way, including chords and melodies.

In guitar tablature, each of the six lines represents one of the guitar's six strings, as shown in Figure 4-5. The top line is the first string, and the bottom line is the sixth string. The numbers on each line represent the fret you need to stop in order to get the desired note—a pretty good system for writing down tunes quickly.

FIGURE 4-5: Guitar tablature

FINDING THE NOTES ON THE GUITAR NECK IN FIRST POSITION

Now that you have a basic foundation in the look of both the music and tablature staves, you should do your first exercise in first position. The purpose of this exercise is to understand the rule of finger per fret (meaning when the left hand is on the guitar, place one finger per fret so that your first finger can play any note along the first fret, the second finger can play any note on the next fret down, etc.).

The left-hand fingers are numbered as shown in Figure 4-6. The open strings are indicated by the number 0, the first finger and first fret by the number 1, the second finger and second fret by the number 2, and the third finger and third fret by the number 3.

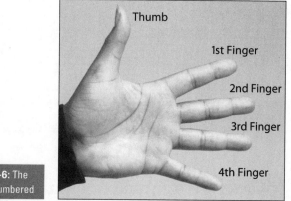

FIGURE 4-6: The left hand, numbered

FIGURE 4-7: Exercise, open position

Now that you have seen where the left hand should stop each string to produce the musical alphabet in first position (as shown in Figure 4-7), the following two figures will show some notes on the fretboard with the fingerings to help you learn the musical alphabet.

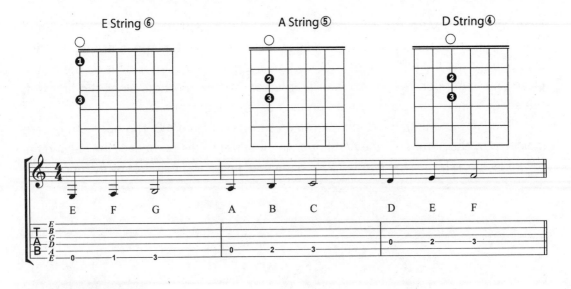

FIGURE 4-8: Bass strings

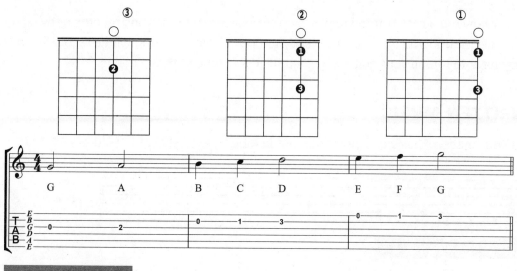

FIGURE 4-9: Treble strings

TIME AND RHYTHM

Having a good knowledge of "where the beat is" and playing in time are paramount for a musician. As Duke Ellington once wrote, "It don't mean a thing, if it ain't got that swing . . ."

Time breaks down into two elements: rhythm, or the "feel" of a piece of music, and tempo, or the speed you play at. Examples of rhythm styles include swing, shuffle, waltz, bossa nova, funk, bop, bluegrass, and so on. Sometimes these rhythms are also the name of the style of music. Music is often marked with a suggested tempo that may look like this: [N] = 120. The number 120 refers to the number of beats per minute (bpm) on a metronome. It denotes how fast (or slow) the piece should be played. The lower the number, the slower the piece of music. The higher the number, the faster the piece of music. In general, these are the accepted tempos (tempi, to be more precise), each of which has an Italian descriptive term, as follows:

- Grave: Very slow (slower than 40 bpm)
- Lento: Slow (40 to 60 bpm)
- Adagio: Slow—literally, "at ease" (60 to 75 bpm)
- Andante: Walking (75 to 100 bpm)
- Moderato: Moderate speed (100 to 120 bpm)
- Allegro: Fast—literally, "cheerful" (120 to 160 bpm)
- Vivace: Lively (150 to 170 bpm)
- Presto: Very fast (170 to 200 bpm)
- Prestissimo: As fast as possible (200 or more bpm)

Many musicians learned to play by playing along with CDs and records or by using a simple metronome that keeps a steady tempo. If you play along with a recording, you may have to retune your guitar slightly until it is in tune with the music.

WRITTEN MUSIC

As you've seen, music can be written out in tablature, as shown in Figure 4-10.

FIGURE 4-10: Music in tablature

The problem is that you can't easily use this kind of chart to show how long you should sound a note. One beat? Two beats? Three beats? How can you tell? While tablature is handy, it has its limitations.

So how do you solve that problem? You split the note up into fractions that each last for a certain portion of the time allotted a whole note. Because these divisions are standard and precise, the fractions retain a predictable, mathematical relationship to one another:

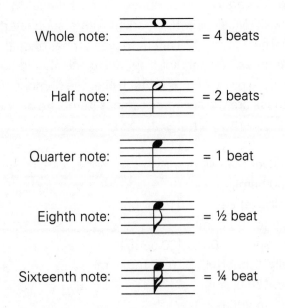

Whole note: = 4 beats

Half note: = 2 beats

Quarter note: = 1 beat

Eighth note: = ½ beat

Sixteenth note: = ¼ beat

You'll notice that eighth notes and sixteenth notes have "flags" attached to the stem. Flags are the little wavy lines at the top (or bottom) of the note stem. The number of flags on a stem tells you the kind of note you're playing.

Time Signatures

Undoubtedly you have seen a marking such as 4/4 at the front of a piece of music (or sometimes 3/4, and so on). This notation is known as the time signature. The top number (4 or 3) tells you how many beats in the bar to count. The bottom number tells you the kind of note you are counting (in this case, a quarter note). So if 4/4 (also known as "common time") means four quarter notes to each bar, and 3/4 means three quarter notes per bar, then 2/2 would be what? You got it: two half notes to the bar. What would 6/8 be? Right—six eighth notes to the bar. And so on.

The notes in the bar have to add up to whatever the time signature says. For example, 3/4 would mean the notes must add up to three. Then a bar line like this " | " is drawn, and you start the next group of three. If the notes had to add up to four, then you would make sure there was a bar line every time the notes added up to four.

For example, the notes in Figure 4-11 all add up to four.

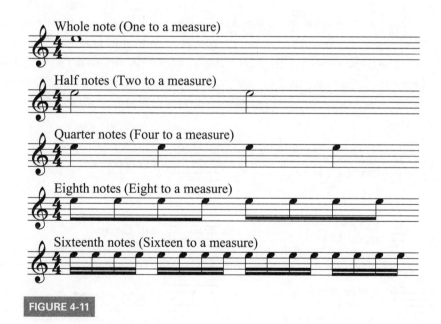

FIGURE 4-11

The notes in Figure 4-12 add up to three.

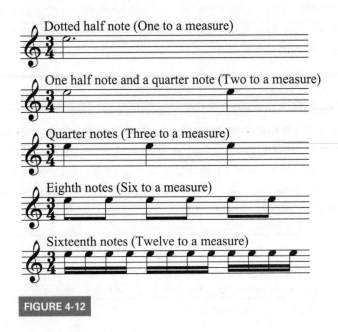

Dotted half note (One to a measure)

One half note and a quarter note (Two to a measure)

Quarter notes (Three to a measure)

Eighth notes (Six to a measure)

Sixteenth notes (Twelve to a measure)

FIGURE 4-12

What if you don't want a note to be played? Or you want one note to last longer than usual? Each of the notes has a corresponding rest note that indicates you should wait that length of time before playing the next note, as shown in Figure 4-13. A quarter-note rest, for instance, indicates that you wait, or "rest," one beat before playing the next note. So in 4/4 time, one bar might consist of a quarter note, a quarter-note rest, and two quarter notes.

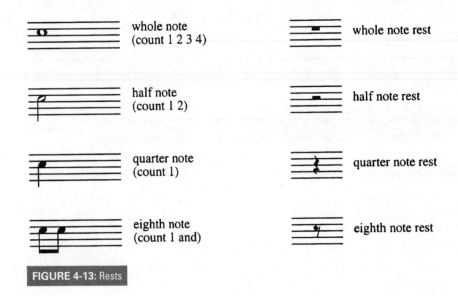

whole note
(count 1 2 3 4)

whole note rest

half note
(count 1 2)

half note rest

quarter note
(count 1)

quarter note rest

eighth note
(count 1 and)

eighth note rest

FIGURE 4-13: Rests

Writing a dot immediately after a note increases that note's duration by half as much again. For example, a dotted whole note would be four beats plus two, totaling six. A dotted half note would be two beats plus one, totaling three. A dotted quarter note would be one beat plus a half of a beat. (In this case, the next note would start on the "off" beat.)

Another way to make a note last longer—and keep everything neatly within the bar lines—is to tie two notes together. In Figure 4-14, for example, notice you play the first note, keep your finger down and continue to count for the length of the second note that is tied to the first with a curved bar connecting the two notes.

count   1 (2   3)   1   2   3   (1 2 3)

FIGURE 4-14: A half note tied to a quarter note

Recap of what you know, using notation.

FIGURE 4-15

DYNAMIC MARKINGS

When musicians talk about dynamics, they are basically referring to how loudly or softly you play a note or chord. Again, the dynamic markings in music have Italian names. Here they are with their symbols:

- pp: Pianissimo (very quiet)
- p: Piano (quiet)
- mp: Mezzo piano (moderately quiet)
- mf: Mezzo forte (moderately loud)
- f: Forte (loud)
- ff: Fortissimo (very loud)

"Staccato" means short and sharp. When you play staccato, you keep the rhythm of the piece, but you play the notes for a shorter duration than you normally would. Staccato notes are often marked with dots underneath.

The opposite of staccato is "legato," which means slurred. Here you slur the notes together, maybe playing one note and hammering down on the next note using left-hand fingering alone.

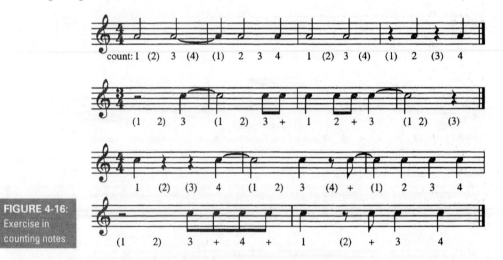

FIGURE 4-16:
Exercise in counting notes

LEFT- AND RIGHT-HAND COORDINATION

People are generally impressed by the fast NASCAR driver, the fast track runner, and the fast-playing guitar master. The one thing all of these examples have in common is coordination. All physical skills are based on coordinated movements. Whether it's learning to walk with one foot after the other or learning to drive a car with a stick shift, all skill sets are series of coordination. In guitar playing, you have to coordinate the left and right hand to the same strings at the same time. Seems easy enough. After you master that, then you have to learn to finger different notes on one string while simultaneously picking the same string and then moving through the other five strings. Whew! Sounds like a lot, but it is more fun than daunting.

INTRODUCTION TO PICKING

There are two distinct ways of hitting the string with a pick: a downstroke and an upstroke. To make a downstroke, use the tip of the pick and push down. Upstrokes are the reverse. The tip of the pick is used to pull up on the string. If you want to master using a pick, you need to become very comfortable mixing downstrokes and upstrokes. Otherwise, you will never get any kind of speed and articulation in your playing. Figure 4-17 shows some exercises to help develop right-hand picking. These exercises use open strings and are written in both music notation and tablature. So one of the great things about this exercise is that you also learn to read music at the same time. Things are a lot more complicated if you're left-handed and choose to use a left-handed guitar. If you get one, then just do everything in a mirror image, substituting left hand for right hand and vice versa.

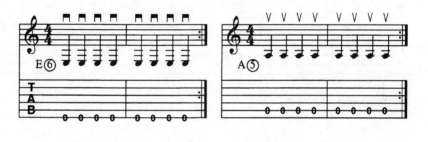

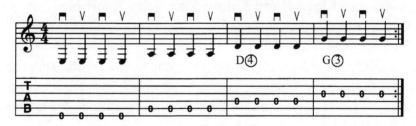

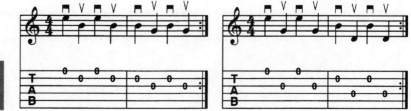

FIGURE 4-17: Right-hand picking exercises

BEGINNING EXERCISES

Figure 4-18 shows a left-hand fingering exercise. Notice that you should play this using each finger to a fret as shown. (Normally, you would not play the B on the fourth fret of the third string or on the open second string. But for the purposes of this exercise go ahead and do it anyway.)

FIGURE 4-18: Left-hand finger exercises

Figure 4-19 shows an exercise enabling you to practice the "finger per fret" rule.

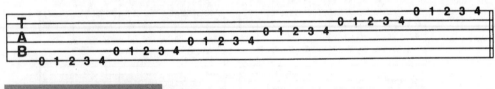

FIGURE 4-19: Each finger to a fret

Left- and Right-Hand Finger-Dexterity Exercise

The exercise shown in Figure 4-20 combines left- and right-hand coordination skills as well as an introduction to finger dexterity. The idea here is to practice slowly. At one point, you will have to use the pinky finger of your left hand. The pinky is a little weaker than the other fingers, so using it will take a little getting used to. Remember, the numbers next to the notes are the fingers to be used on the left hand.

FIGURE 4-20: Octave scale

PRACTICE TIPS

The key to good practice habits is consistency. Ten minutes a day—every day—is better than eight hours all at once on Saturday afternoon. Your fingers have to develop a muscle memory of how to form the chords and where to go and what to do, and you have to get over the slight soreness of your fingertips until calluses build up. (A hint: If your fingertips get sore, take a break.)

Knowing how to practice, and what to practice, can mean the difference between spending hours spinning your wheels in one place and advancing by leaps and bounds with only an hour or two a day.

5

Introduction to Simple Songs

Now you're going to learn to strum some songs and play some simple melodies. To do this, you'll need to learn a few chords first. A chord is made when three or more strings are played together, usually by strumming down with plectrum (more commonly known as a pick) or by using your thumb. Playing a chord is one of the most basic and important guitar-playing concepts, which is why it is taught before any other technique.

CHORDS C AND G7

The chords you are going to learn now are easy versions of basic chords. (You'll learn the more complex forms later.) The chords are C (shown in Figures 5-1 and 5-2) and G7 (shown in Figures 5-3 and 5-4). Memorize the names of the chords and the shapes they make.

FIGURE 5-1: Basic C chord

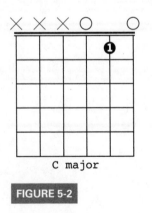

C major

FIGURE 5-2

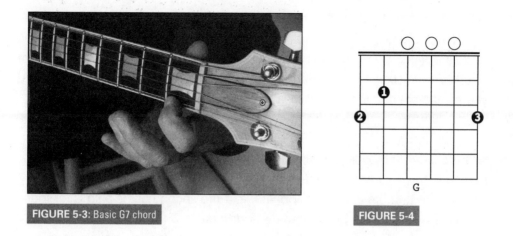

FIGURE 5-3: Basic G7 chord

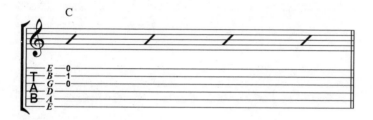

FIGURE 5-4

To play the C chord, put your first finger on the second string at the first fret. Press hard. Strum the first, second, and third strings together to sound the C chord. Do this four times. You've now strummed four beats. When these four beats are written as shown in Figure 5-5, they make one bar (or measure) of music.

FIGURE 5-5: Four-beat bar

Strum the chord four more times. You've now strummed two bars of C.

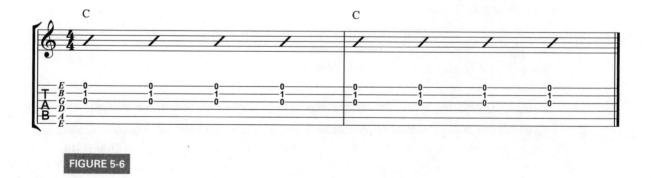

FIGURE 5-6

To play the G7 chord, put your first finger on the first string at the first fret. Strum the first three strings together, and do this four times. Play the C chord four times, and then another four times. Play G7 four times. Now play C four times.

Surprise! You've successfully played the song "Merrily We Roll Along." The 4/4 at the beginning means count and play four beats in every bar. (If the time signature was 3/4, what would that mean? Answer: You would play and count three beats in the bar instead of four.)

The bars are created by bar lines that look like this: " | " It is usual to write four bars per line and then go to another line. In "Merrily We Roll Along," for example, as Figure 5-7 shows, the first bar is C for four beats, and the second bar is also C for four beats. The third bar is G7 for four beats, and the fourth bar is C for four beats. The next line is a repeat of the first line, so that the song has a total of eight bars altogether.

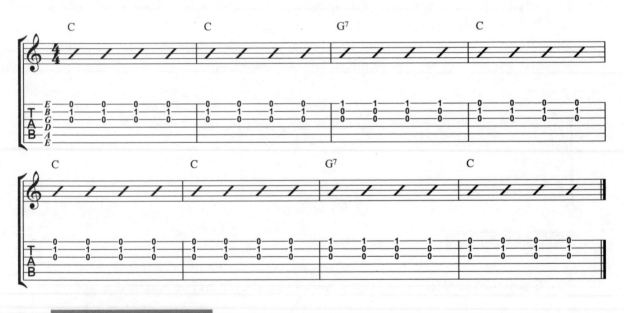

FIGURE 5-7: Merrily We Roll Along

Merrily we roll along, roll along, roll along,
Merrily we roll along, over the deep blue sea.

Changing chords to play this song is going to take some practice. You may find that your fingertips get sore. The strings will buzz if you stop them in the wrong part of the fret or don't press hard enough. As you change chords while you strum, it's a challenge to jump your finger smoothly from the first string to the second string and back again. But don't get disheartened. Remember, everyone who has ever played the guitar—from

Segovia to Pat Metheny to Eric Clapton—has had to go through this stage, and every one of them found it just as awkward and just as frustrating as you do.

The trick again is to practice slowly and try to aim for good technique. Slightly arch your wrist, use your fingertips, and press firmly with your thumb in the middle of the back of the neck as you press down with your fingertip to stop the string. Try to eliminate all sounds of buzzing. Keep your other fingers out of the way.

Now try another old folk song, "Go Tell Aunt Rhodie," shown in Figure 5-8.

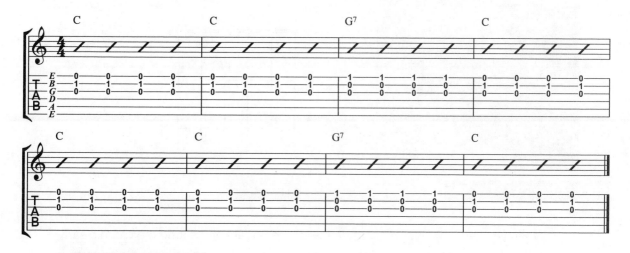

FIGURE 5-8: Go Tell Aunt Rhodie

Go tell Aunt Rhodie, go tell Aunt Rhodie,
Go tell Aunt Rhodie, the old grey goose is dead.

Once you can play these two simple tunes with smooth chord changes from C to G7, it is time to move on and learn two more important chords.

CHORDS D7 AND G

The next chord to learn is D7. This chord uses three fingers. Study the chord chart shown in Figures 5-9 and 5-10. Remember, the numbers represent the finger you should use on each string (third finger on second fret of first string; first finger on first fret of second string; second finger on second fret of third string).

It will probably take some practice before you make the D7 chord sound clearly. Work at it. A good exercise is to first press hard and play the chord. Next, relax your hand

and lift your fingers slightly off the guitar strings but keep them in the shape of the chord. Then put your fingers back on the strings—again, pressing hard. This helps build muscle memory, so that the fingers remember where they should go to form this chord.

FIGURE 5-9: Basic D7 chord

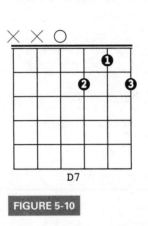

FIGURE 5-10

When you can hold the D7 chord with all three fingers and sound the chord clearly, with no buzzing strings, it is time to move on and learn the basic G chord. The form is shown in Figures 5-11 and 5-12. If you have trouble with this, just play the note on the first string and strum the first four open strings.

FIGURE 5-11: Basic G chord

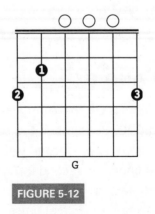

FIGURE 5-12

In the next song, "Twinkle, Twinkle Little Star," shown in Figure 5-13, you'll have to move back and forth among the different chords you've learned so far.

Notice that in this song, in the second and third bars and elsewhere, you'll play two beats of C and then two beats of G. This is a hard tune to play, so practice it a lot. The whole idea is for you to get comfortable changing chords.

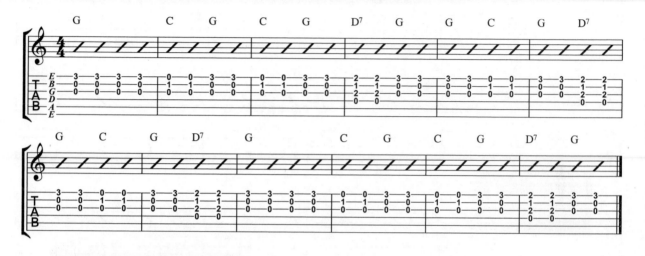

FIGURE 5-13: Twinkle, Twinkle Little Star

Twinkle, twinkle little star, how I wonder where you are
Up above the world so high, like a diamond in the sky,
Twinkle, twinkle little star, how I wonder where you are.

"Amazing Grace," shown in Figure 5-14, has a time signature of 3/4. This means you strum three beats to the bar.

FIGURE 5-14: Amazing Grace

To keep notation simple, instead of writing out measures that are simply repeats of the previous measure, you can use a repeat measure sign. This sign indicates that you should repeat the previous measure. (See the way it is used in "She'll Be Comin' Round the Mountain," shown in Figure 5-23.)

FIGURE 5-15: Repeat measure sign

Try the fuller versions of the C and G7 chords (shown in Figures 5-16 through 5-19).

FIGURE 5-16: C chord full

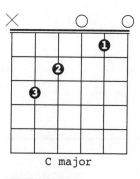

C major

FIGURE 5-17

FIGURE 5-18: G7 chord full

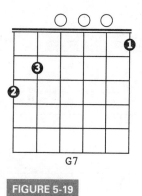

G7

FIGURE 5-19

SONGS ON THE FIRST TWO STRINGS

The following are the full versions of "Merrily We Roll Along" and "Go Tell Aunt Rhodie." Both of these songs are played on the first two strings. Figures 5-20 and 5-21 show these songs with the melody included. Use the tablature if necessary.

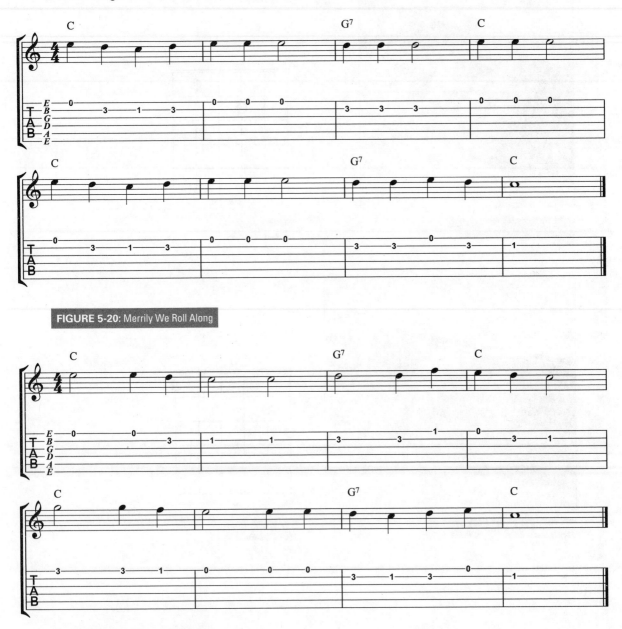

FIGURE 5-20: Merrily We Roll Along

FIGURE 5-21: Go Tell Aunt Rhodie

SONG ON THE FIRST THREE STRINGS

"Twinkle, Twinkle Little Star" is played on the first three strings. Figure 5-22 shows this song along with the melody.

FIGURE 5-22: Twinkle, Twinkle Little Star

SONGS ON THE FIRST FOUR STRINGS

Figures 5-23 and 5-24 show "She'll Be Comin' Round the Mountain" and "Amazing Grace," both played on the first four strings.

FIGURE 5-23: She'll Be Comin' Round the Mountain

FIGURE 5-24: Amazing Grace

BASS PATTERNS ON THE FIFTH AND SIXTH STRINGS

Just as an extra exercise, try playing "She'll Be Comin' Round the Mountain" on the fifth and sixth strings, as shown in Figure 5-25. You've just transposed the song down one whole octave—see how far you have come? Good work.

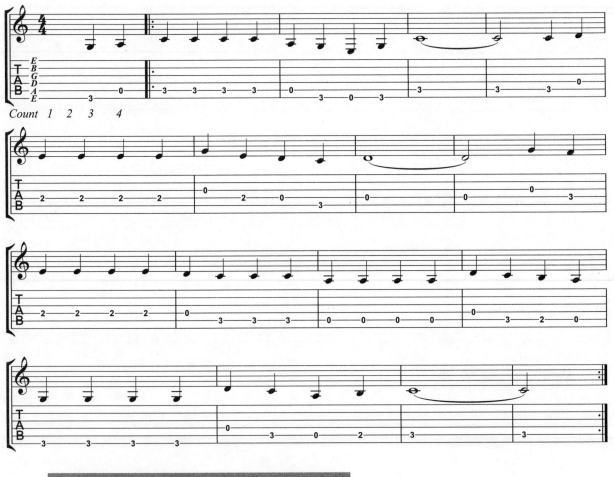

FIGURE 5-25: She'll Be Comin' Round the Mountain down one octave

PART 2

Scales

6

What Is a Scale?

A scale is simply an organization of music notes or tones. There are literally thousands of scales if you start combining all twelve chromatic notes from the musical alphabet together in various ways. What you'll learn in this chapter is a great collection of useful scales to get you through many musical situations. Within each section, you'll learn some important info about the scale in question, what style(s) of music use(s) that scale, and, where applicable, which chords correlate with those scales.

For the purposes of this chapter, a scale is defined as musical material that you can use to create melodies, whether composed or improvised. As your knowledge of scales grows deeper, you can learn to make chords and harmony from these scales. No guitarist gets through even his first month of guitar lessons without learning at least one scale!

In this chapter, we'll cover six scales that are frequently used:

- Major pentatonic
- Minor pentatonic
- Major

- Minor
- Dorian
- Mixolydian

KEY SIGNATURES

In Chapter 3, you learned that on the music staff, notes can be shown on the lines (E-G-B-D) or the spaces (D-F-A-C-E-G) and you can raise or lower these notes using sharp ♯ and flat ♭ signs. (Flattening—or diminishing—a note means dropping it down a semitone or fret. Augmenting—or raising—a note means sharpening or raising it a semitone or fret.) Instead of placing lots of sharps or flats into the notation, which can look cluttered and confusing, you can instead put them at the beginning of a piece of music. This method tells you that all the notes that have a sharp or flat sign in front of them should be played that way unless a natural sign ♮ tells you otherwise.

KEY SIGNATURES

A key signature is a series of sharps or flats at the beginning of a staff showing which notes are to be played higher or lower than the natural notes. Depending on how many sharps or flats there are at the beginning of a piece of music, you can tell which key the music is written in.

The list below shows the correspondence between sharps and flats and key signatures (shown in Figure 6-1):

- No sharps or flats = Key of C
- One sharp = Key of G
- Two sharps = Key of D
- Three sharps = Key of A
- Four sharps = Key of E
- Five sharps = Key of B
- Six sharps = Key of F♯

- One flat = Key of F
- Two flats = Key of B♭
- Three flats = Key of E♭
- Four flats = Key of A♭
- Five flats = Key of D♭
- Six flats = Key of G♭

Six flats (or altered notes) are just about as many notes as you need to remember. After this you'll learn about "enharmonic" notes, or notes that have the same name. An example of this would be C flat, which is really B natural.

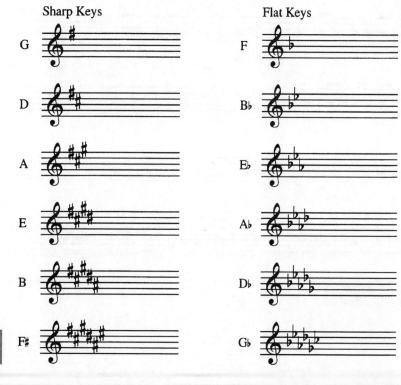

FIGURE 6-1: Key signatures

When you're comfortable with all this, try playing the tunes shown in Figures 6-2 through 6-4.

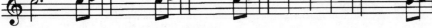

FIGURE 6-2: Polly Wolly Doodle

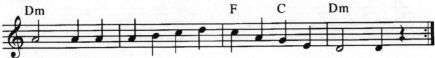

FIGURE 6-3: Drunken Sailor

FIGURE 6-4: We Wish You a Merry Christmas

INTERVALS

The distance between two notes is called an interval. The frets of a guitar are a half-step or half-tone apart (same thing, different name). A half-tone or semitone (again, same thing, different name) is the smallest interval, or distance, between two notes—at least in Western music. This is the distance from C to C♯. (C♯ is one half-step up from C, and D♭ is enharmonically the same note, a half-step down from D.)

A whole step or whole tone (usually just called a tone), which is two semitones, would be from C to D. This would be the equivalent of jumping to a note two frets away on the guitar.

It's very helpful not only to know this information intellectually but also to see how you can apply it to your instrument. To see how intervals look in the flesh, look at your fifth string. The following examples are all counted from C, which is played at the third fret of the fifth string:

Names of Intervals

- The interval from C to C♯ (fourth fret, also known as D♭) is a semitone—the interval known as a minor second.
- The interval from C to D (fifth fret) is a whole tone, or two semitones—the interval known as a second.
- The interval from C to E♭ (sixth fret) is three semitones—the interval known as a minor third.

- The interval from C to E (seventh fret) is four semitones—the interval known as a major third.
- The interval from C to F (eighth fret) is five semitones—the interval known as a fourth.
- The interval from C to G♭ (ninth fret) is six semitones—the interval known as a diminished or flatted fifth. Alternately, you can say that this interval is from C to F♯ (enharmonically the same note as G♭). In that case, this interval is called an augmented fourth.
- The interval from C to G (tenth fret) is seven semitones—the interval known as a fifth.
- The interval from C to G♯ (eleventh fret) is eight semitones—the interval known as an augmented fifth (also called a raised fifth). If you say the interval is from C to A♭ (enharmonically the same note), it is known as a minor sixth.
- The interval from C to A (twelfth fret) is nine semitones—the interval known as a major sixth.
- The interval from C to A♯ (thirteenth fret) is ten semitones—the interval known as an augmented sixth. If you say the interval is from C to B♭, the interval is called a minor seventh.
- The interval from C to B (fourteenth fret) is eleven semitones—the interval known as a major seventh.
- The interval from C to C (fifteenth fret) is twelve semitones—the interval known as an octave.

Figure 6-5 shows the intervals written as notation.

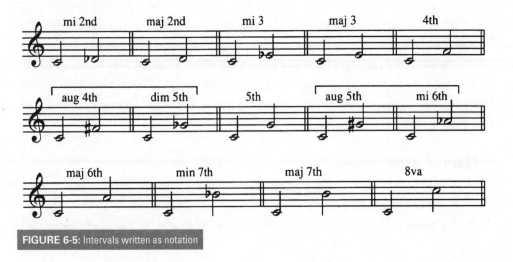

FIGURE 6-5: Intervals written as notation

CIRCLE OF FIFTHS

If you follow the key signatures carefully, you'll see that from C to G is a fifth, G to D is a fifth, D to A is a fifth, and so on through the sharp keys. Similarly, C to F is a fourth, and from F to B♭ is a fourth, and so on through the flat keys. Essentially, the pattern is a fifth in one direction, a fourth in the other. Called the circle of fifths, this pattern is illustrated in Figure 6-6.

The circle of fifths is an easy but important way to learn the key of a piece of music because it tells you how many sharps or flats are in the key. C has no sharps or flats.

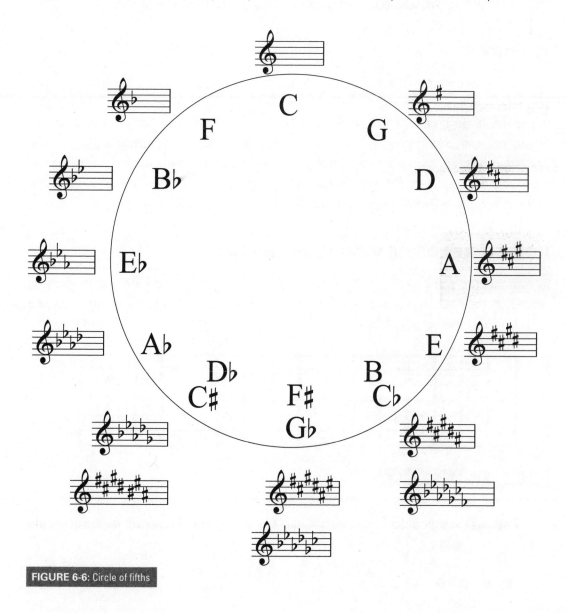

FIGURE 6-6: Circle of fifths

The circle of fifths shows how when you go clockwise around the circle you go up a fifth. For example, the fifth note of the C major scale is G. The fifth note of the G major scale is D, and so on. Also notice how there are twelve notes on the circle of fifths, corresponding to twelve numbers on a clock.

How is this information helpful? Take any chord progression, for example, C major to F major. Now, suppose you'd switch that to A. In other words, you want the same exact same sounding chord progression, you just want it in A instead of C. Since F is in the position that is one turn counterclockwise of C, then all you have to do is go to A, and then go one turn counterclockwise to D. That how easy it is to use the circle of fifths.

THEORY

Before you see any of the scales, you'll see a bit of background information on the scale. One of the things you'll see is a sample of the musical notes contained within the scale. In each case, you'll see this in relation to the C scale only (rather than all twelve chromatic spellings). This is to serve as a reference for you. You'll also see the *scale degrees,* which is a way of identifying the scale tones by numbers. Knowing the scale degrees, coupled with knowledge of key signatures, will allow you to spell all the notes in any scale you see in this book.

HOW TO READ THE VISUAL DIAGRAMS

In this chapter, you'll see an overview of the guitar's fingerboard with dots/fingerings placed on the neck to indicate where to press. Let's start with a blank diagram (Figure 6-7) and explain what you're looking at.

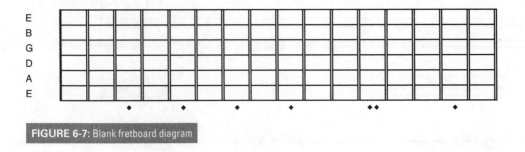

FIGURE 6-7: Blank fretboard diagram

Each fretboard contains six strings, just like your guitar. To the left of the scale are the following notes:

E B G D A E

These notes correspond to the names of the open strings of the guitar. With that said, the diagrams are laid out with the low strings on the bottom of the diagrams and the high strings on the top of the diagrams. If you set your guitar in your lap, with the fingerboard up, you'll be looking down at the fretboard diagram you'll see throughout this book.

Below each diagram is a group of what look like diamonds. These diamonds are located at the following frets:

- 3rd fret
- 5th fret
- 7th fret

- 9th fret
- 12th fret (double diamonds)
- 15th fret

Each of these diamonds corresponds to the typical position markers that you find inlaid into your fingerboard. Most guitars have them as circles, but some have more ornate shapes (and many of them diamonds). In any case, they are there to help you find your way on the fretboard. On the diagrams in this book, you'll see them on the bottom of the fingerboard because you'll need to keep the actual fingerboard free for the notes you'll play. The diamonds are there to show you on which fret the scale shape will occur.

The fret-board diagram itself is a grid of 6 × 16 boxes, with each box designating a fret. This diagram provides a simple explanation of how to read the diagrams. (See Figure 6-8.)

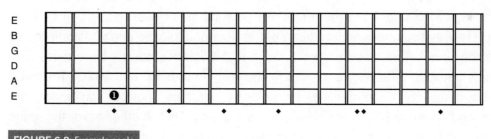

FIGURE 6-8: Example scale

This scale isn't really a scale, but it does provide us a great way to illustrate how the system works. The single dot (in this case a 1) is on the bottom row, on the lowest space, which designates that it's the sixth string. The dot is placed on the 3rd fret (also designated by a diamond). Press down the third fret of the sixth string, and you'll have read your first diagram.

Full Diagrams

Now that you understand how the diagrams are put together, let's look at a sample scale. (See Figure 6-9.)

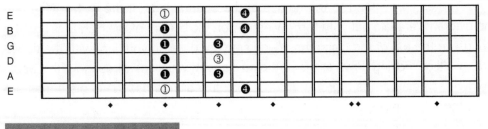

FIGURE 6-9: A minor pentatonic scale

You can see that this scale has two notes on each string and that every string is used. How do you play this? This is the fun part! A scale has no start and no end. A scale is just showing you what you *can* play to make the sound of A minor pentatonic happen. There is no right or wrong way to play it. It's analogous to an alphabet. You can make words as you please and organize them into sentences. What a scale is *not* is a rote pattern that you'll ever play the same way twice. Think of each scale in this book as a vast array of possibilities. Mix them up, play them out of order, skip around. The more you experiment, the more fun you'll have, and the more original your solos and riffs will sound.

The Dots

Throughout this part, there are dots placed on the fingerboard to indicate which fingers you should use. Firstly, the fingerings are merely a suggestion. You'll find that the fingerings in this book are there to make your life as a player easier. But if at any point you feel that you have figured out a better fingering, please don't hesitate to use it—only the sound of the scale comes through to the listener, not the fingers used!

You'll see two different color dots in the diagrams: black and white. The black dots are the majority of the markings on the scale diagrams. They tell you what finger to press, and where to play them; their color is arbitrary. On the other hand, the white dots indicate the root of the scale. (For instance, if you're playing a C major scale, all of the Cs will be in white.) This will help you learn the notes on your fingerboard as you progress throughout the chapter. Since all of the scales in this chapter progress in more than one octave, you'll see more than one white circle (indicating the root). This will give you a chance to anchor the root of the scale from more than one place on your neck, greatly speeding up your learning of the notes on the fingerboard—a task that every guitarist should take seriously!

A Sample Page

Let's look at a sample page, so you can see what you'll encounter. Figure 6-10 shows the C major scale that you'll find within this book.

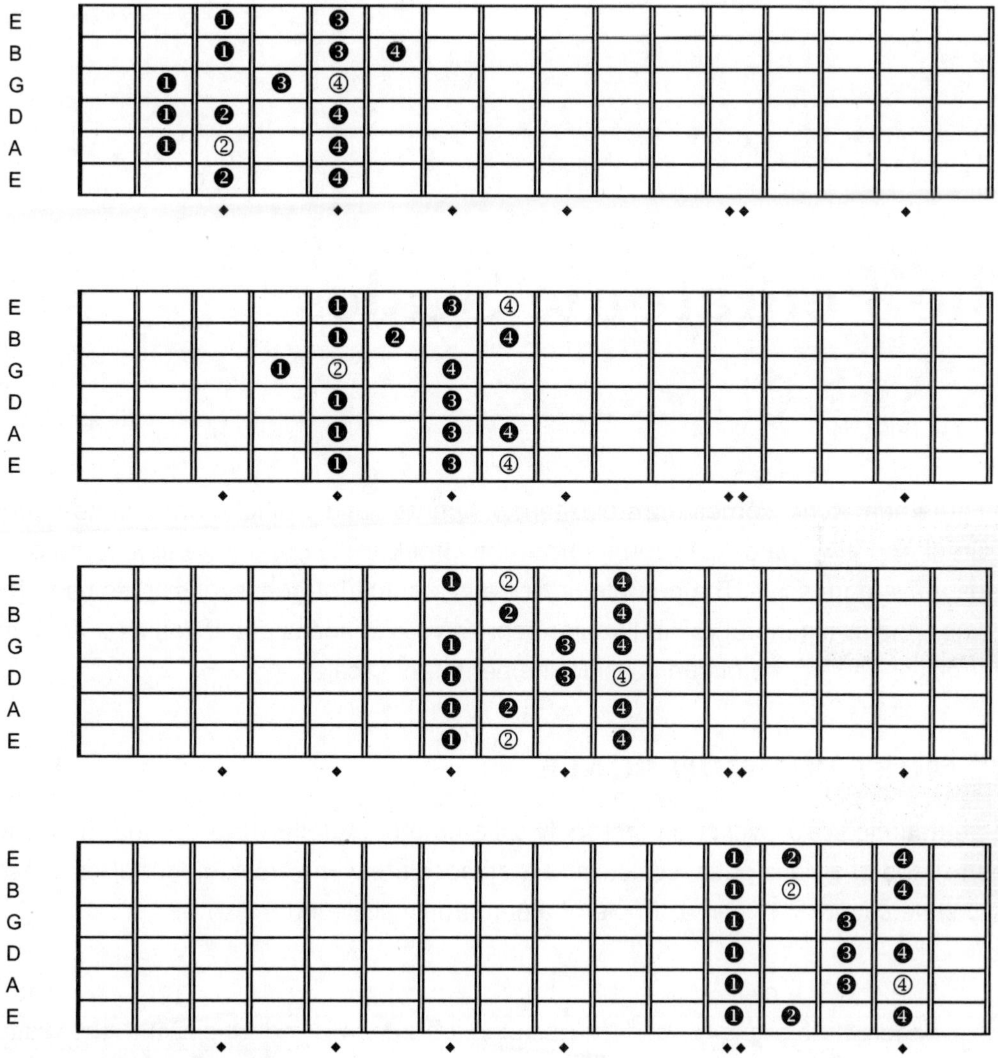

FIGURE 6-10: The C major scale

What you're looking at is four different variations of the same scale. Each scale pattern contains the exact same pitches (C, D, E, F, G, A, B, C). What each diagram shows you is how to play those same pitches, and more importantly, the sounds of those scales in a few spots on your neck. You can start in any position on the neck you choose and go back and forth as you please. Think of them, once again, as a set of possibilities.

7

The Pentatonic Scales

The name pentatonic comes from two terms: "penta" and "tonic." Penta comes from the Greek for "five," and tonic comes from the Greek for "notes." Literally, pentatonic means a five-note scale. The pentatonic scale is a staple of guitar music; it's used for melodies and as a general vocabulary for improvising. Chances are, if you hear another guitar player soloing, he or she is using the pentatonic scale.

THE MOST COMMON SCALE

The pentatonic scale, which is commonly called the pentatonic "box," is the most frequently used of all lead guitar scales, and is an absolutely universal tool for playing lead in any style. Figure 7-1 is an example of a pentatonic scale in the key of A.

FIGURE 7-1

You can see from the music there are only five notes, and they repeat in the same sequence. As you play it, try to visualize the shape your fingers make on the fret board. It's essential to memorize the pattern up and down, because this scale will be your main lead scale.

The example in Figure 7-2 is the same scale shape with the note names (pitches) written beneath. Now you can track which five notes make up the scale, and how they repeat.

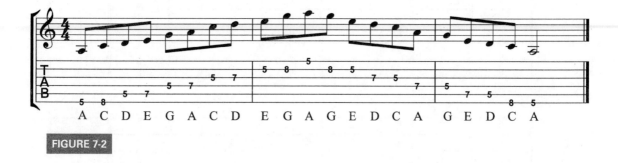

A C D E G A C D E G A G E D C A G E D C A

FIGURE 7-2

No scale is more closely tied to guitar than the pentatonic scale, which you will learn in two varieties: major and minor. These are the most standard pentatonic scales. No mater what style of music you play, you're going to play the pentatonic scales!

THE MAJOR PENTATONIC SCALE IN ALL TWELVE KEYS

The major pentatonic scale is a five-note scale, which in the key of C would contain the notes (C, D, E, G, A), which are also the scale degrees of (1, 2, 3, 5, 6). The major pentatonic scale is immensely popular in practically all genres of music. It's particularly prevalent in folk, bluegrass, country, and rock. You'd use this scale when playing over major chord progressions, or major chord vamps. It's a lovely scale that's hard to make sound bad. See Figure 7-3.

THE MINOR PENTATONIC SCALE IN ALL TWELVE KEYS

There is no scale more important to guitarists than the minor pentatonic scale. The minor pentatonic scale in the key of C would contain the notes (C, E♭, F, G, B♭), which are the scale degrees of (1, ♭3, 4, 5, ♭7). This scale is used in every genre of music, and is the sound of rock 'n' roll and the blues. You'll be hard pressed to find a scale more widely used than the minor pentatonic scale. See Figure 7-4.

FIGURE 7-3: C MAJOR PENTATONIC

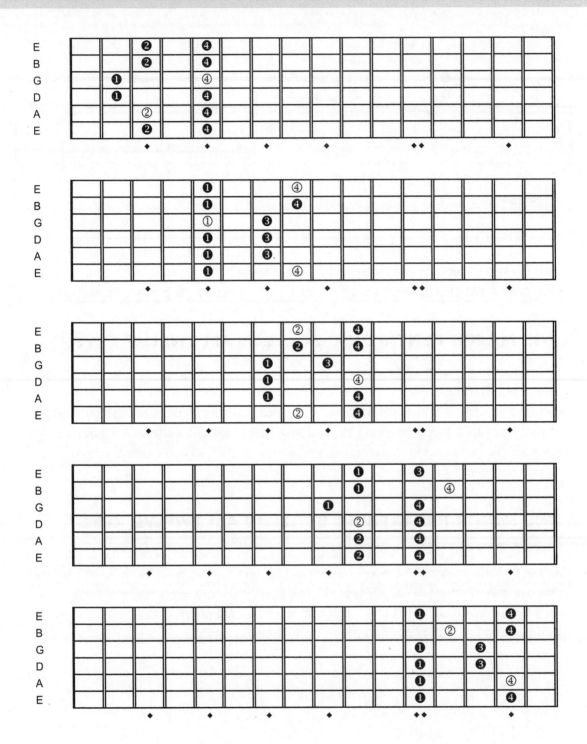

FIGURE 7-3: C#/D♭ MAJOR PENTATONIC

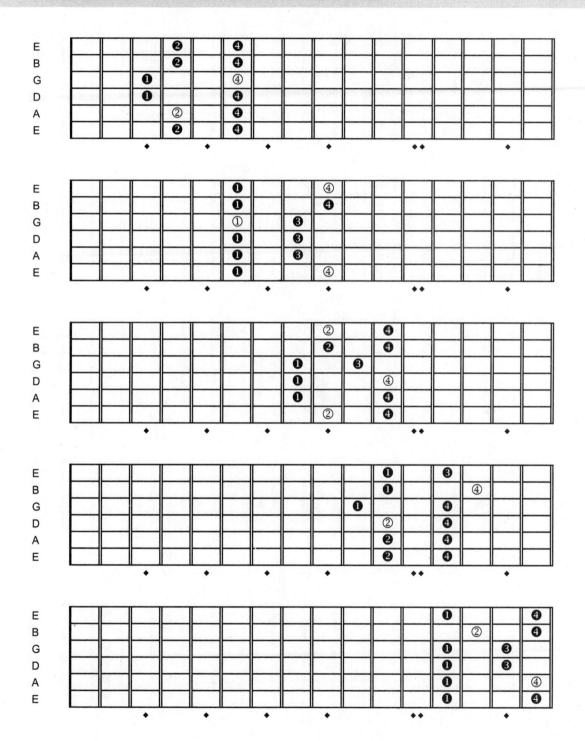

FIGURE 7-3: D MAJOR PENTATONIC

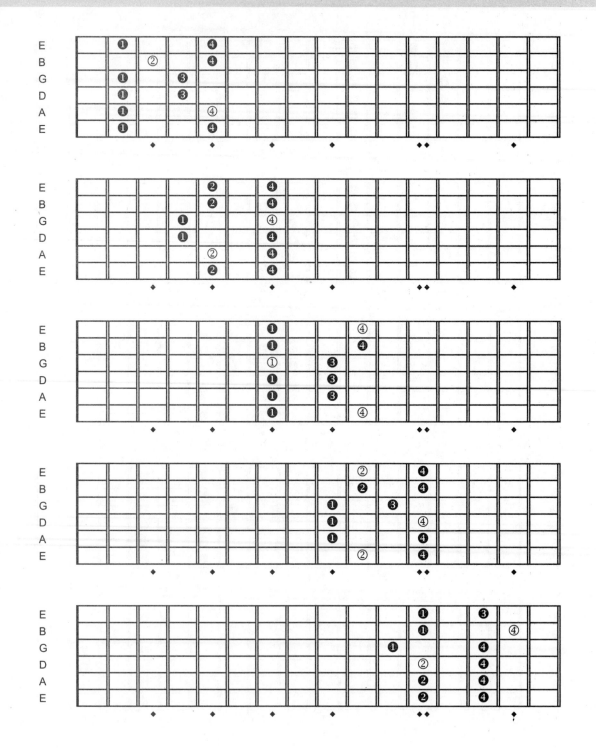

FIGURE 7-3: D♯/E♭ MAJOR PENTATONIC

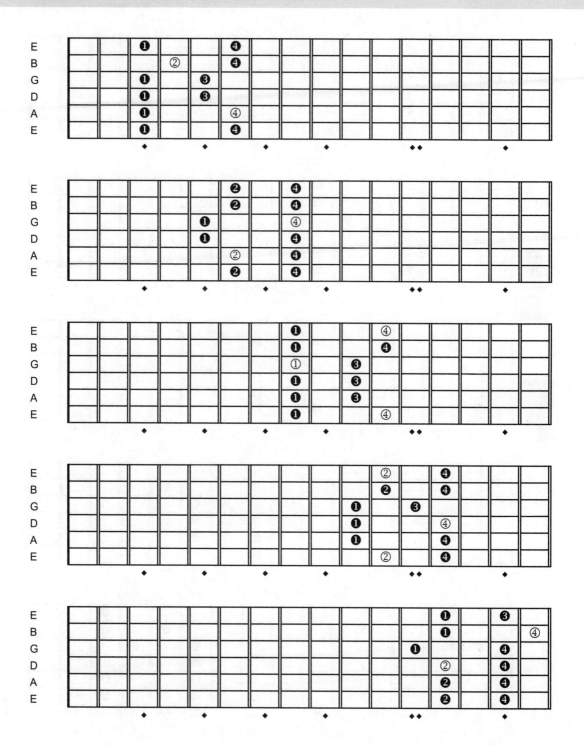

FIGURE 7-3: E MAJOR PENTATONIC

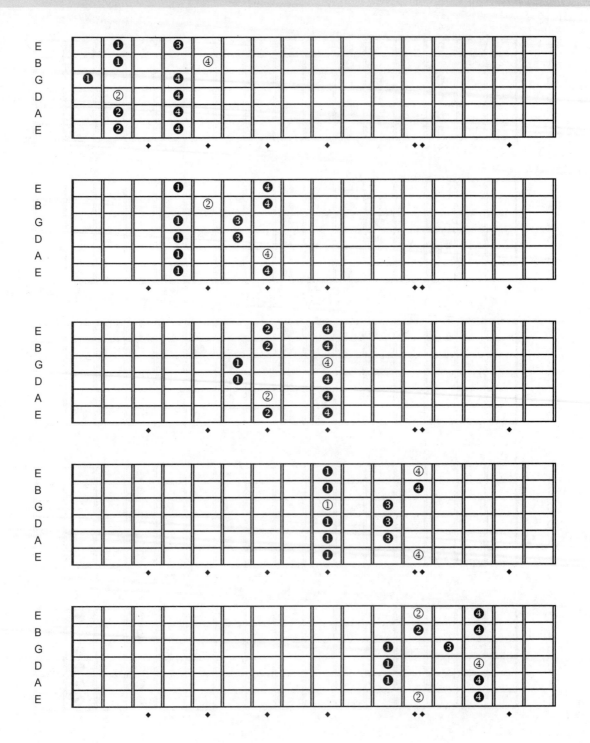

FIGURE 7-3: F MAJOR PENTATONIC

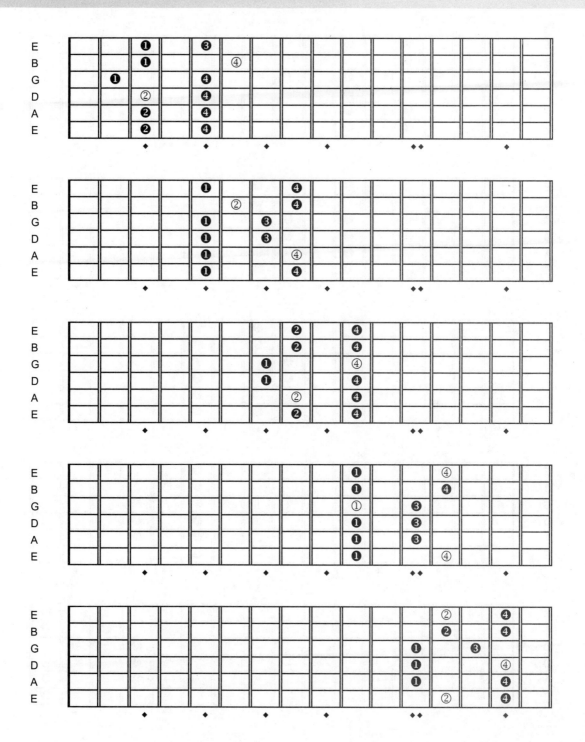

FIGURE 7-3: F#/G♭ MAJOR PENTATONIC

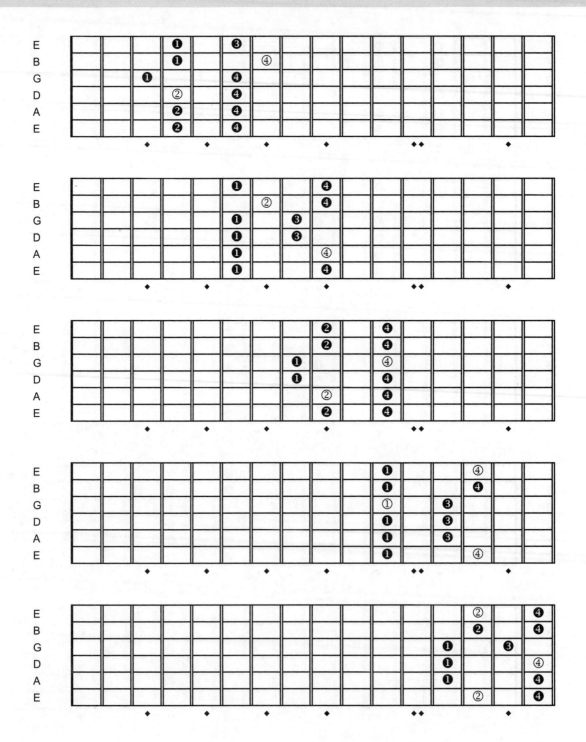

FIGURE 7-3: G MAJOR PENTATONIC

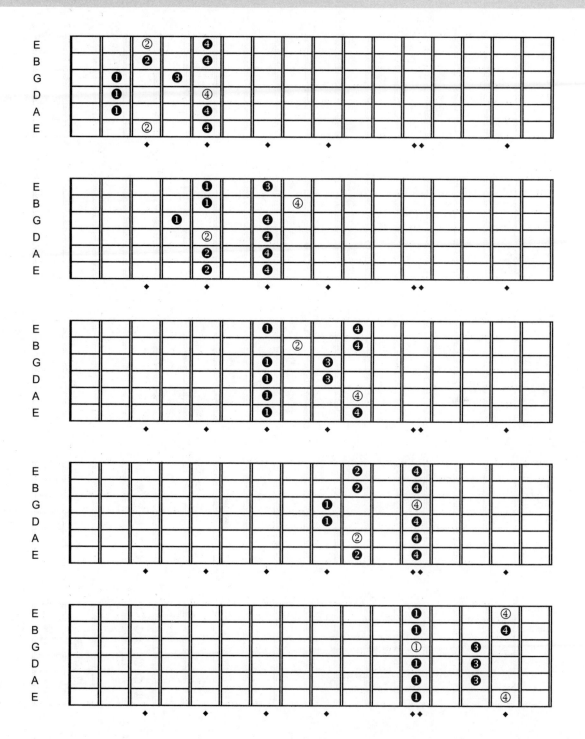

FIGURE 7-3: G♯/A♭ MAJOR PENTATONIC

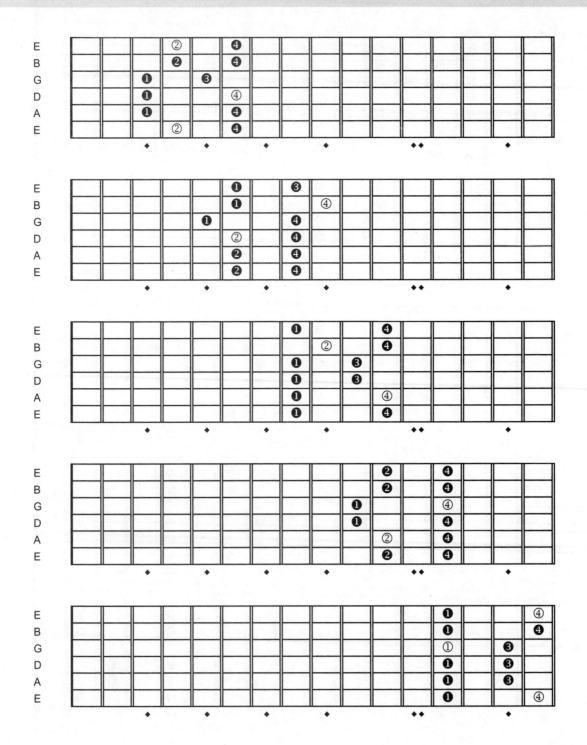

FIGURE 7-3: A MAJOR PENTATONIC

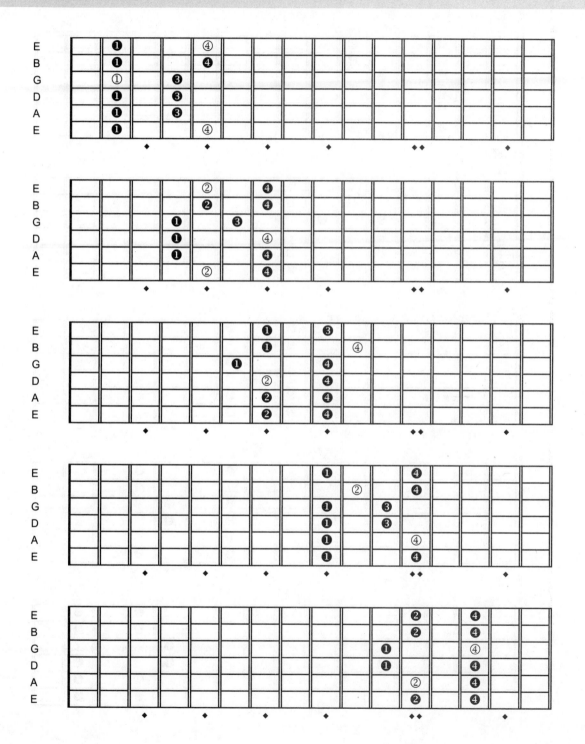

FIGURE 7-3: A♯/B♭ MAJOR PENTATONIC

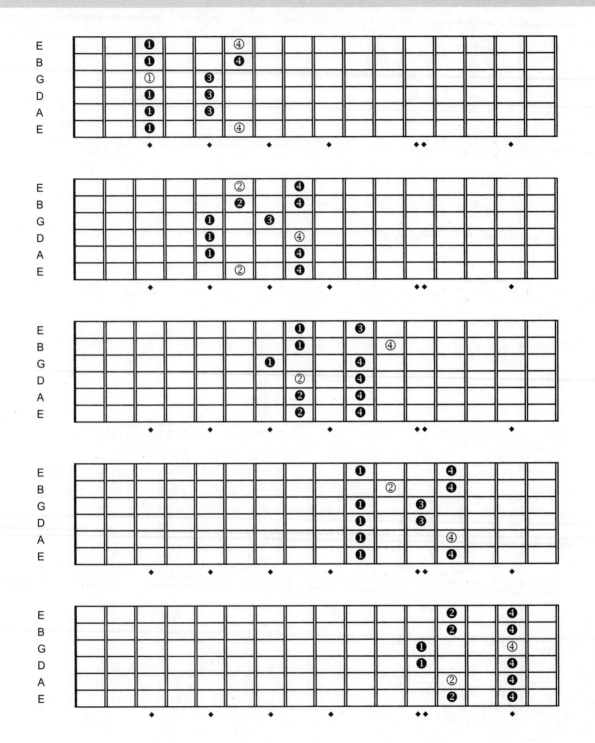

FIGURE 7-3: B MAJOR PENTATONIC

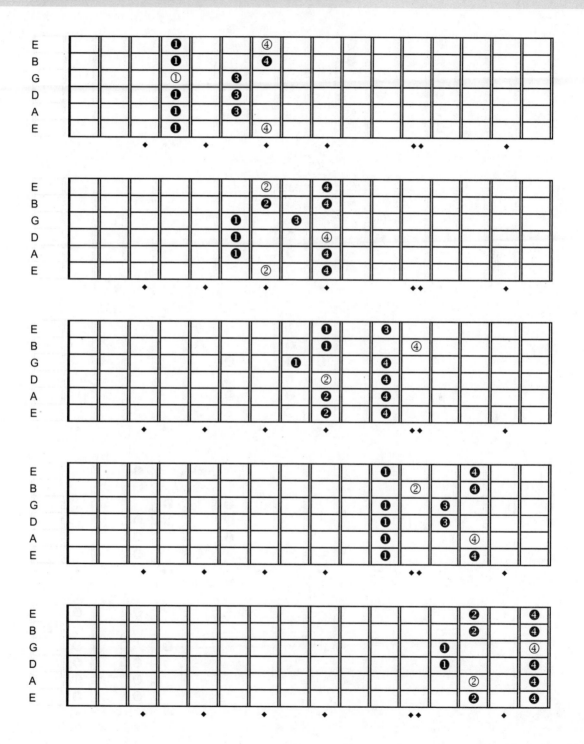

FIGURE 7-4: C MINOR PENTATONIC

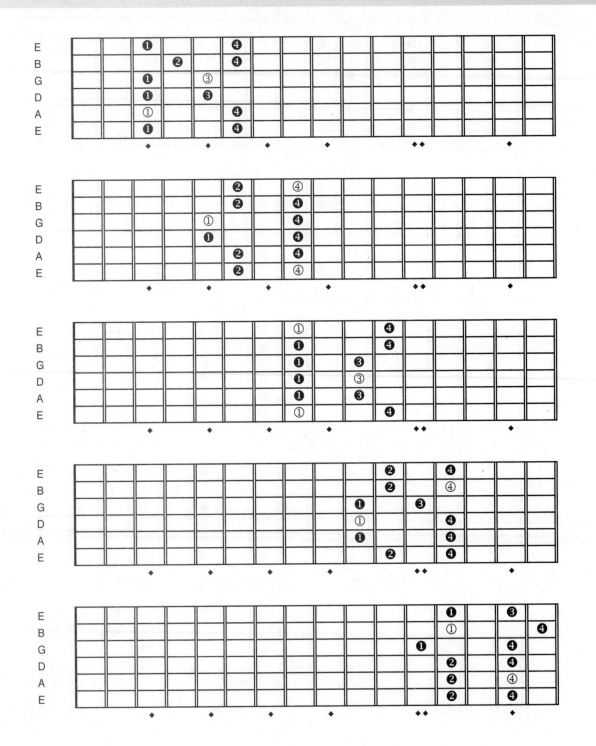

FIGURE 7-4: C#/D♭ MINOR PENTATONIC

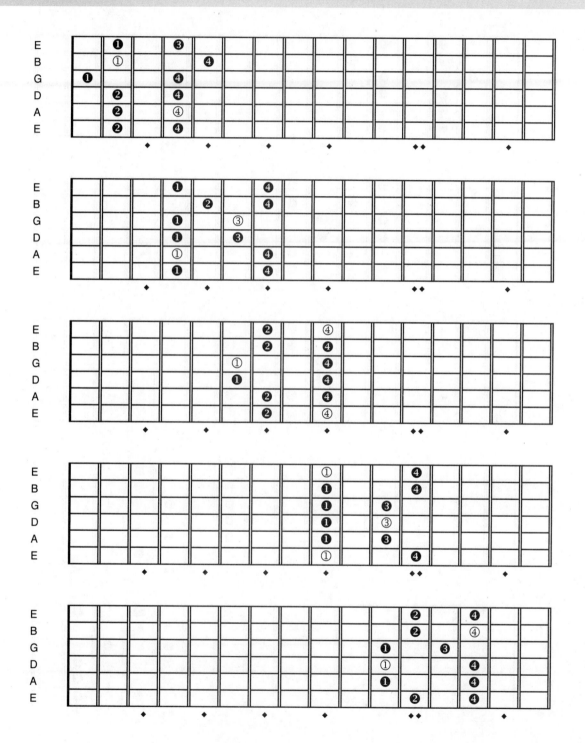

FIGURE 7-4: D MINOR PENTATONIC

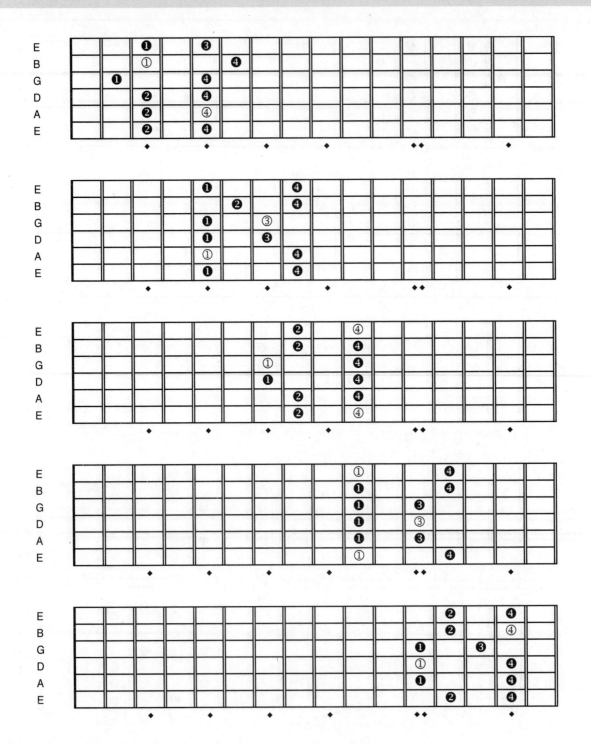

FIGURE 7-4: D♯/E♭ MINOR PENTATONIC

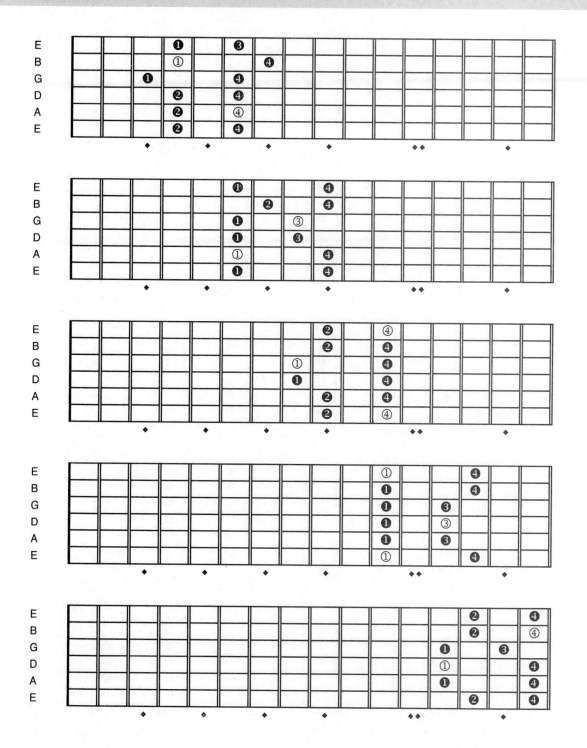

FIGURE 7-4: E MINOR PENTATONIC

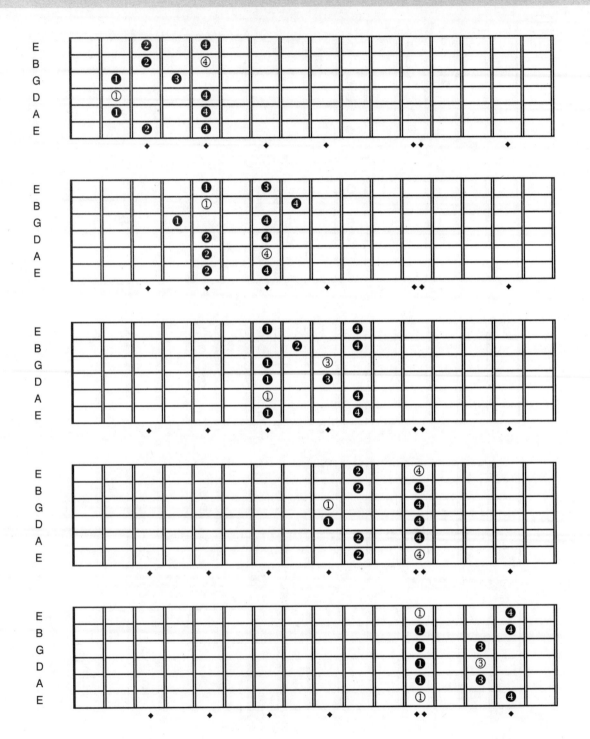

FIGURE 7-4: F MINOR PENTATONIC

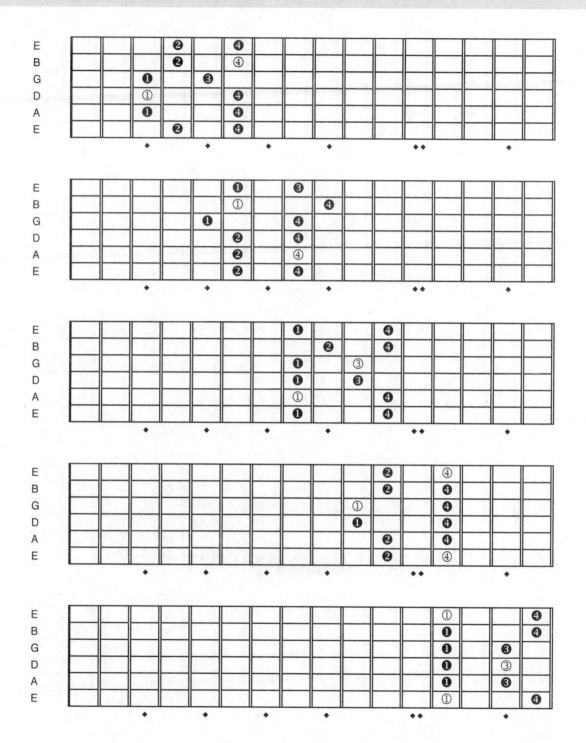

FIGURE 7-4: F♯/G♭ MINOR PENTATONIC

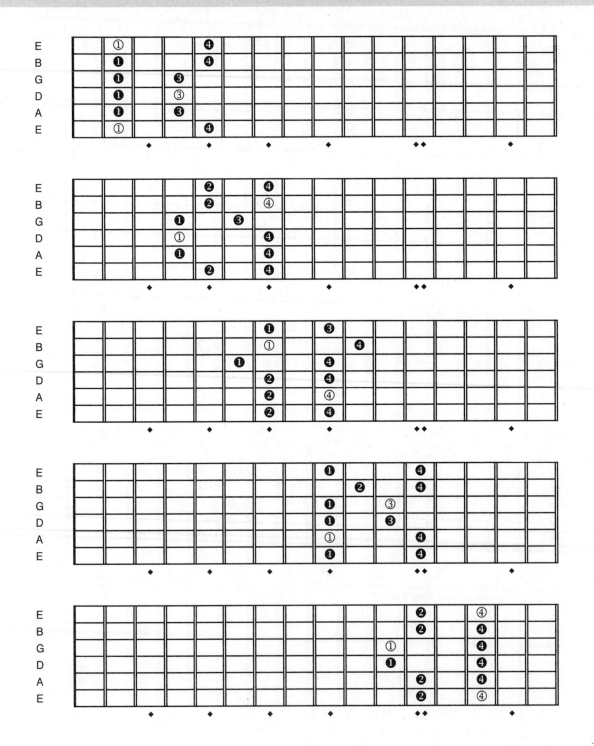

FIGURE 7-4: G MINOR PENTATONIC

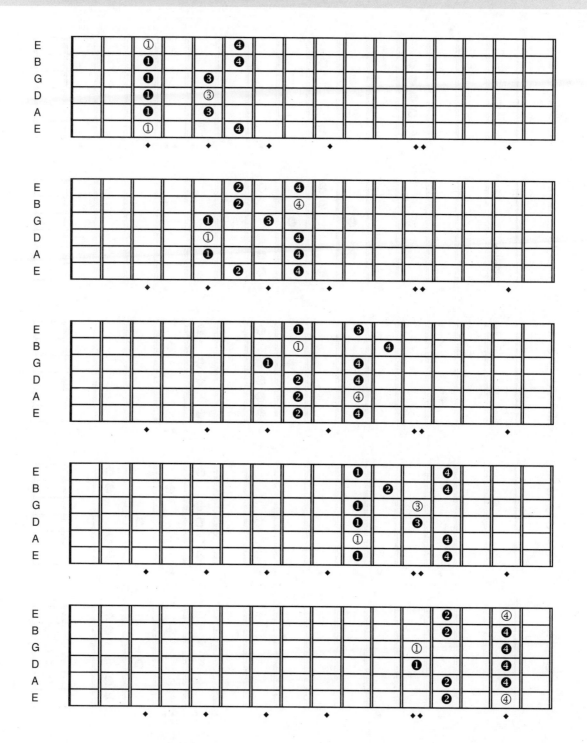

FIGURE 7-4: G♯/A♭ MINOR PENTATONIC

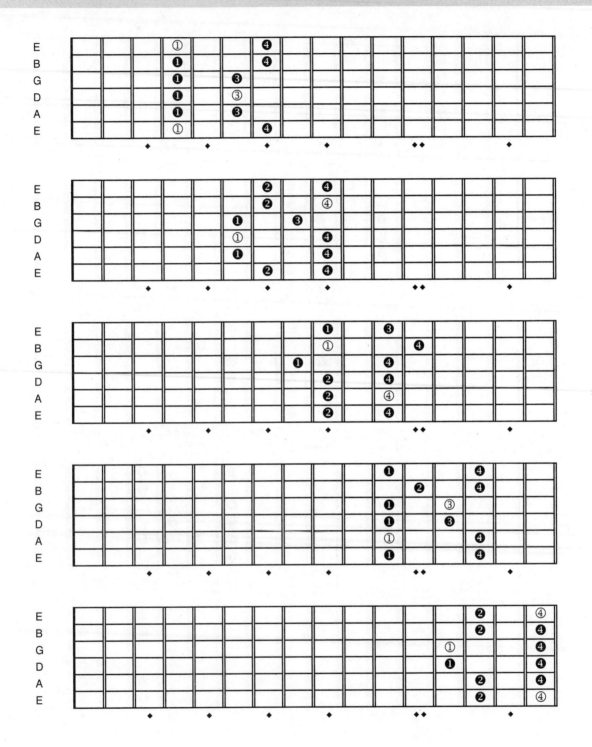

FIGURE 7-4: A MINOR PENTATONIC

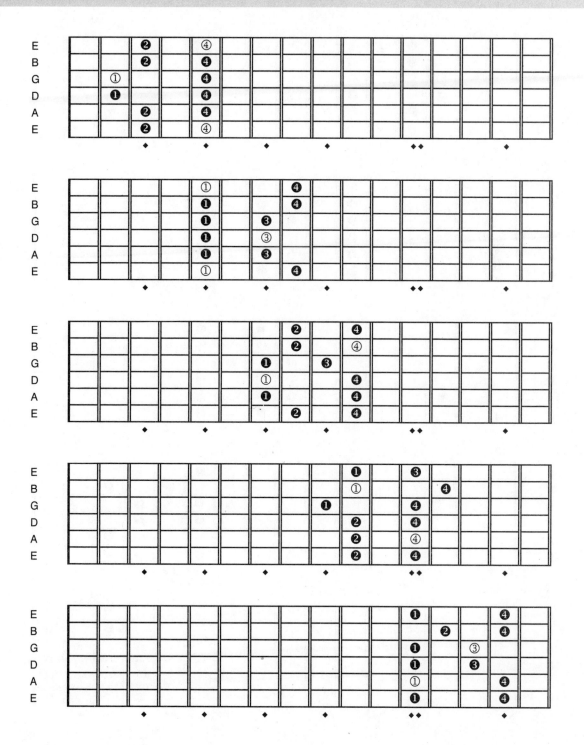

FIGURE 7-4: A♯/B♭ MINOR PENTATONIC

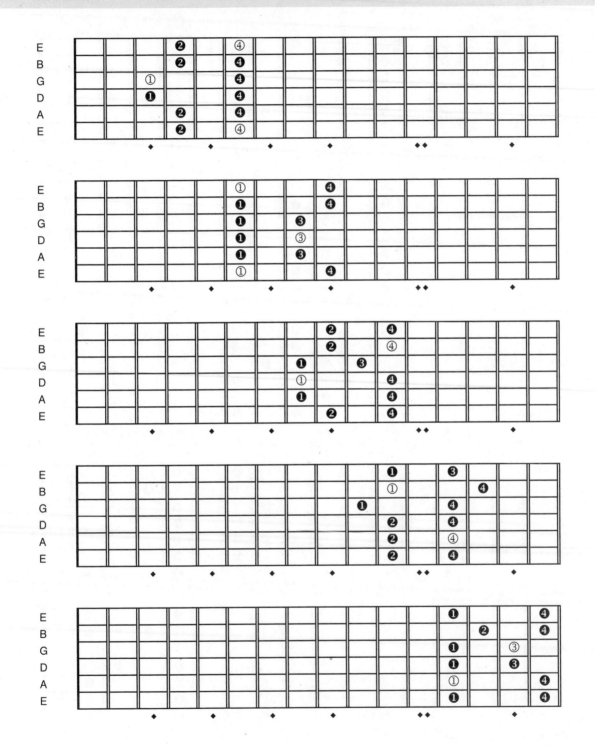

FIGURE 7-4: B MINOR PENTATONIC

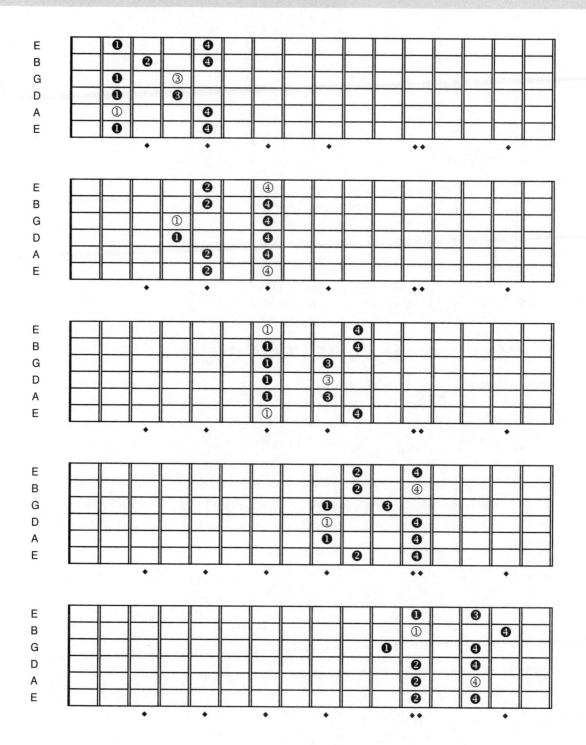

8

The Major Scale

The major scale, a seven-note scale, is one of the underpinnings of traditional harmony and is a great resource for melodies. The major scale is thousands of years old, and you'll find it in literally all genres of music. Being able to play major scales could well be your first step into music theory and to unlocking your guitar.

THE MAJOR/IONIAN SCALE IN ALL TWELVE KEYS

The major scale in C would spell as (C, D, E, F, G, A, B, C). Since every scale in this book relates to the major scale, its scale degrees are (1, 2, 3, 4, 5, 6, 7). This scale has ties to the old church modes, which originate from the Greek music system. Due to this fact, you'll see this scale referred to as "the major scale" and as "the Ionian mode." Either way, it's the same scale.

The major scale is used for soloing and creating melodies in major keys. You hear it in virtually every style of music, and it's got that calming, yet happy feeling when you play it. It's also a staple of classical music melodies, so don't be surprised if you accidentally find some familiar melodies! See Figure 8-1.

FIGURE 8-1: C MAJOR

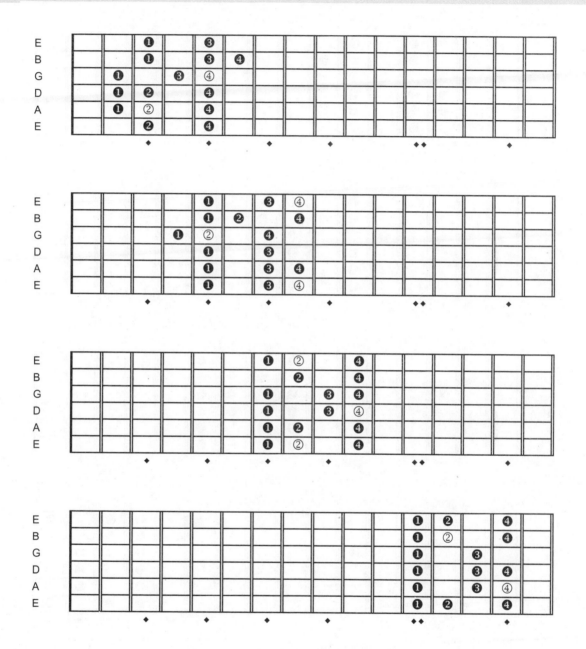

FIGURE 8-1: C♯/D♭ MAJOR

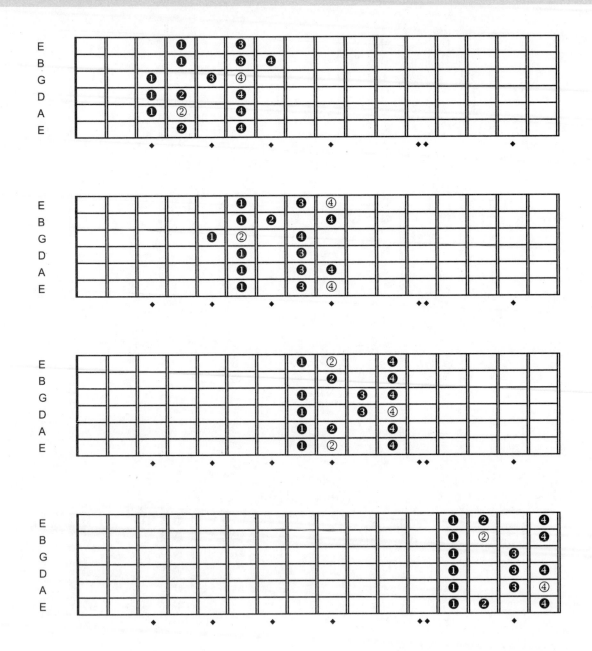

FIGURE 8-1: D MAJOR

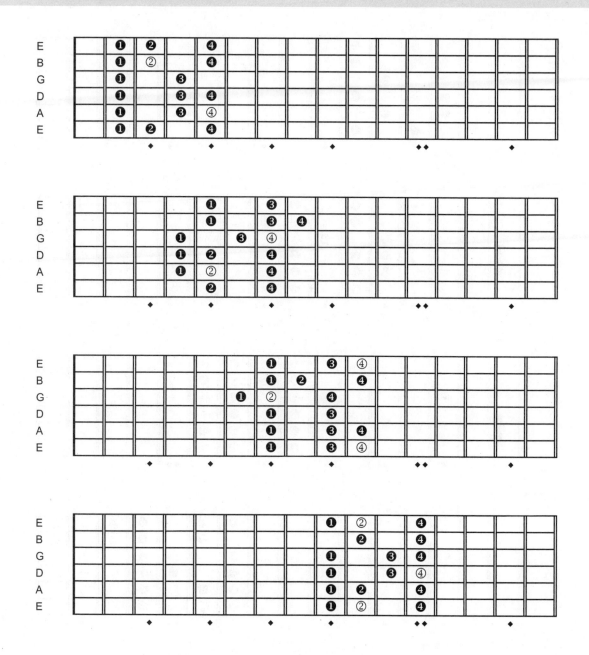

FIGURE 8-1: D♯/E♭ MAJOR

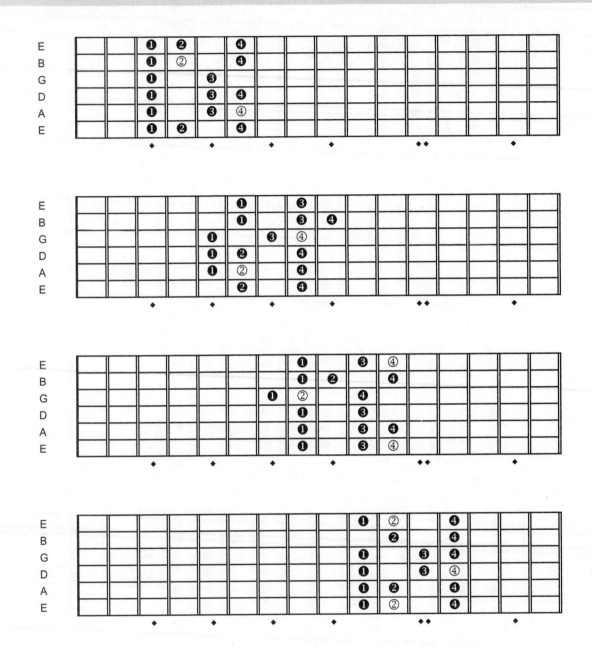

FIGURE 8-1: E MAJOR

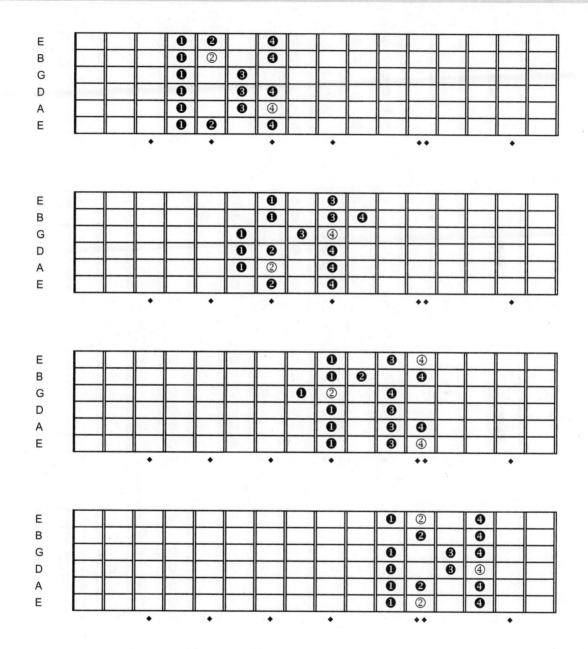

FIGURE 8-1: F MAJOR

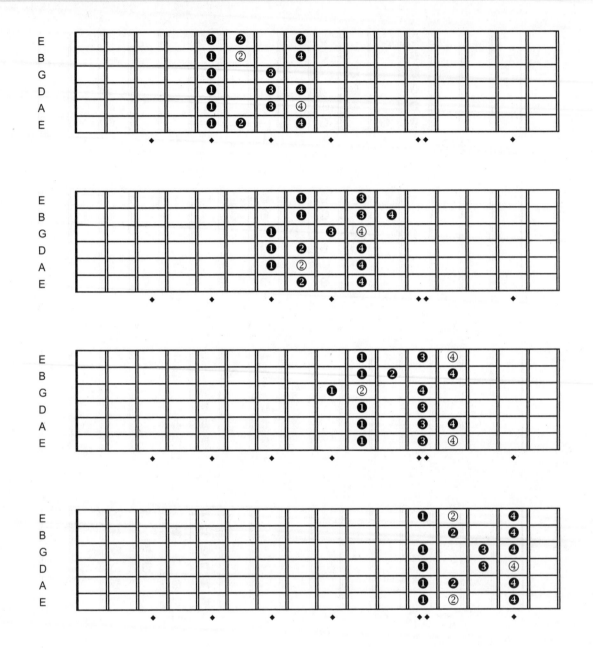

FIGURE 8-1: F♯/G♭ MAJOR

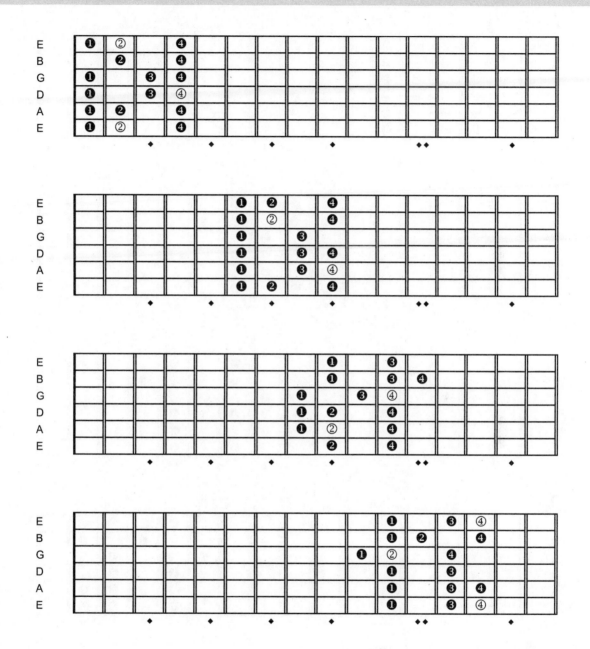

FIGURE 8-1: G MAJOR

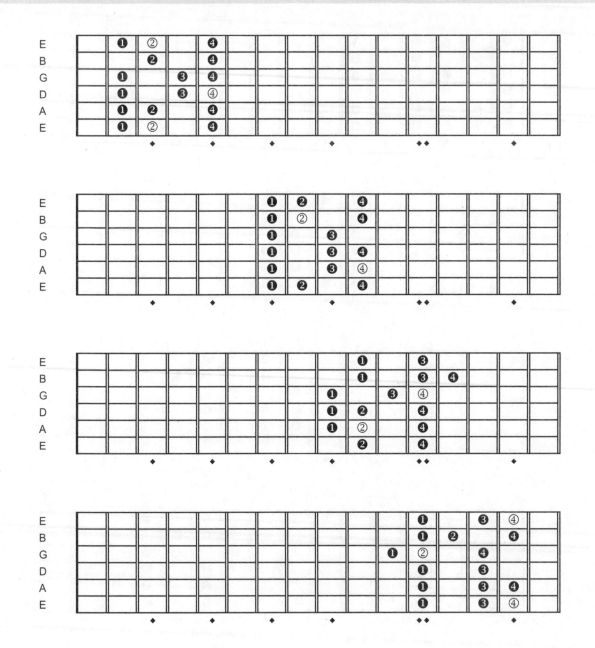

FIGURE 8-1: G♯/A♭ MAJOR

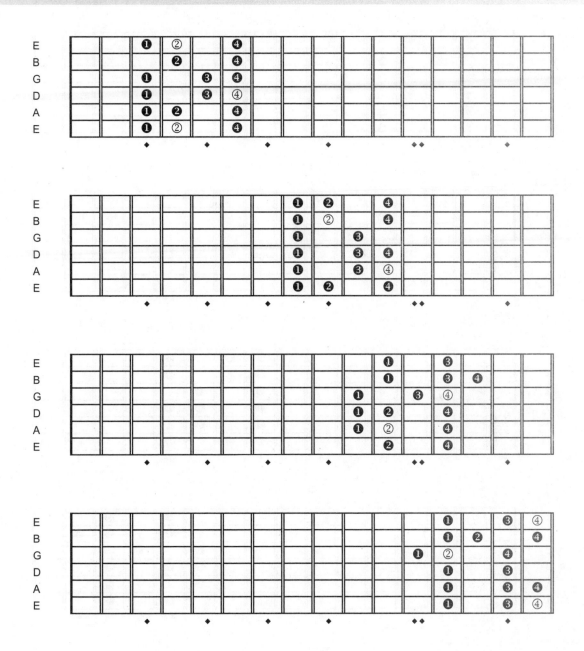

FIGURE 8-1: A MAJOR

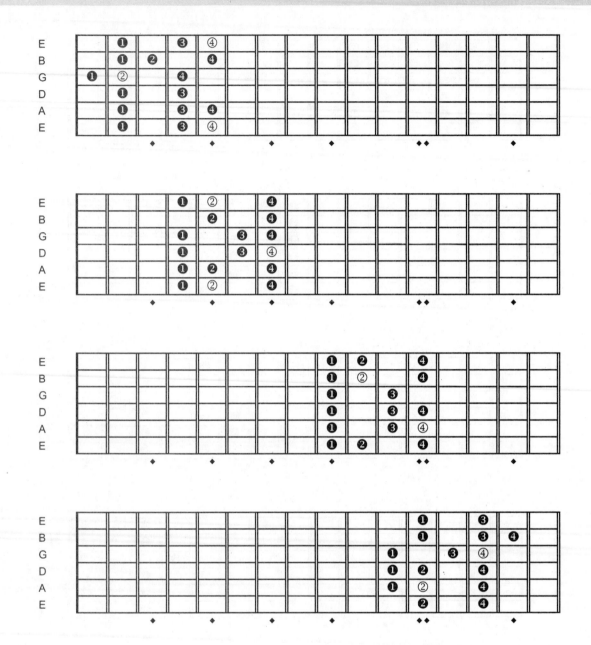

FIGURE 8-1: A♯/B♭ MAJOR

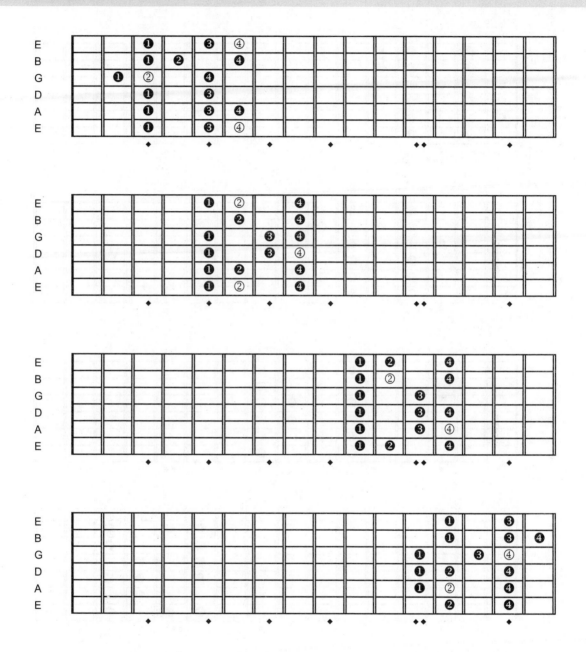

FIGURE 8-1: B MAJOR

9

The Minor Scale

The other staple of music theory is the minor scale/key, which is the other most commonly used scale and tonality in all of music. Minor scales encompass the darker, sadder sounds in music. You'll find minor scales in almost all styles of music, especially rock, jazz, and classical. No player's repertoire would be complete without some knowledge of the minor scale.

THE MINOR/AEOLIAN SCALE IN ALL TWELVE KEYS

If the major scale is the calming and happy scale, then the minor scale is its alter-ego—darker and more melancholy. The minor scale in C would use the notes (C, D, E♭, F, G, A♭, B♭, C), and its formula in scale degrees would be (1, 2, ♭3, 4, 5, ♭6, ♭7). You find the minor scale (yet again) in almost all styles of music, but you hear it in rock, hard rock, metal, Latin, jazz, and classical most often. You'd use it to improvise over minor chord progressions/keys. The minor scale is another vestige from the ancient church modes, and it goes by the alternate name "the Aeolian mode." Both names refer to the same scale. See Figure 9-1.

FIGURE 9-1: C MINOR

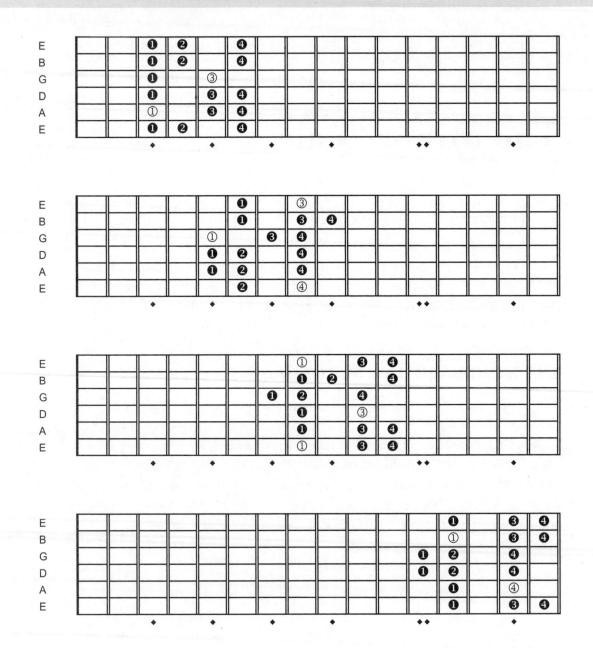

FIGURE 9-1: C♯/D♭ MINOR

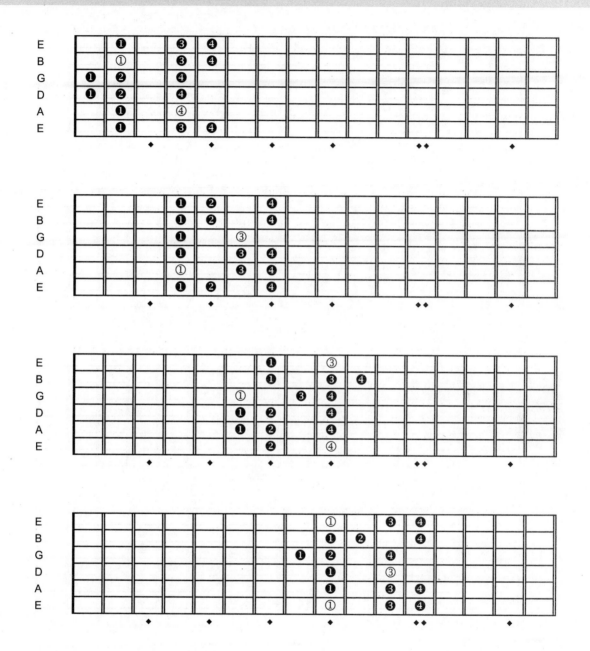

FIGURE 9-1: D MINOR

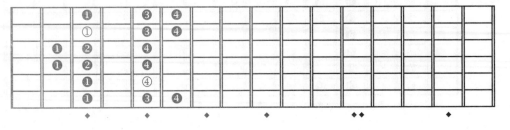

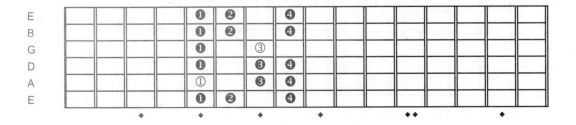

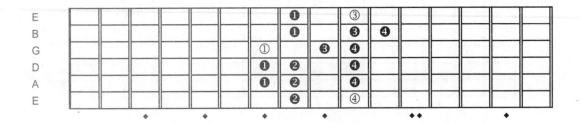

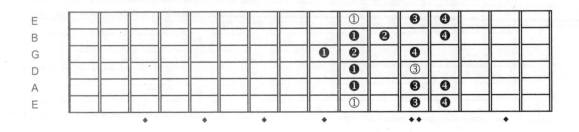

FIGURE 9-1: D♯/E♭ MINOR

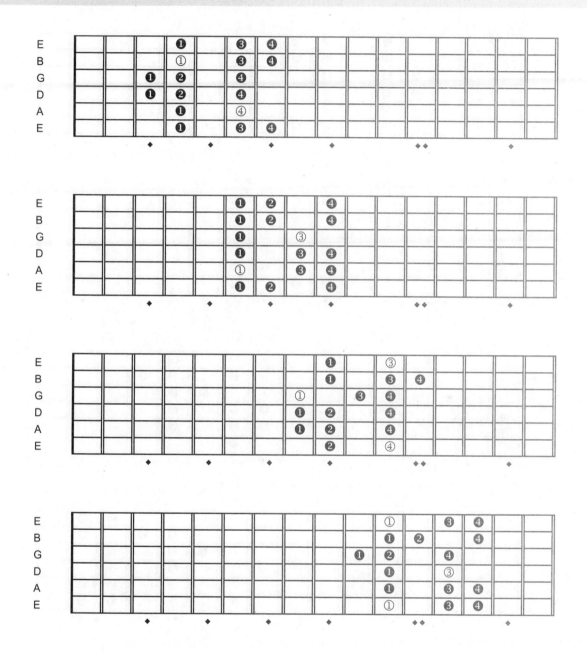

FIGURE 9-1: E MINOR

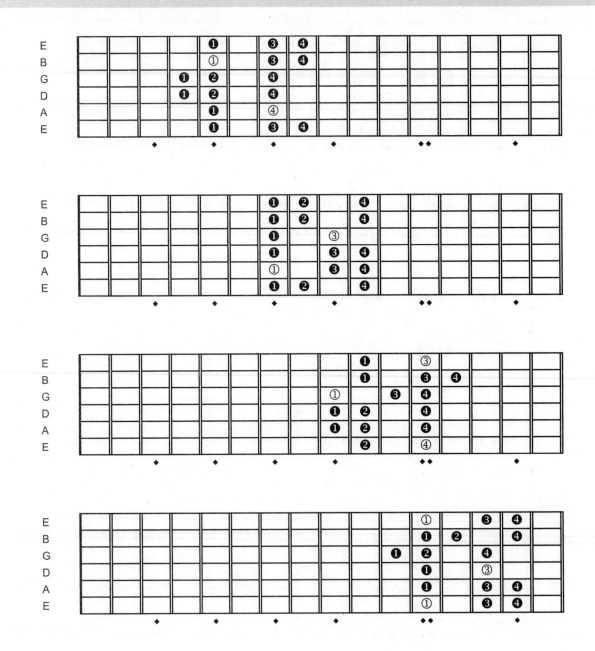

FIGURE 9-1: F MINOR

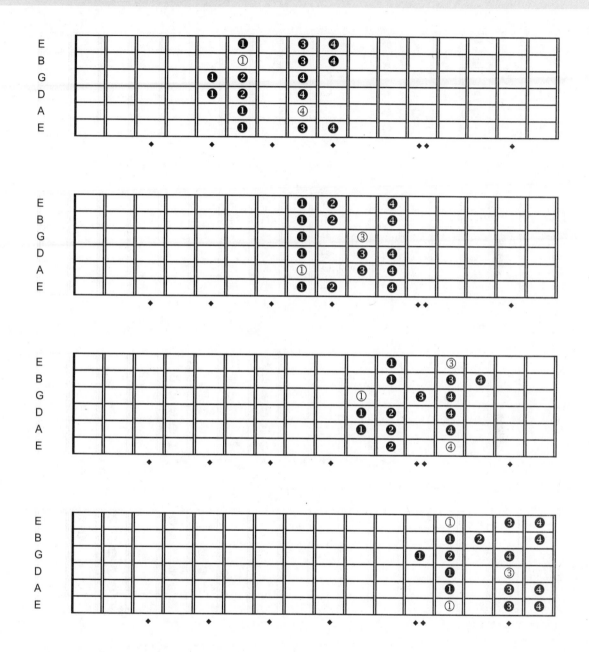

FIGURE 9-1: F♯/G♭ MINOR

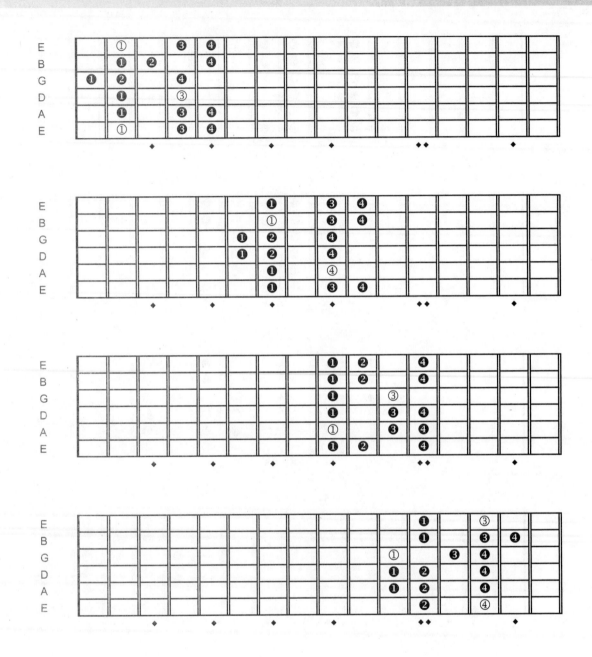

FIGURE 9-1: G MINOR

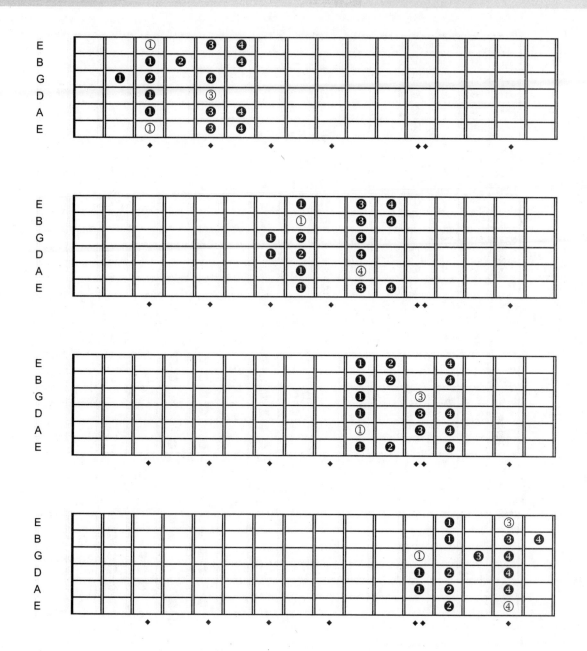

FIGURE 9-1: G♯/A♭ MINOR

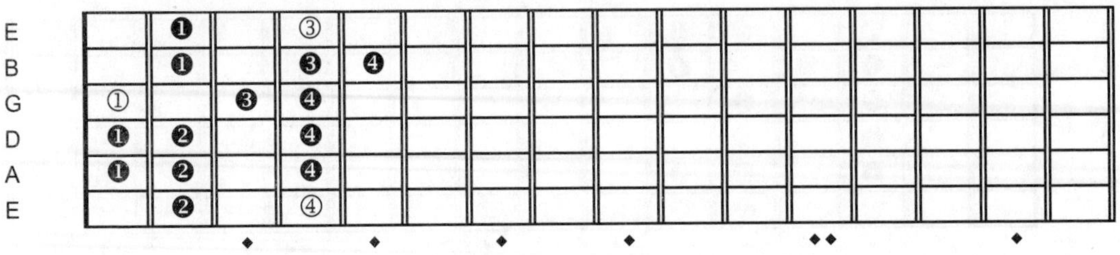

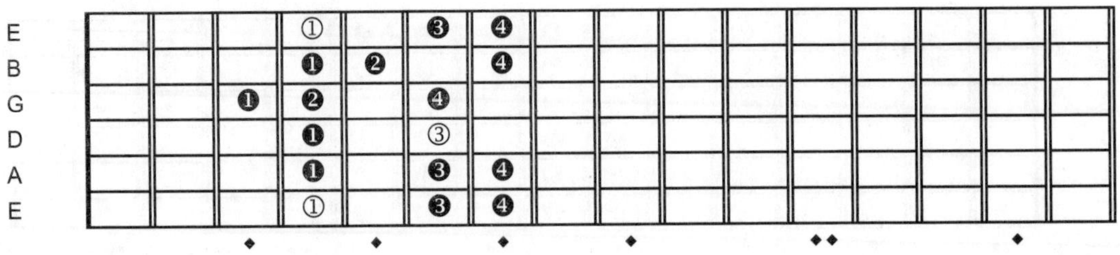

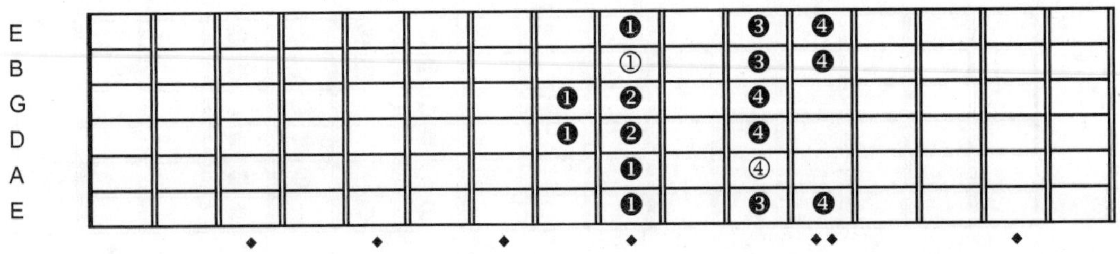

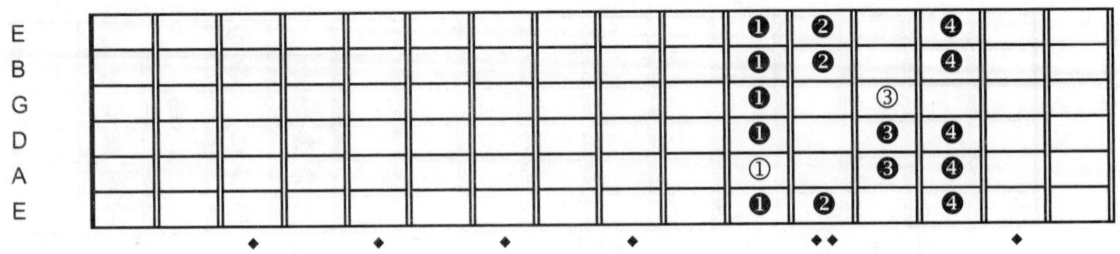

FIGURE 9-1: A MINOR

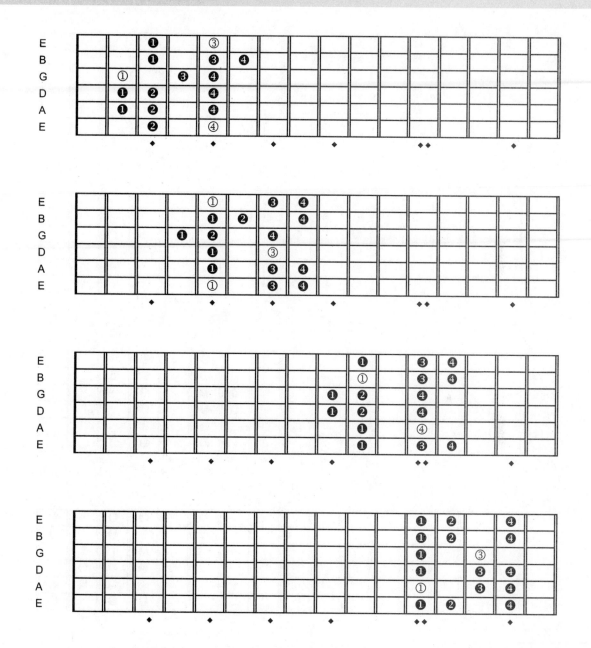

FIGURE 9-1: A♯/B♭ MINOR

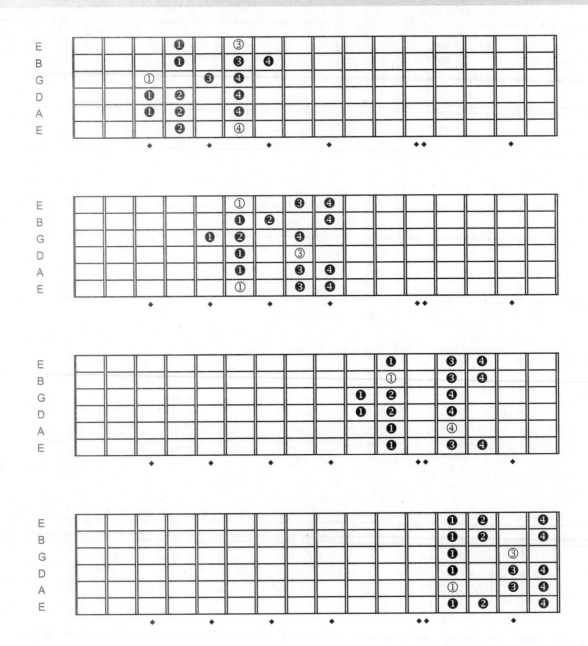

FIGURE 9-1: B MINOR

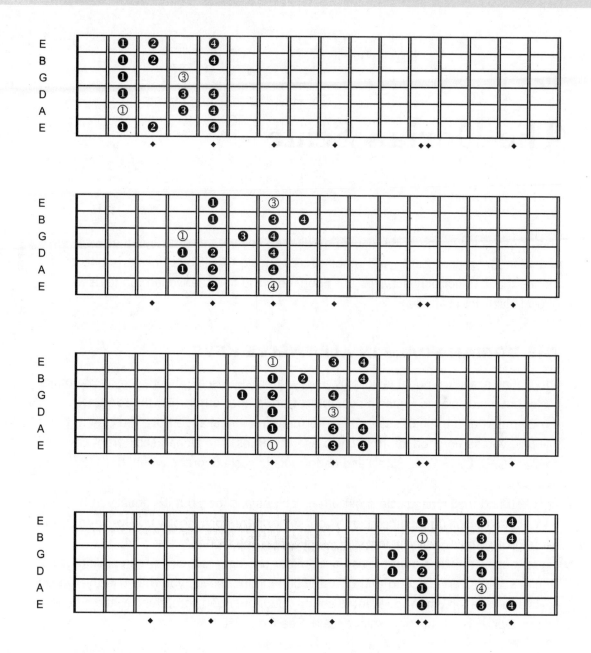

10

The Dorian Scale

The Dorian scale is one of the church modes, an ancient set of scales that were used widely in Gregorian chants and other sacred music. The Dorian scale is one of the modes that has not only survived but flourished. You find the Dorian mode use extensively in jazz, for example.

THE DORIAN SCALE IN ALL TWELVE KEYS

The Dorian scale (or mode) is actually a very interesting scale. It's based on the major scale, but it's displaced (meaning you start from a note other than the root). Dorian is the 2nd mode of the major scale. This information won't change how you play it, but it will give you some good information to use at parties! The Dorian scale from C would spell as (C, D, E♭, F, G, A, B♭, C) and its formula in scale degrees would be (1, 2, ♭3, 4, 5, 6, ♭7).

You find the Dorian scale most often in blues and jazz, but it's equally at home in rock. If you're looking to supercharge your minor pentatonic scale, try Dorian from the same root instead. Typically, most musicians play the Dorian scale when they are trying to create melodies or improvise over minor chords. Also, since the spelling of the Dorian scale is very close to that of a traditional minor scale, you may use the Dorian scale as a variation when you want to sound minor but need something a little different. In jazz, Dorian is the de facto minor scale. See Figure 10-1.

FIGURE 10-1: C DORIAN

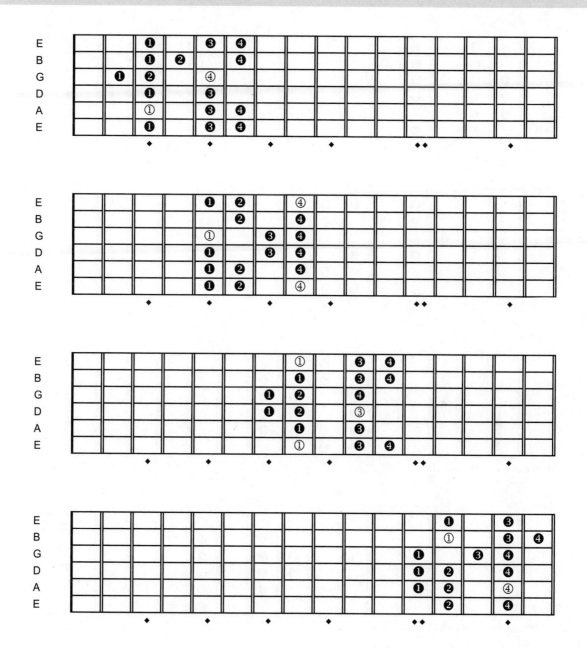

FIGURE 10-1: C#/Db DORIAN

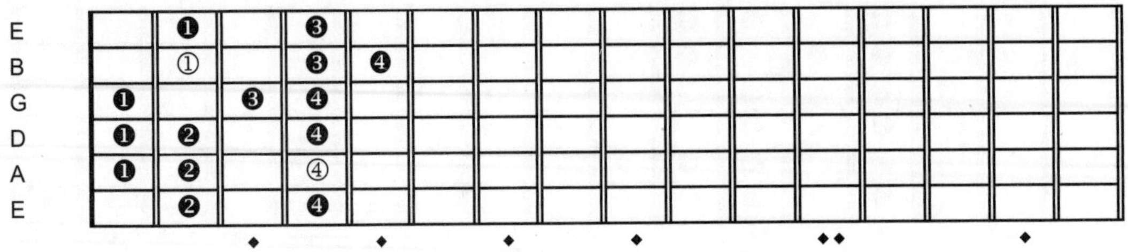

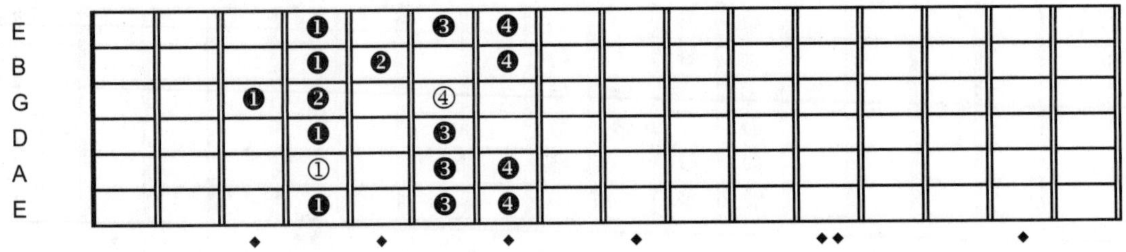

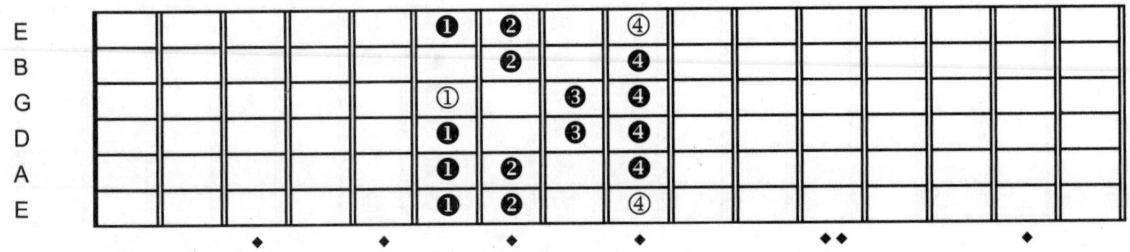

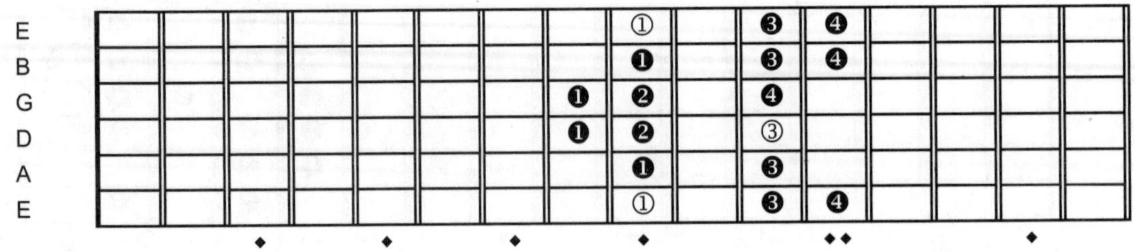

FIGURE 10-1: D DORIAN

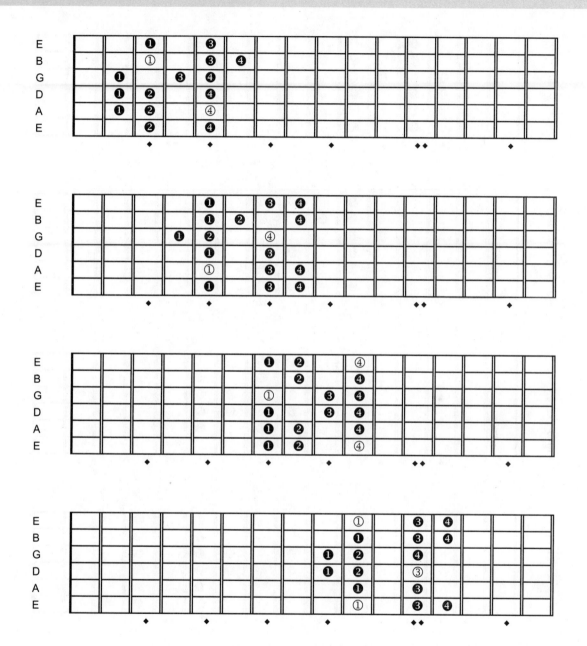

FIGURE 10-1: D♯/E♭ DORIAN

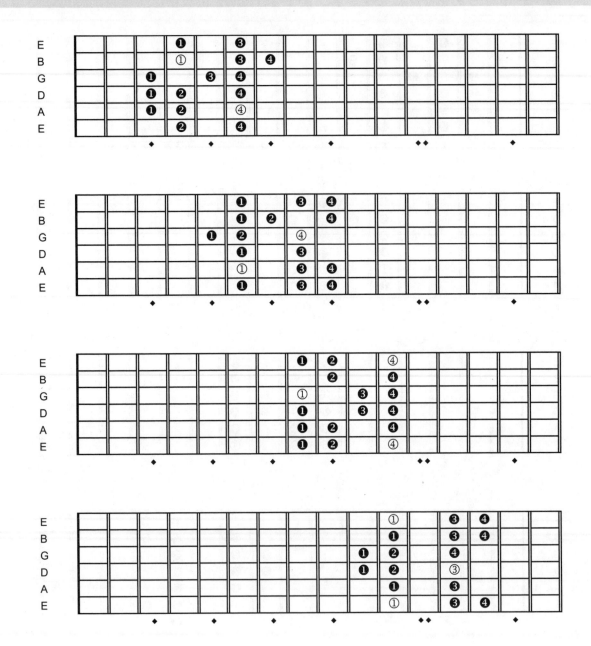

FIGURE 10-1: E DORIAN

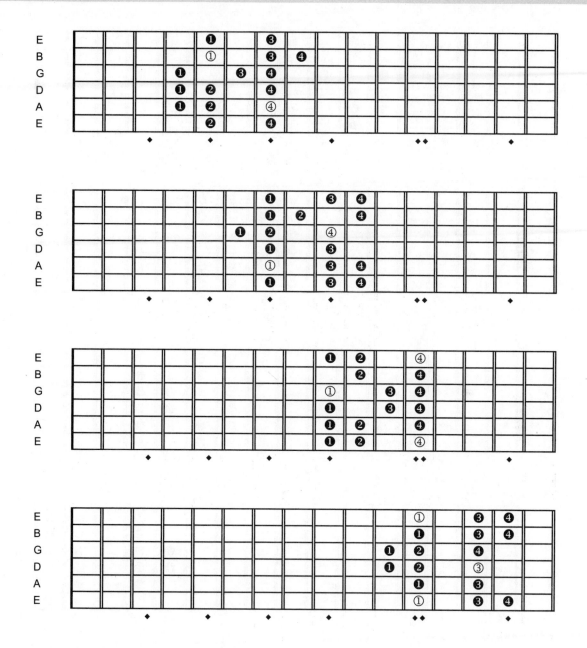

FIGURE 10-1: F DORIAN

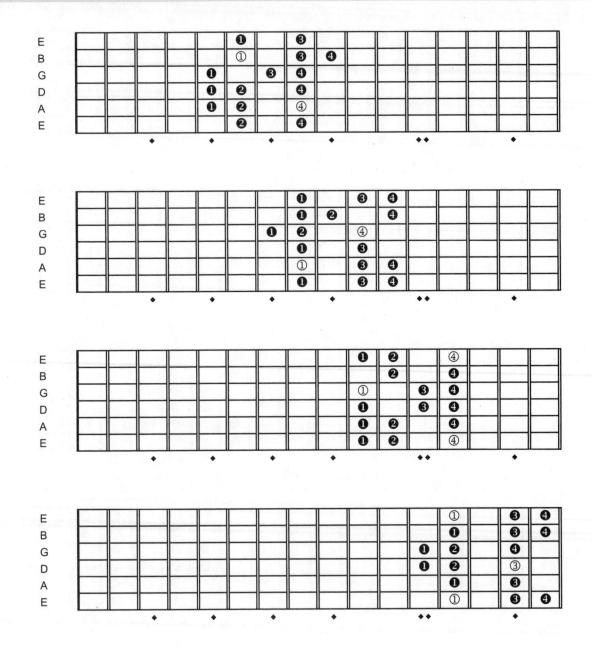

FIGURE 10-1: F♯/G♭ DORIAN

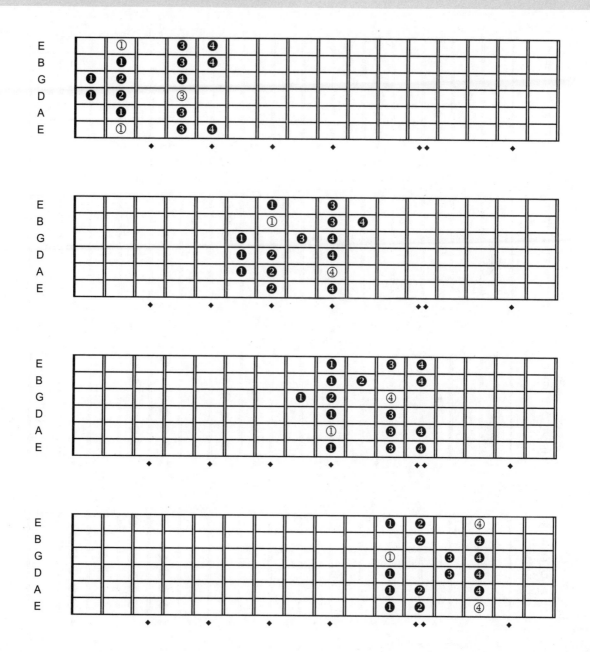

FIGURE 10-1: G DORIAN

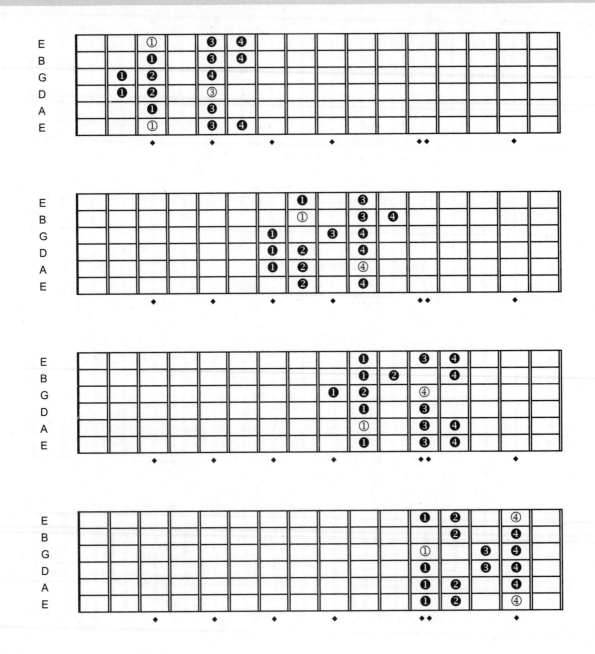

FIGURE 10-1: G♯/A♭ DORIAN

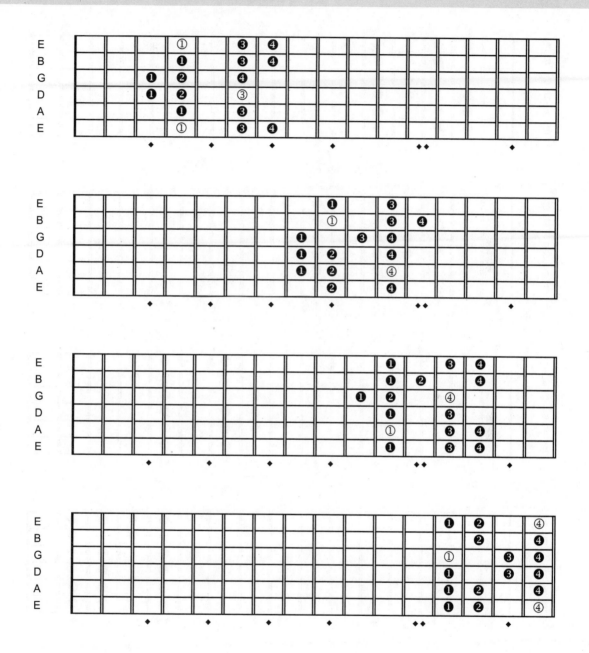

FIGURE 10-1: A DORIAN

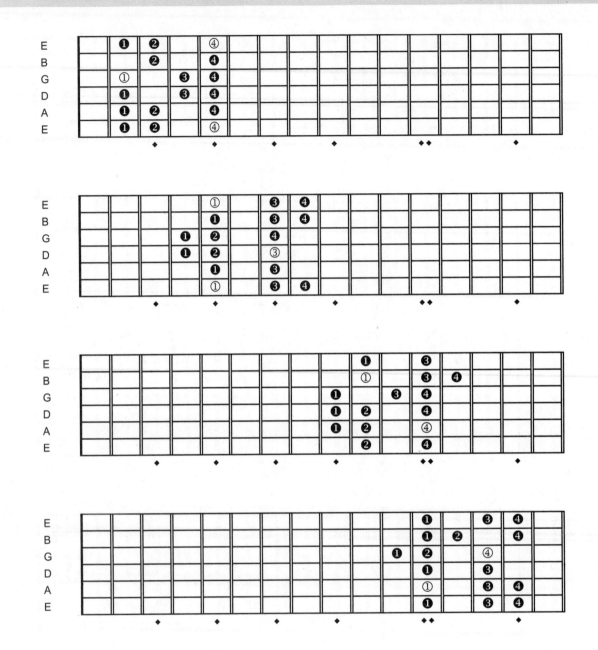

FIGURE 10-1: A#/B♭ DORIAN

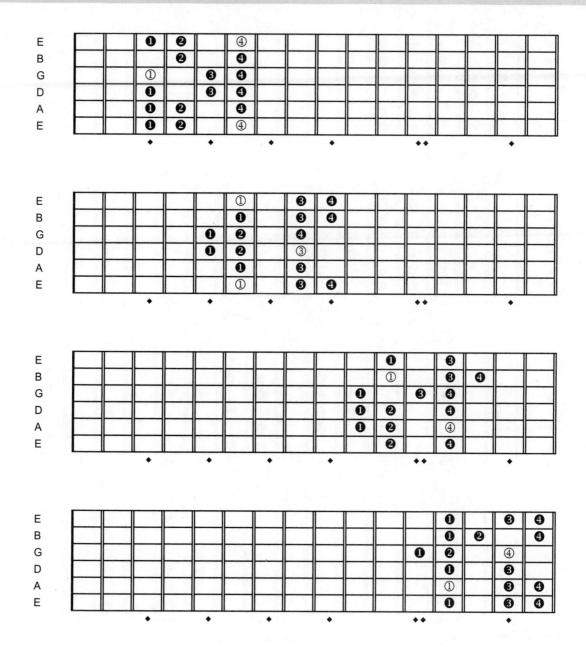

FIGURE 10-1: B DORIAN

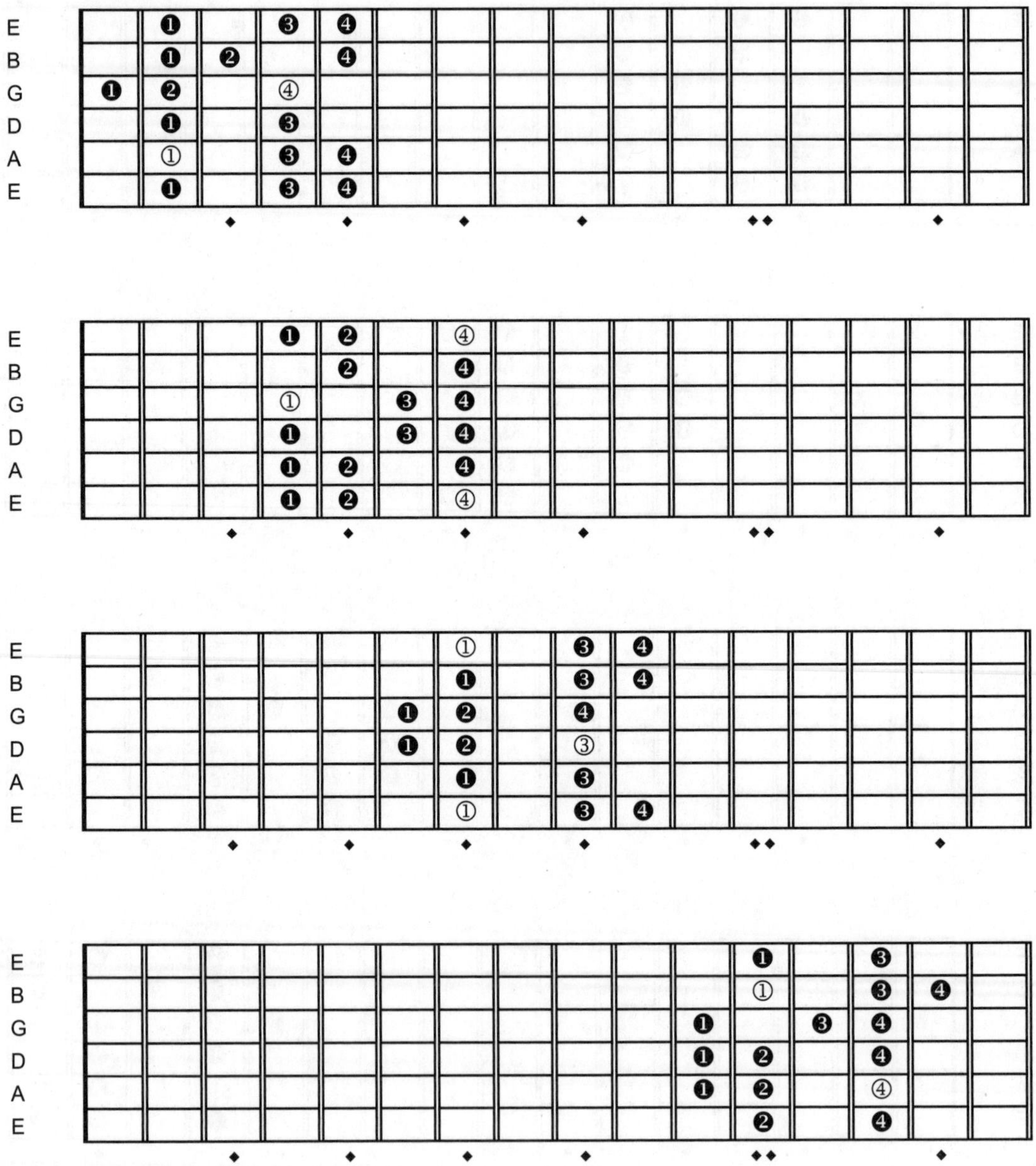

11

The Mixolydian Scale

The Mixolydian scale is another of the church modes, an ancient set of scales that were used widely in Gregorian chants and other sacred music. The Mixolydian is an extremely popular scale that has seen adoption in rock and blues music. The Mixolydian mode is a darker, blusier major scale that highlights the dominant, or flat, seventh scale degree. Not just for jazz and blues musicians, this mode is a staple of Celtic and other traditional northern European music.

THE MIXOLYDIAN SCALE IN ALL TWELVE KEYS

The Mixolydian scale is another really old scale that refuses to go away. The Mixolydian scale is derived from a single major scale, just displaced. (Mixolydian is the 5th mode of the major scale.) In C, the scale spells as (C, D, E, F, G, A, B♭, C) and its formula in scale degrees is (1, 2, 3, 4, 5, 6, ♭7).

The Mixolydian scale sounds like a bluesy major scale and is used in rock, blues, jazz, and jam band music. It's a favorite scale of Jerry Garcia and others in the jam band movement. It's a perfect blues scale, ripe with possibilities and beautiful melodic tools. In addition to its bluesy vibe, it's one of the best scales you can play over the equally bluesy dominant seventh chord (such as C7). See Figure 11-1.

FIGURE 11-1: C MIXOLYDIAN

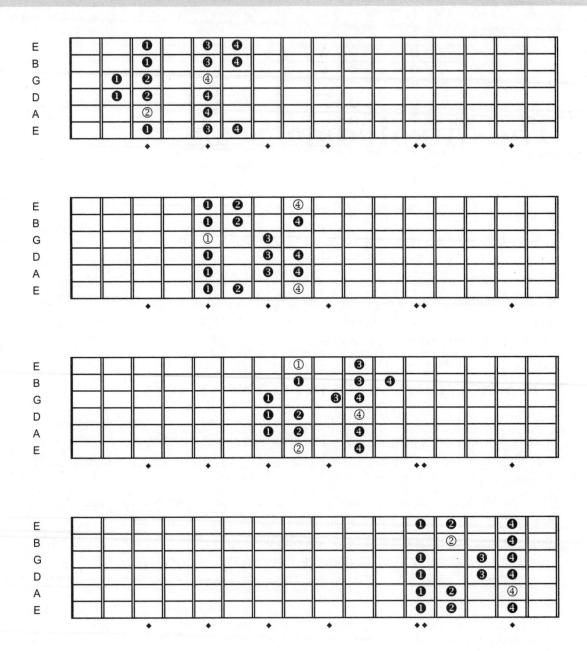

FIGURE 11-1: C#/D♭ MIXOLYDIAN

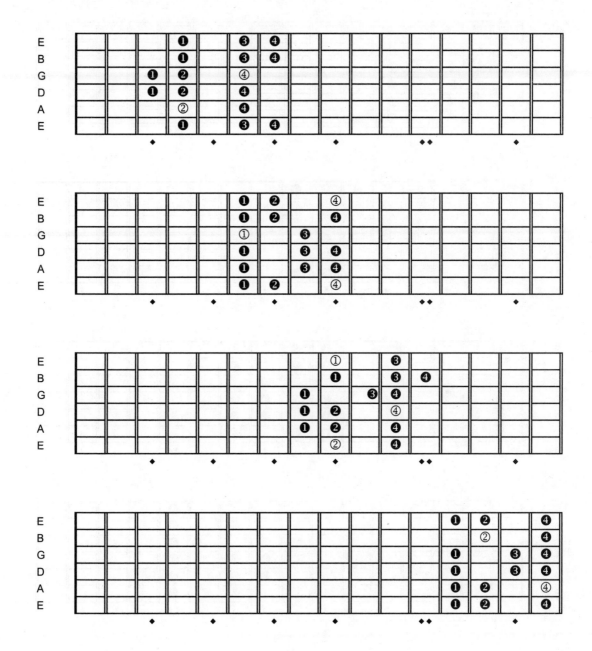

FIGURE 11-1: D MIXOLYDIAN

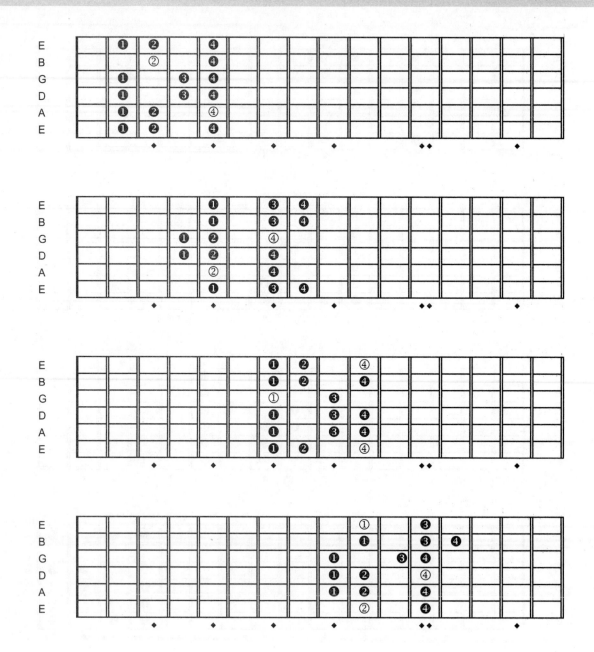

FIGURE 11-1: D♯/E♭ MIXOLYDIAN

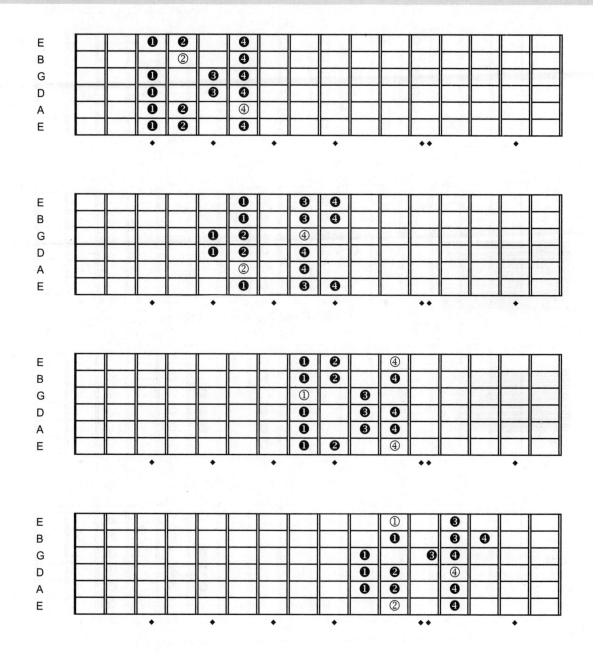

FIGURE 11-1: E MIXOLYDIAN

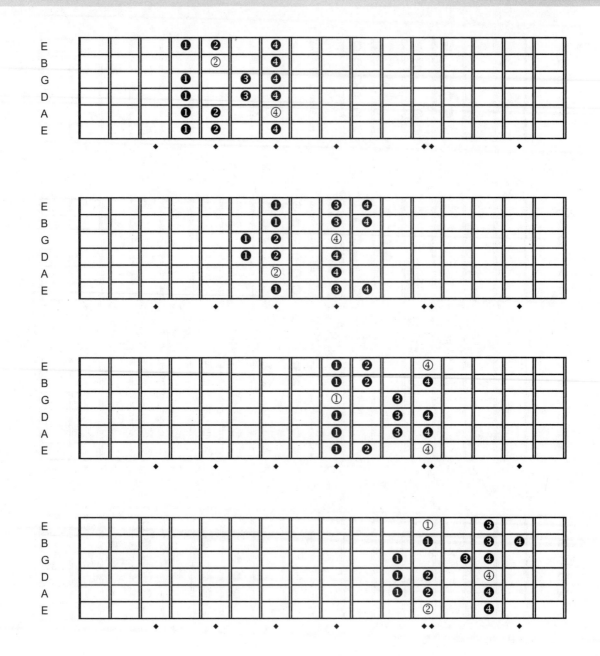

FIGURE 11-1: F MIXOLYDIAN

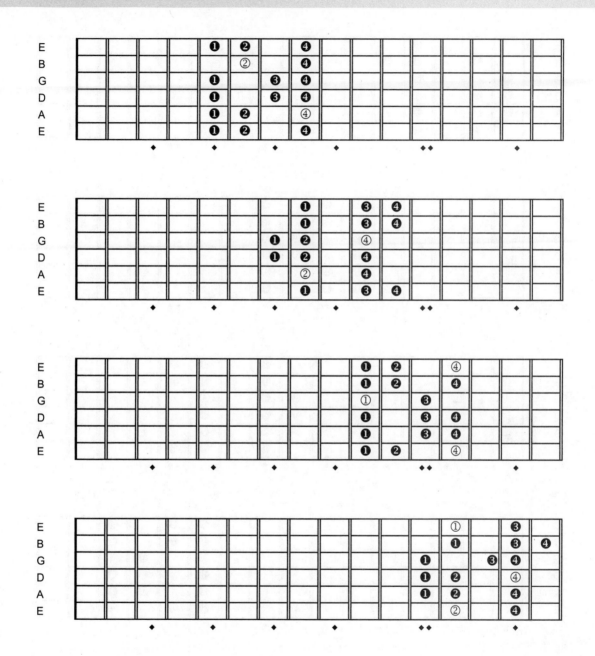

FIGURE 11-1: F#/G♭ MIXOLYDIAN

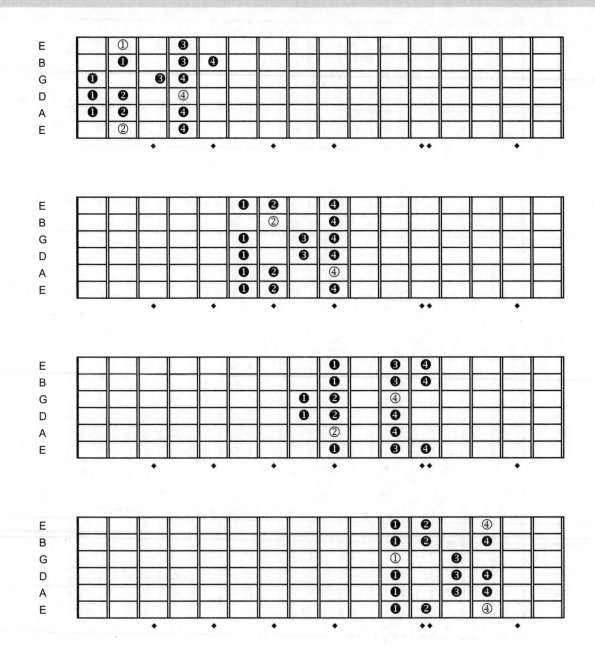

FIGURE 11-1: G MIXOLYDIAN

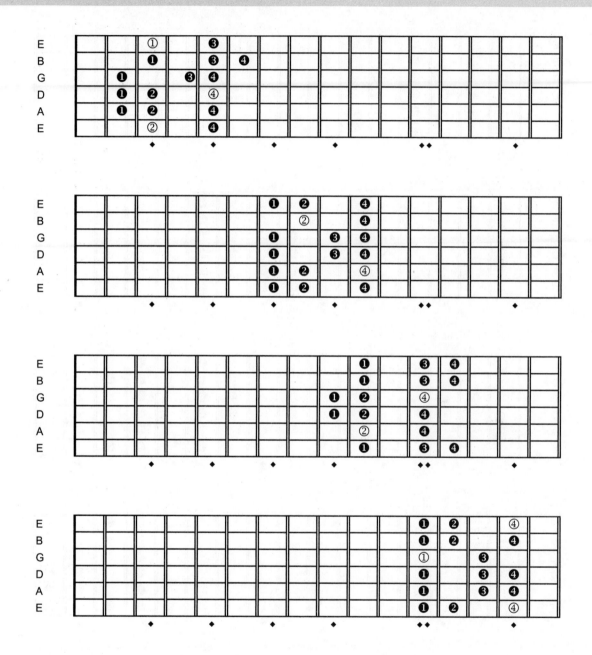

FIGURE 11-1: G#/Ab MIXOLYDIAN

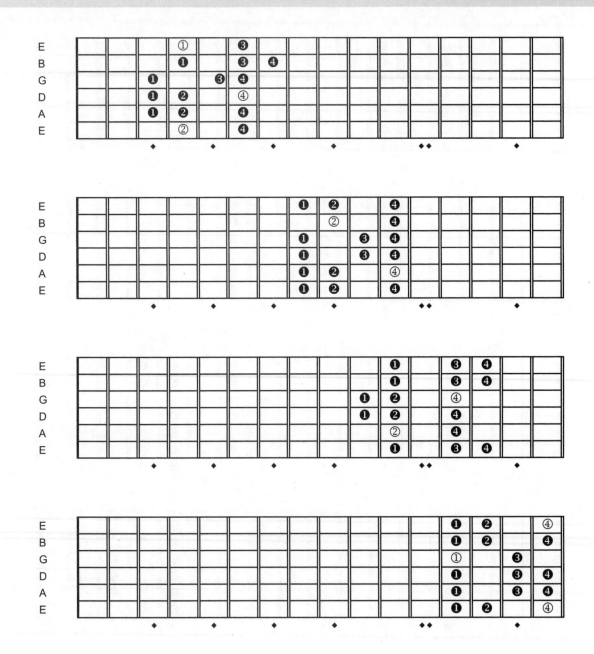

FIGURE 11-1: A MIXOLYDIAN

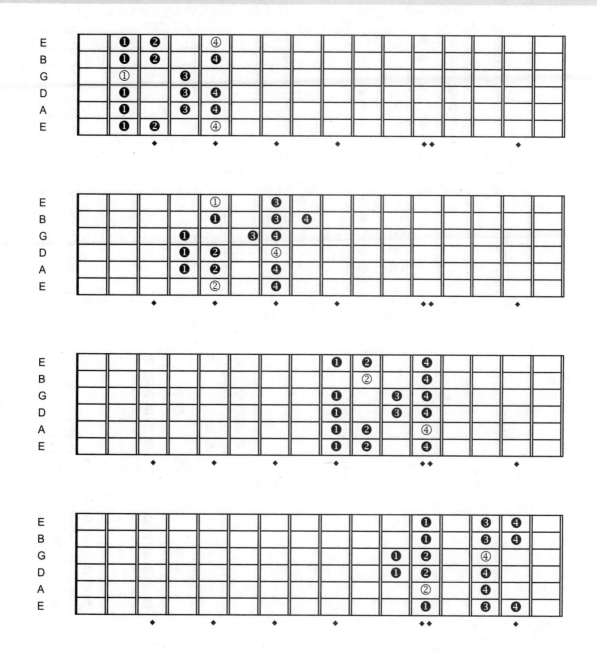

FIGURE 11-1: A♯/B♭ MIXOLYDIAN

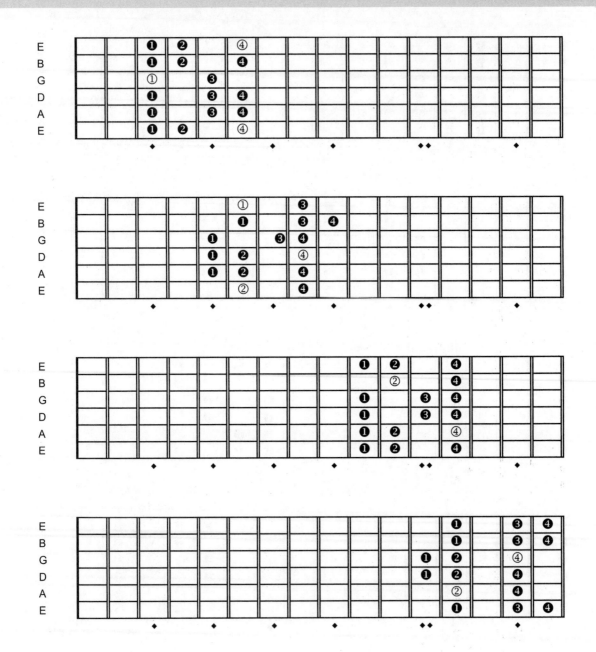

FIGURE 11-1: B MIXOLYDIAN

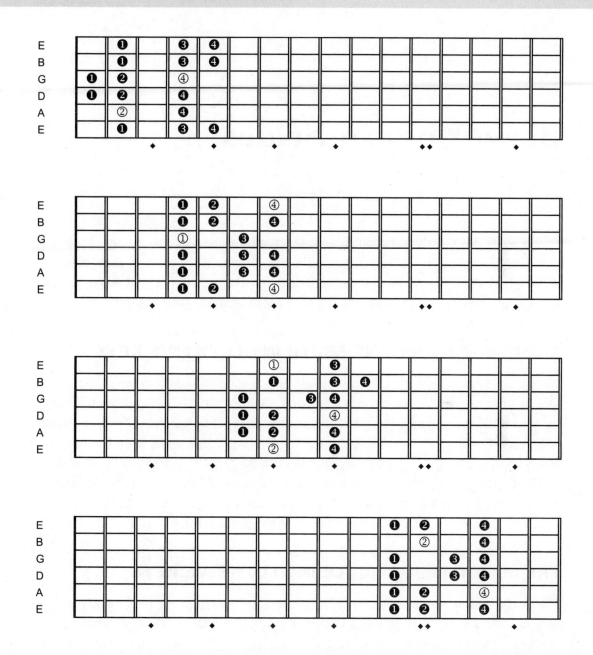

12

Jazz/Modern Scales

This chapter deals with some unusual scales that are used mostly in jazz improvisation. The five scales in this chapter help take care of jazz music's occasional "difficult" chords. They also provide some of the sounds that make jazz what it is! If you're looking to take your playing into the modern era, take a look at these new scales!

THE BEBOP DOMINANT SCALE IN ALL TWELVE KEYS

The bebop dominant scale probably really isn't a scale in the traditional sense, but if you look at (or better yet, transcribe) jazz solos from the bebop era (such as those of Charlie Parker and Dizzy Gillespie), you'll see this configuration of notes all the time. The scale is essentially a Mixolydian scale, but it adds a natural 7th passing tone. In C, this scale spells as (C, D, E, F, G, A, B♭, B, C), and its formula in scale degrees is (1, 2, 3, 4, 5, 6, ♭7, 7). Most jazz players will use this over a standard dominant seventh chord (such as C7), and it's important to note that most jazz players play this scale descending only. You can, however, use it any way you want! See Figure 12-1.

THE MAJOR BEBOP SCALE IN ALL TWELVE KEYS

The next bebop scale is the major bebop scale, and—you guessed it—jazz players like to use this over major chords. It's essentially a major scale, with an additional note between 5 and 6 (a passing tone), to give it the typical chromatic sound that you hear in jazz. In C, the major bebop scale spells as (C, D, E, F, G, G♯, A, B, C), and its formula in scale degrees is (1, 2, 3, 4, 5, ♯5, 6, 7). See Figure 12-2.

FIGURE 12-1: C BEBOP DOMINANT

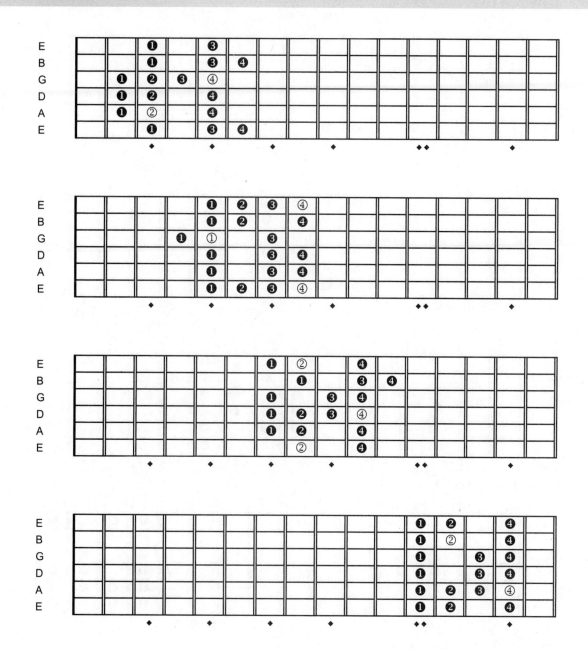

FIGURE 12-1: C♯/D♭ BEBOP DOMINANT

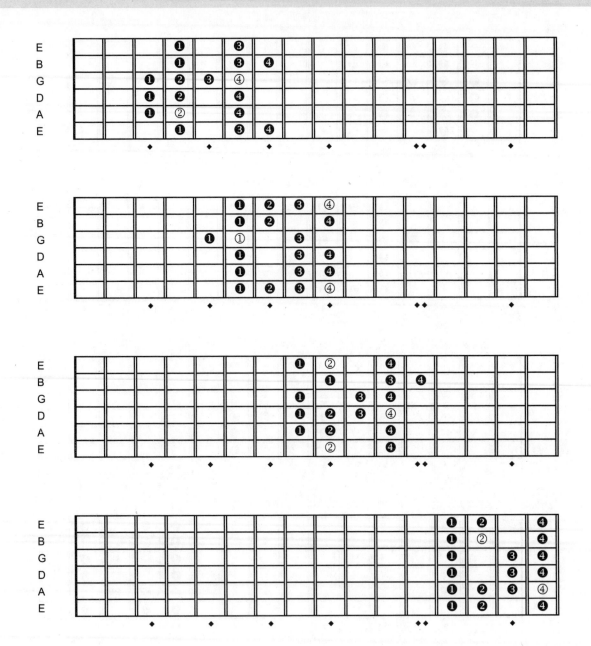

FIGURE 12-1: D BEBOP DOMINANT

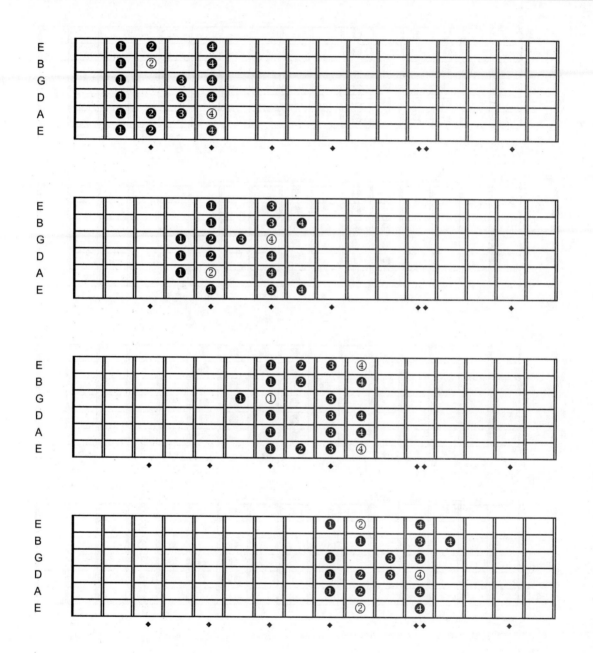

FIGURE 12-1: D♯/E♭ BEBOP DOMINANT

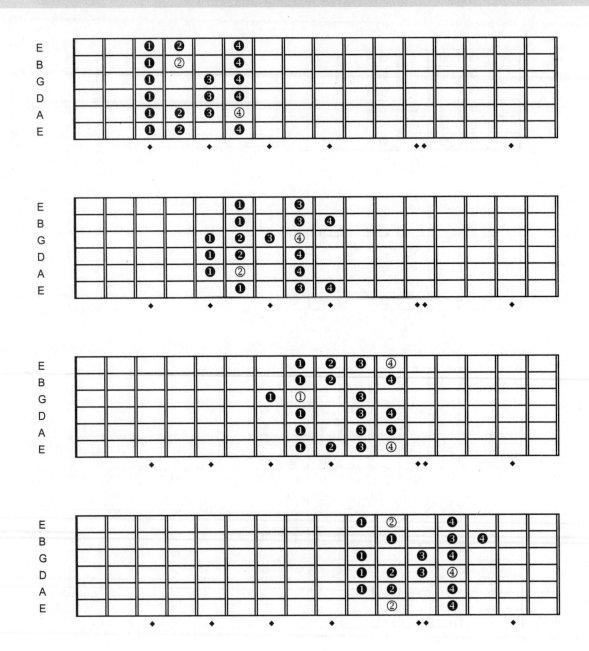

FIGURE 12-1: E BEBOP DOMINANT

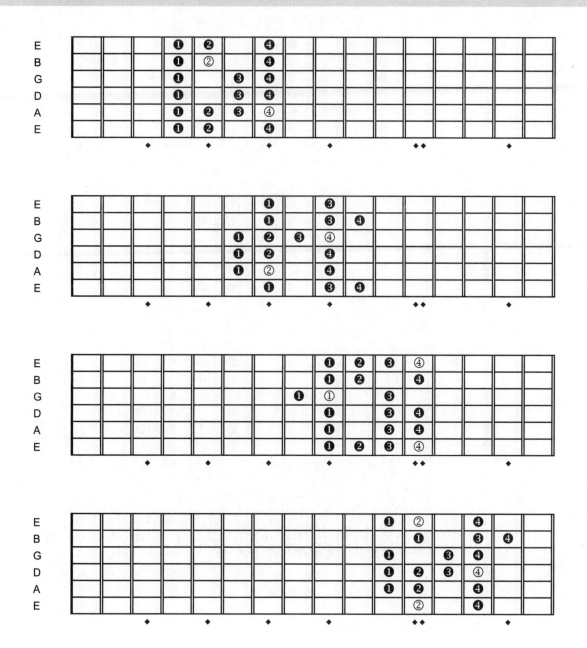

FIGURE 12-1: F BEBOP DOMINANT

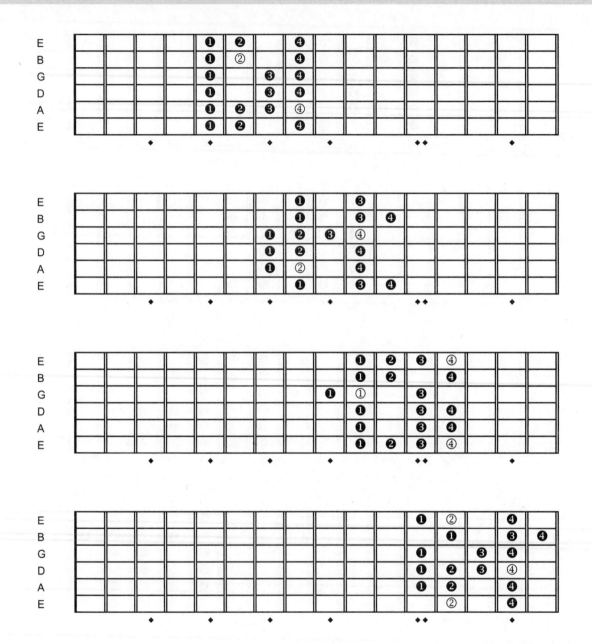

FIGURE 12-1: F#/Gb BEBOP DOMINANT

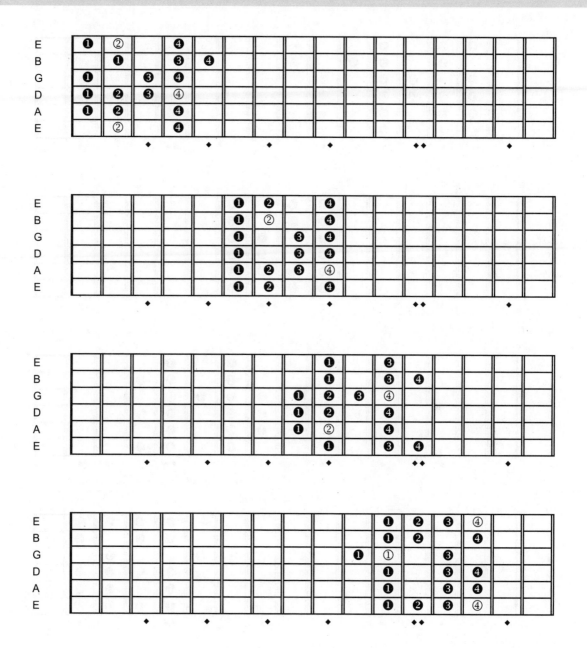

FIGURE 12-1: G BEBOP DOMINANT

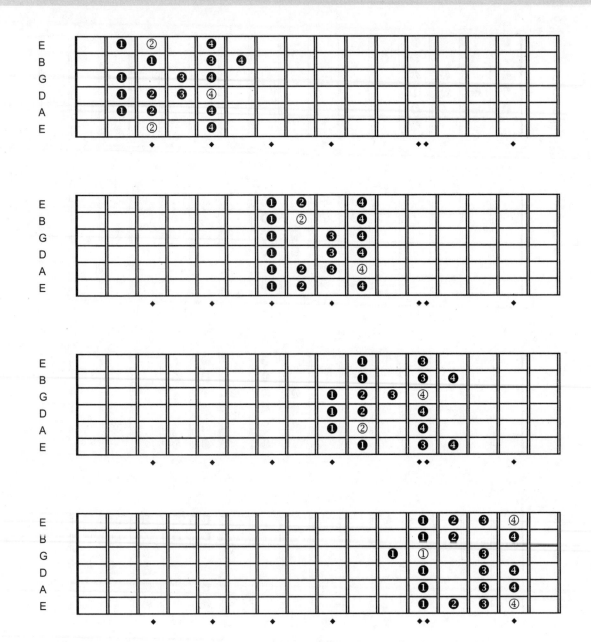

FIGURE 12-1: G♯/A♭ BEBOP DOMINANT

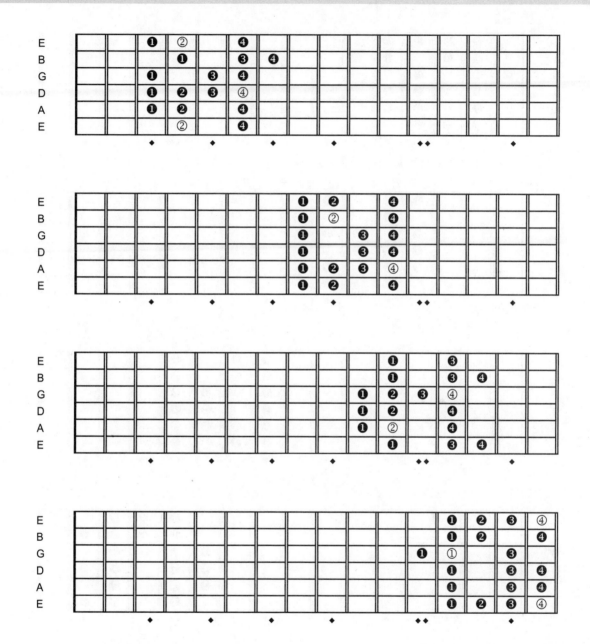

FIGURE 12-1: A BEBOP DOMINANT

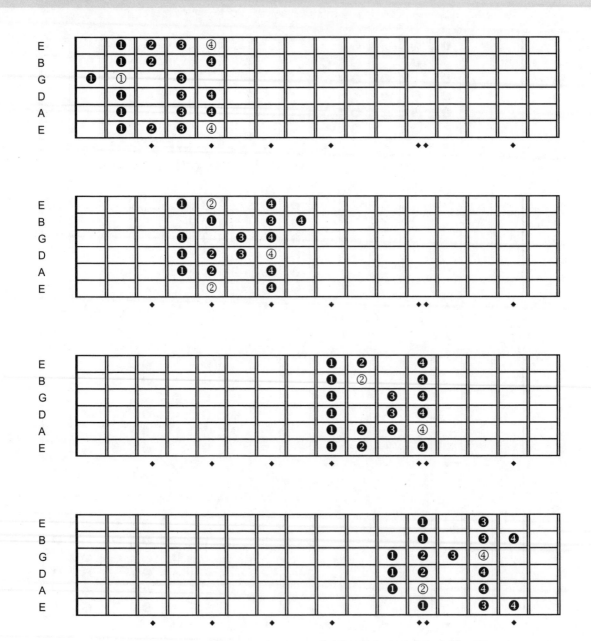

FIGURE 12-1: A♯/B♭ BEBOP DOMINANT

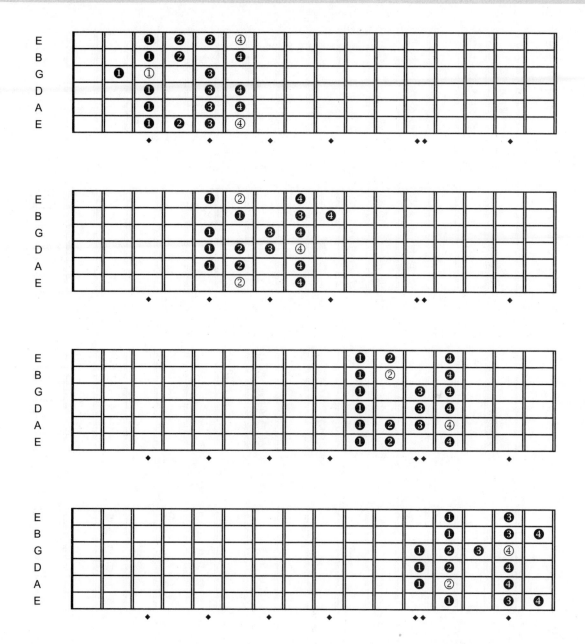

FIGURE 12-1: B BEBOP DOMINANT

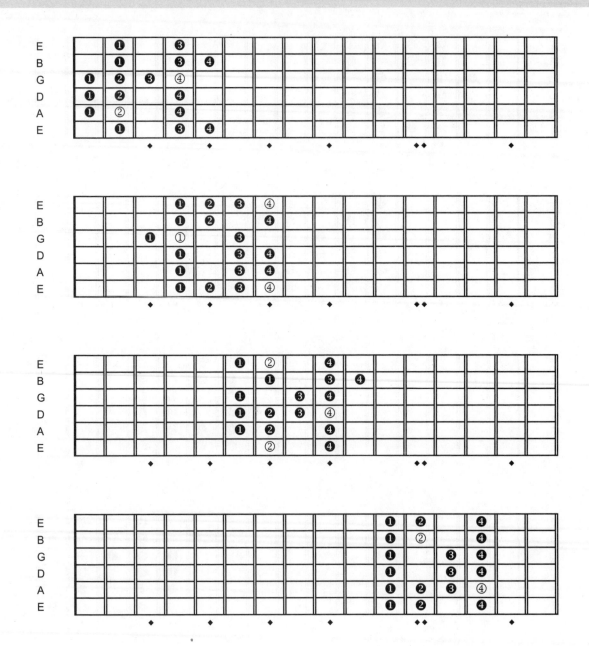

FIGURE 12-2: C BEBOP MAJOR

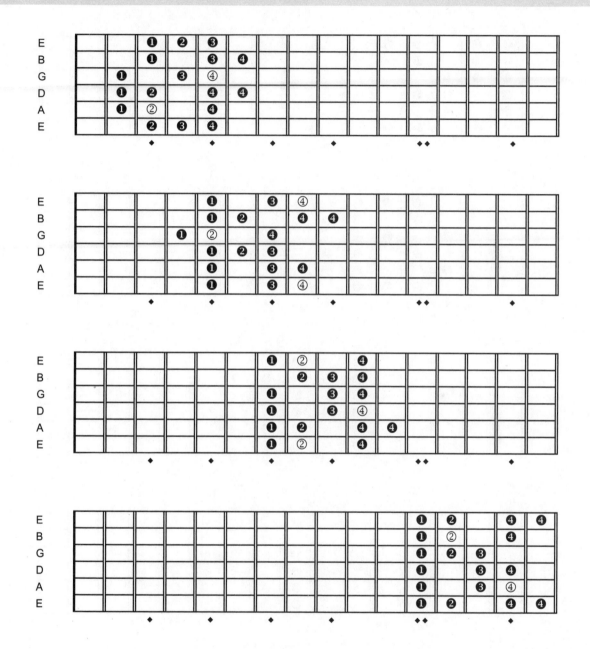

FIGURE 12-2: C#/D♭ BEBOP MAJOR

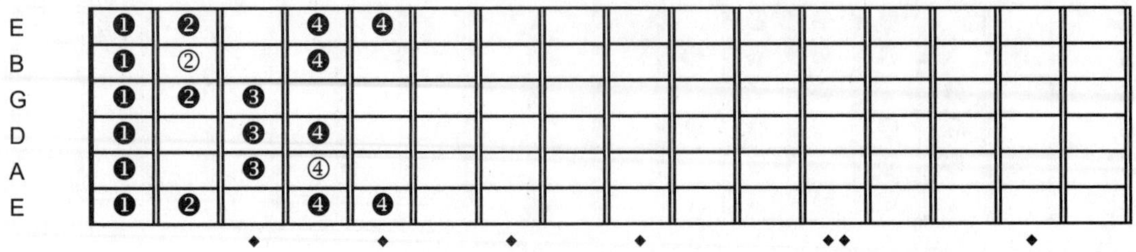

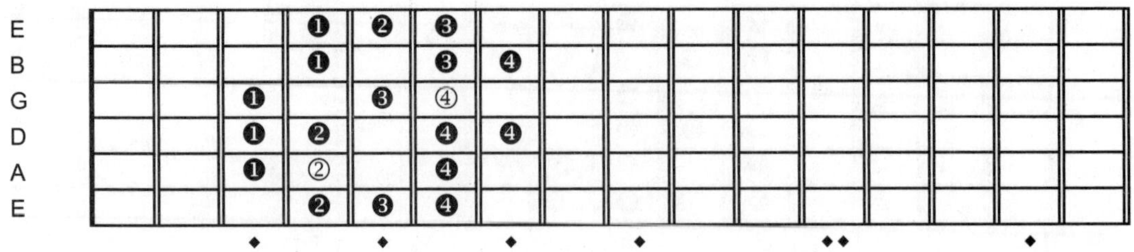

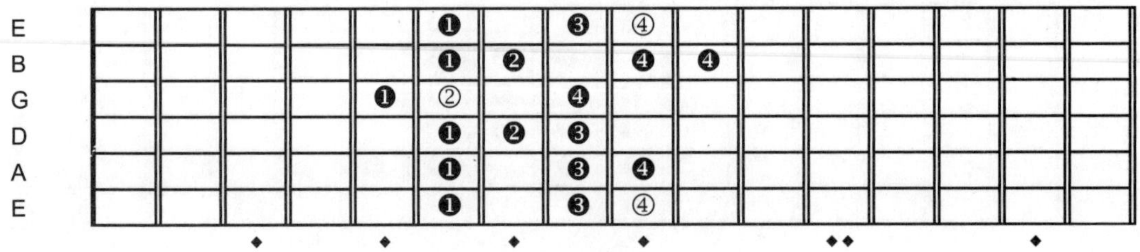

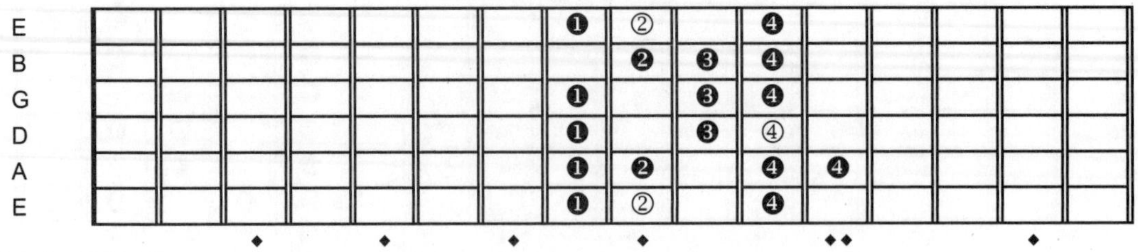

FIGURE 12-2: D BEBOP MAJOR

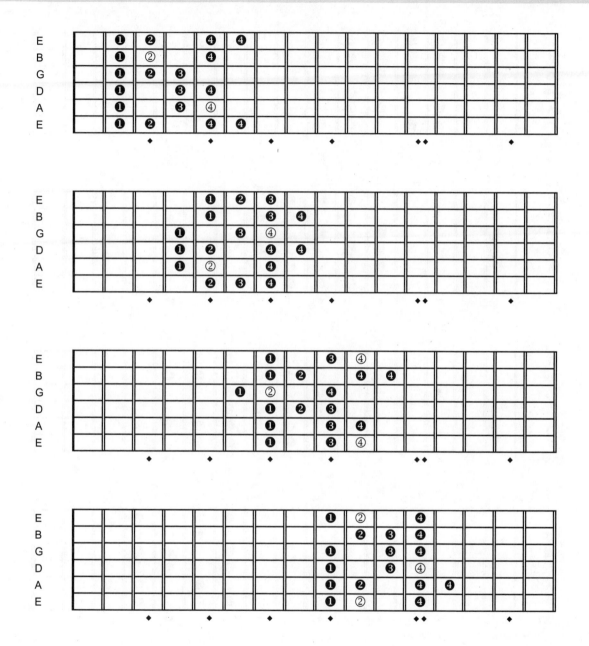

FIGURE 12-2: D♯/E♭ BEBOP MAJOR

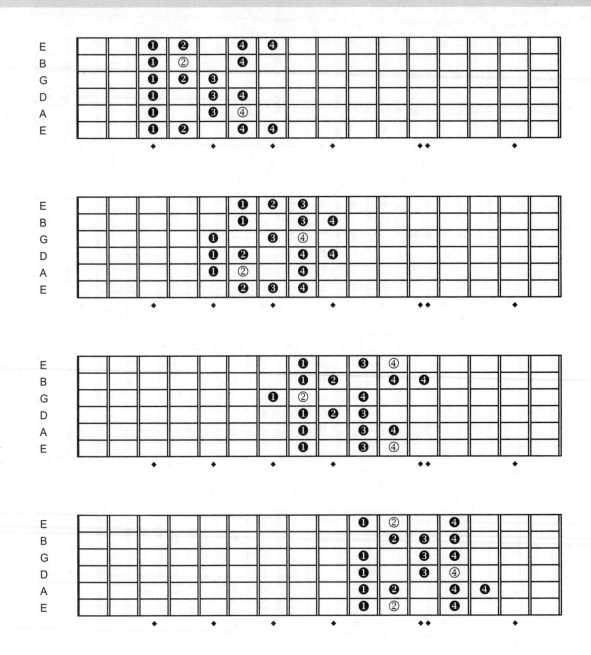

FIGURE 12-2: E BEBOP MAJOR

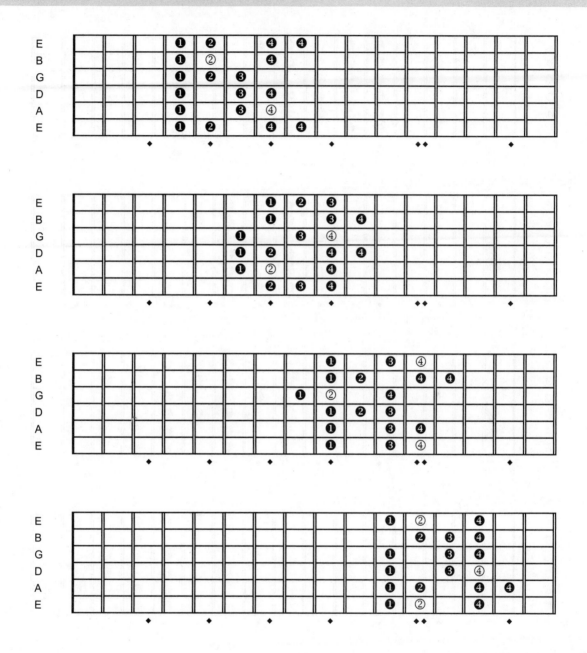

FIGURE 12-2: F BEBOP MAJOR

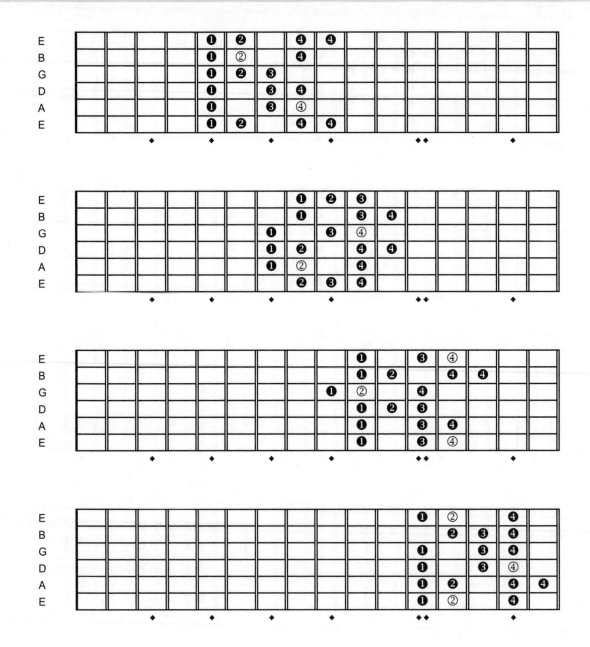

FIGURE 12-2: F#/Gb BEBOP MAJOR

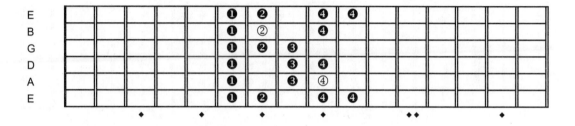

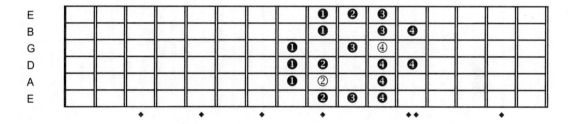

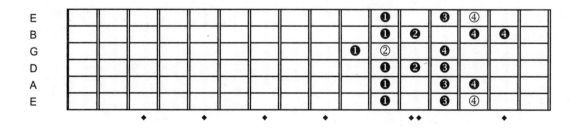

FIGURE 12-2: G BEBOP MAJOR

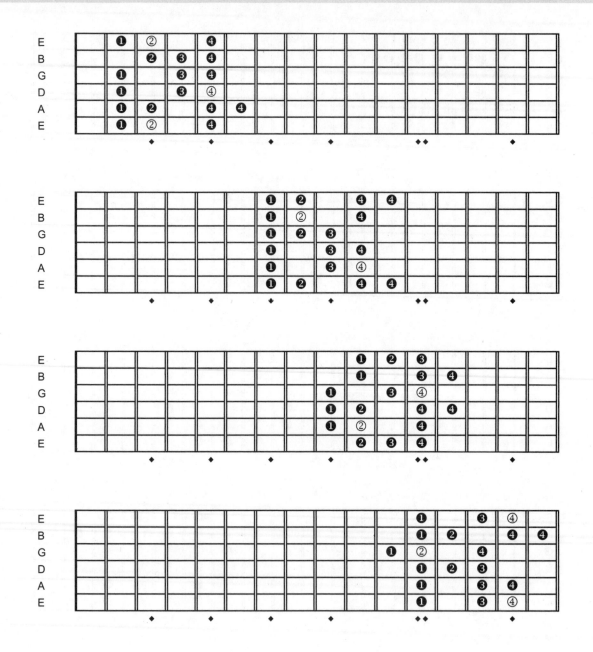

FIGURE 12-2: G♯/A♭ BEBOP MAJOR

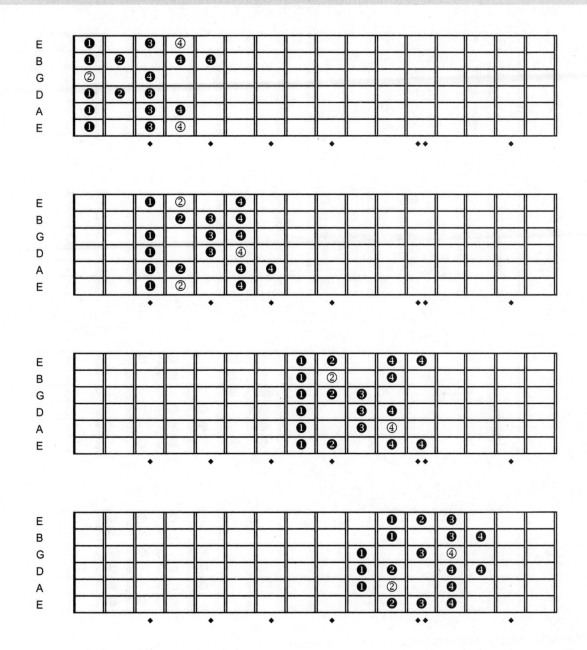

FIGURE 12-2: A BEBOP MAJOR

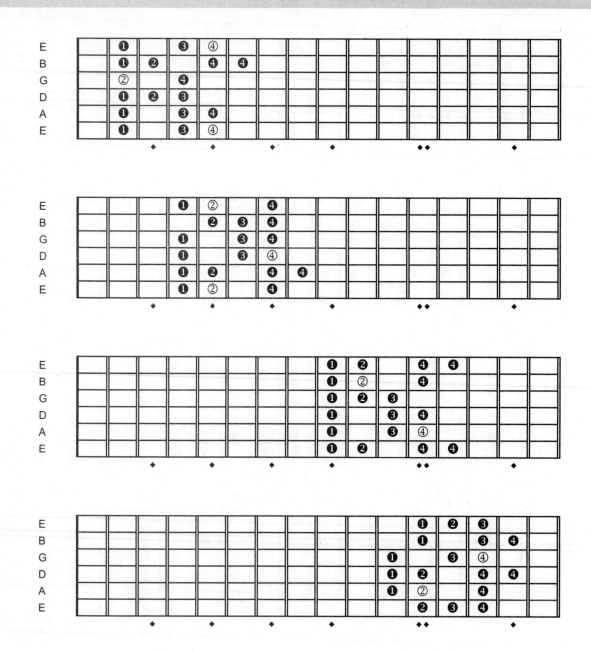

FIGURE 12-2: A#/Bb BEBOP MAJOR

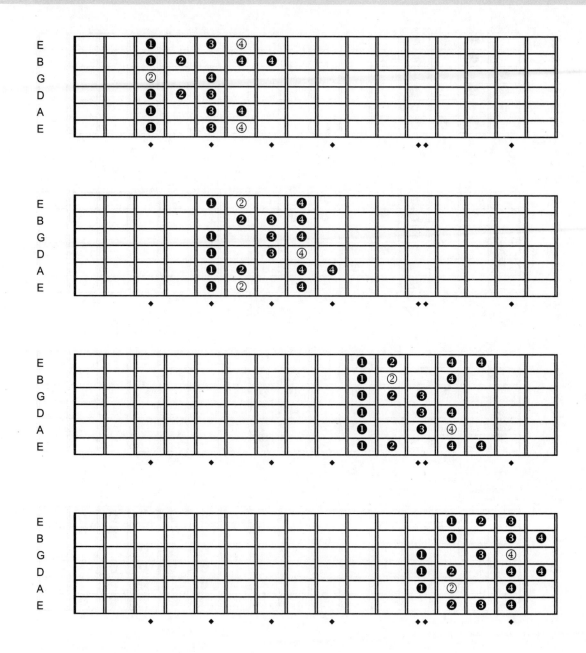

FIGURE 12-2: B BEBOP MAJOR

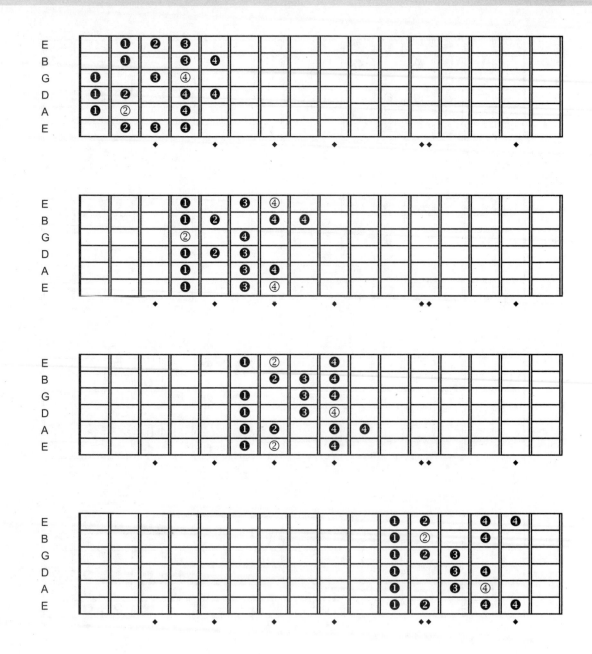

THE ALTERED DOMINANT SCALE IN ALL TWELVE KEYS

In jazz, you're faced with some very odd chords, and no chord or type of chord is mutilated as often as the poor old dominant seventh (such as C7). In a jazz tune, that C7 may appear as a C7#9♭5♭13, and it's totally at the discretion of the pianist playing at the time how "outside" they may push that chord. Of course, when you add odd notes into chords, you're going to need scales that contain those notes in order to make cogent melodies. The altered dominant scale is a scale that contains every possible alteration jazz players put into dominant chords.

In C, the altered dominant scale spells as (C, D♭, E, ♭E, F#, A♭, B♭) or in scale degrees as (1 ♭2/♭9, ♭3/#9, 3, #4/#11/♭5, #5/♭13, ♭7). When nothing else works, try this scale. It's meant for those impossible dominant chords. Jazz players also love to use this scale over normal dominant chords (that is, unaltered) just to create tension. See Figure 12-3.

THE LOCRIAN ♮2 SCALE IN ALL TWELVE KEYS

Jazz players deal with the minor7♭5 (half diminished) chord on a regular basis. Normally, the scale of choice is the Locrian mode, but over the years, the dissonance of the Locrian mode gave players the impetus to seek out other scales. By raising the second note of the Locrian mode half a step (it's flat normally in Locrian), many jazz players found a nicer-sounding scale over the very prevalent min7♭5 (half diminished) chord. In C, this scale spells as (C, D, E♭, F, G♭, A♭, B♭, C) and its interval scale degrees are (1, 2, ♭3, 4, ♭5, ♭6, ♭7). Try this scale out the next time you have to play over a min7♭5 chord—it's a really lovely sound. See Figure 12-4.

FIGURE 12-3: C ALTERED DOMINANT

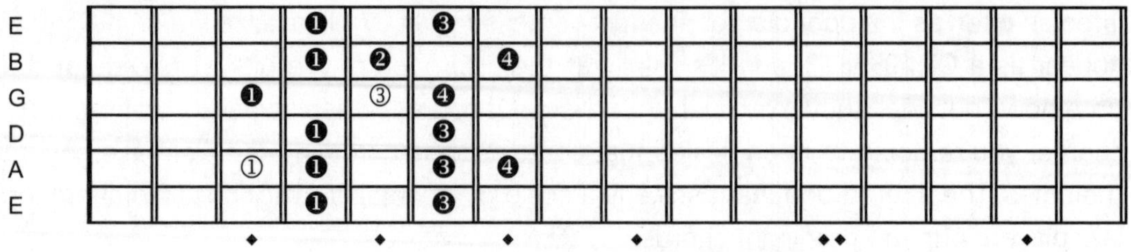

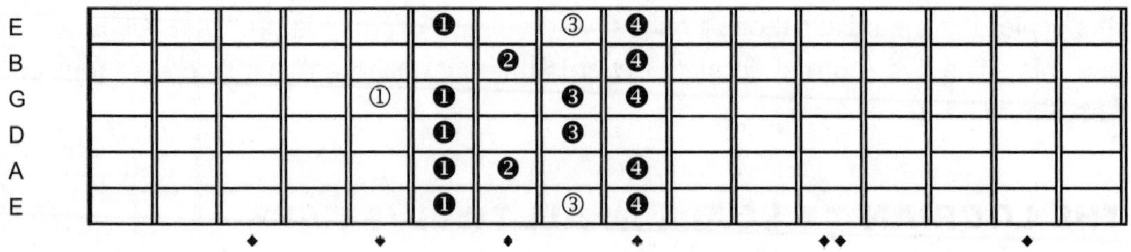

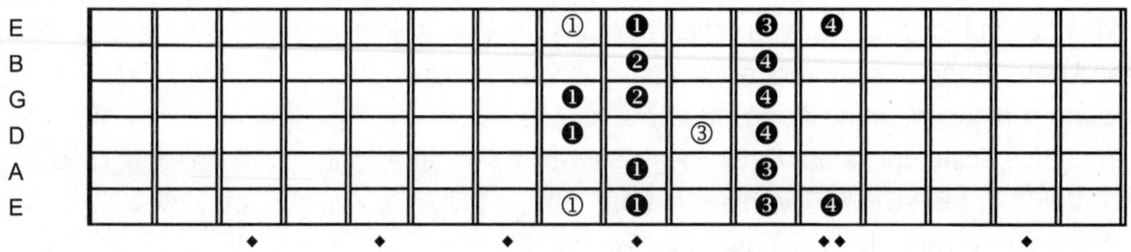

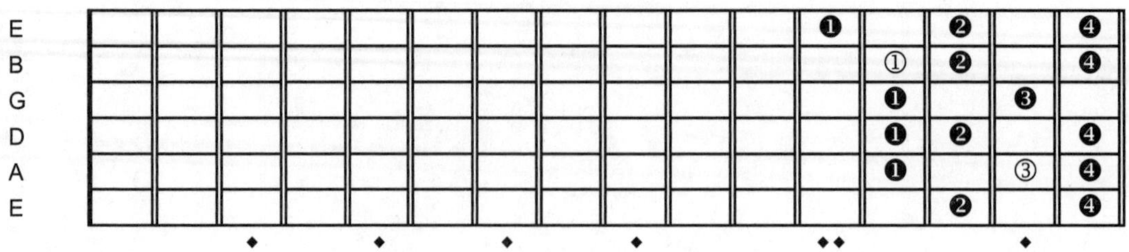

FIGURE 12-3: C♯/D♭ ALTERED DOMINANT

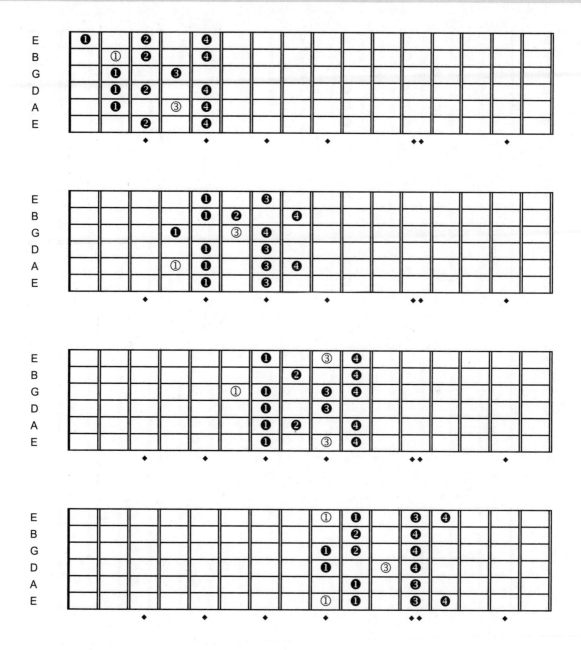

FIGURE 12-3: D ALTERED DOMINANT

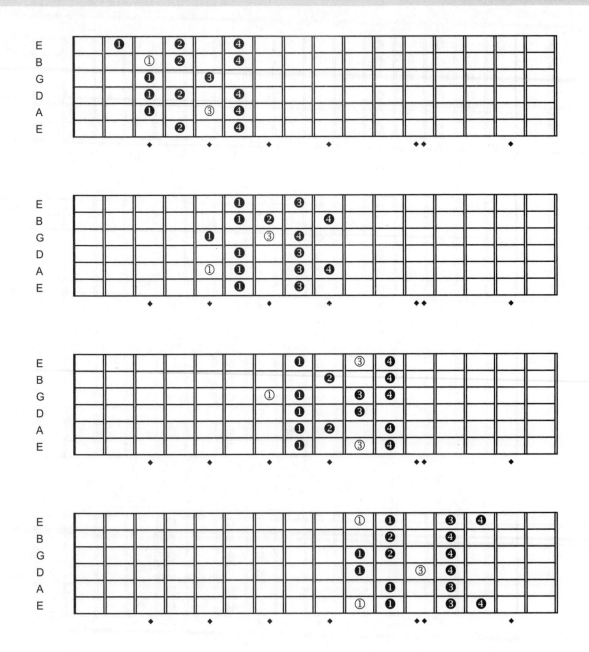

FIGURE 12-3: D♯/E♭ ALTERED DOMINANT

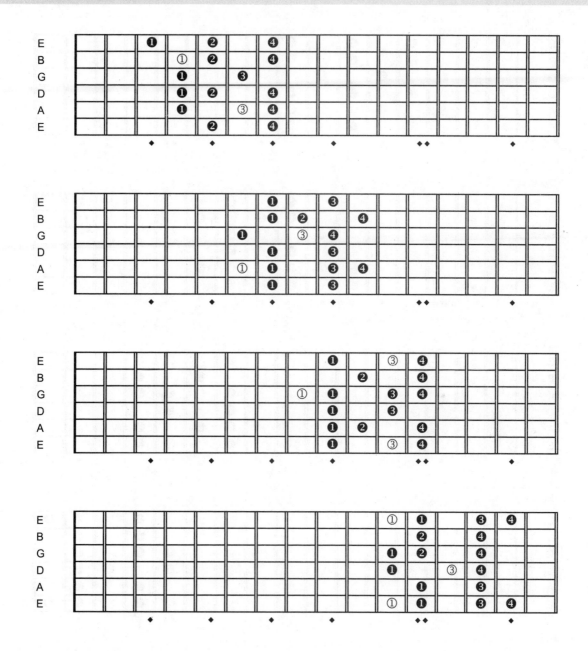

FIGURE 12-3: E ALTERED DOMINANT

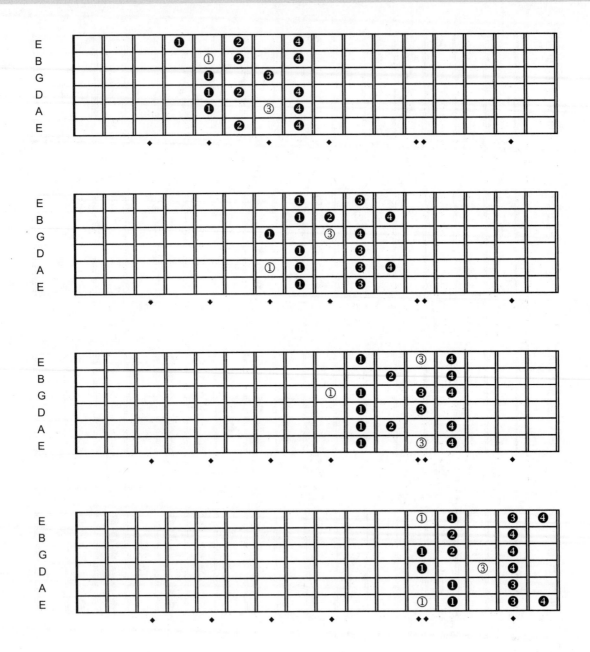

FIGURE 12-3: F ALTERED DOMINANT

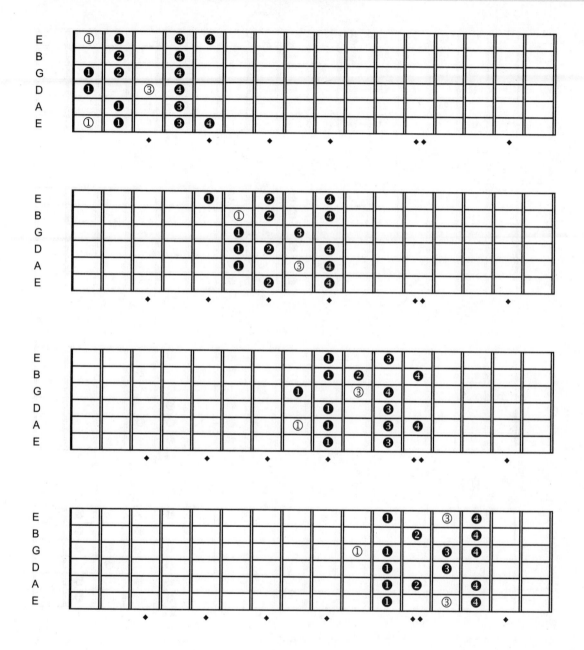

FIGURE 12-3: F♯/G♭ ALTERED DOMINANT

FIGURE 12-3: G ALTERED DOMINANT

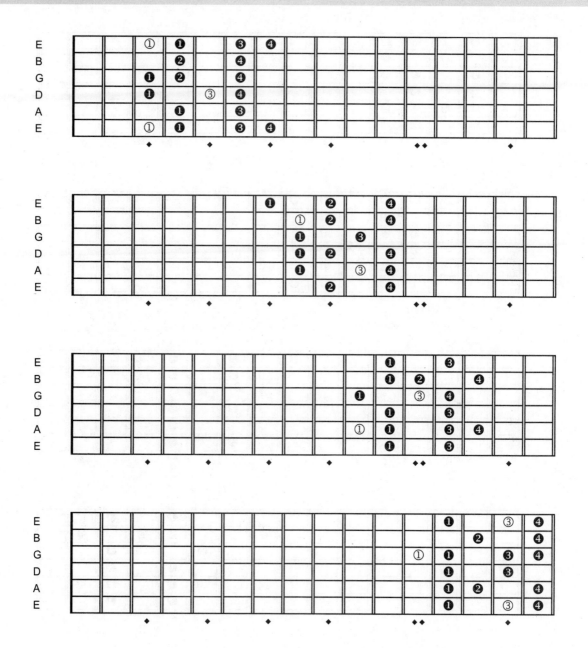

FIGURE 12-3: G#/A♭ ALTERED DOMINANT

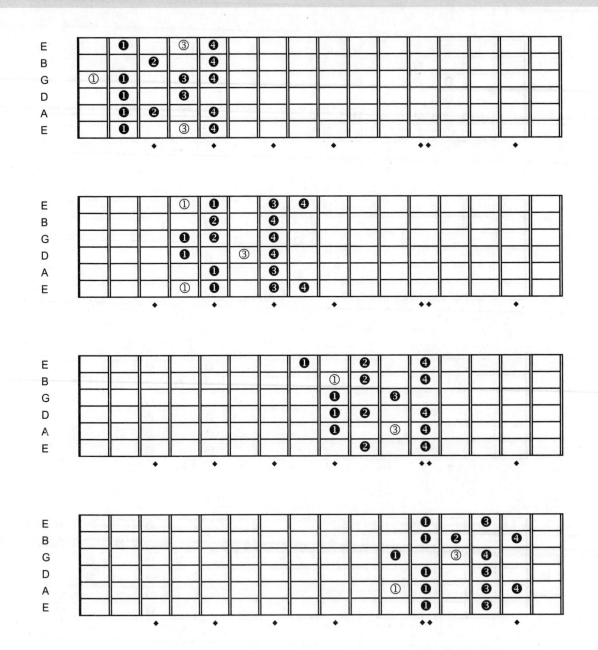

FIGURE 12-3: A ALTERED DOMINANT

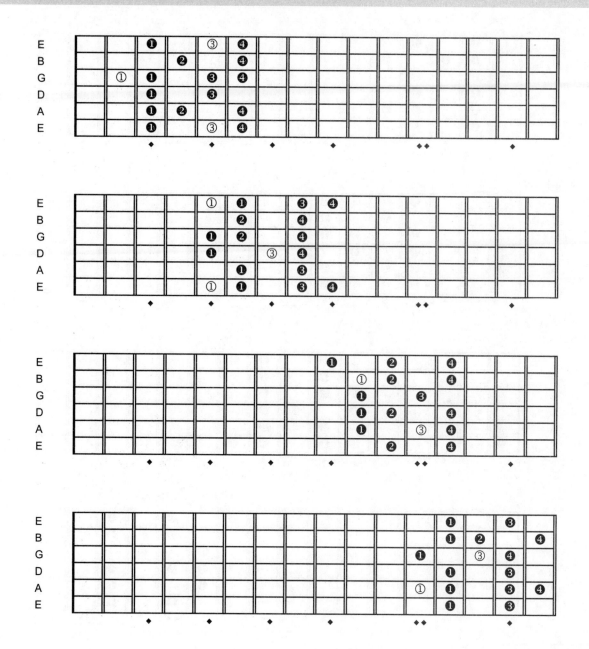

FIGURE 12-3: A♯/B♭ ALTERED DOMINANT

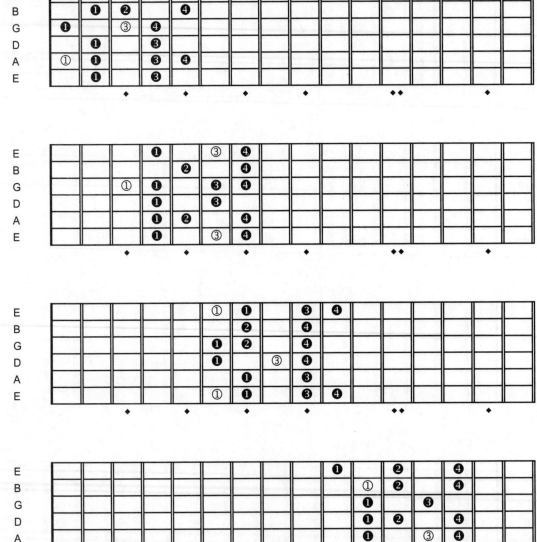

FIGURE 12-3: B ALTERED DOMINANT

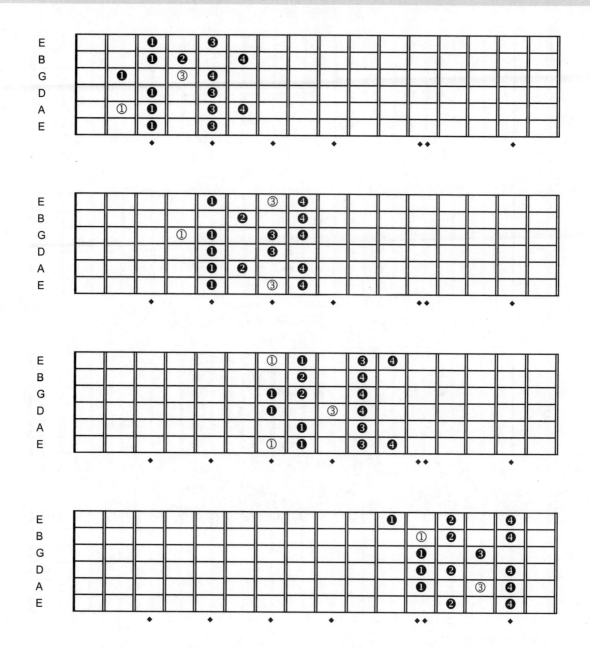

FIGURE 12-4: C LOCRIAN #2

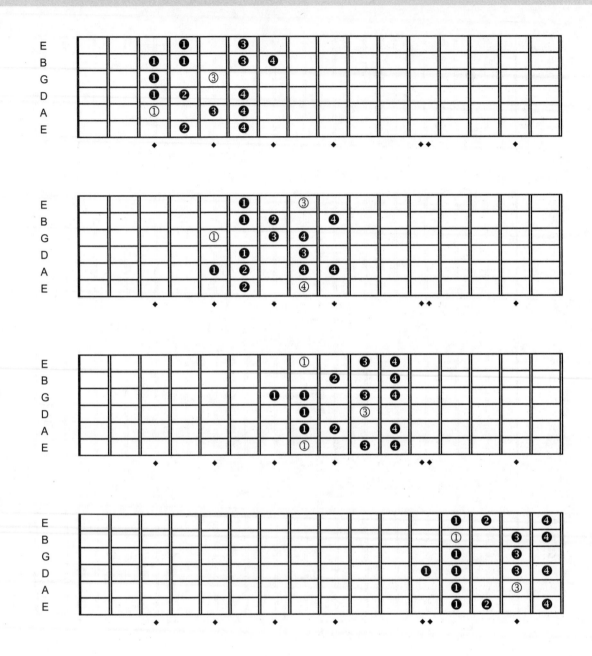

FIGURE 12-4: C♯/D♭ LOCRIAN #2

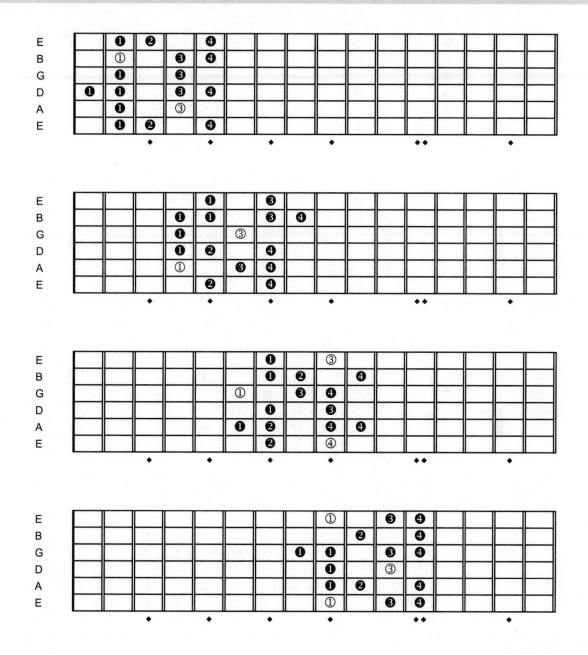

FIGURE 12-4: D LOCRIAN #2

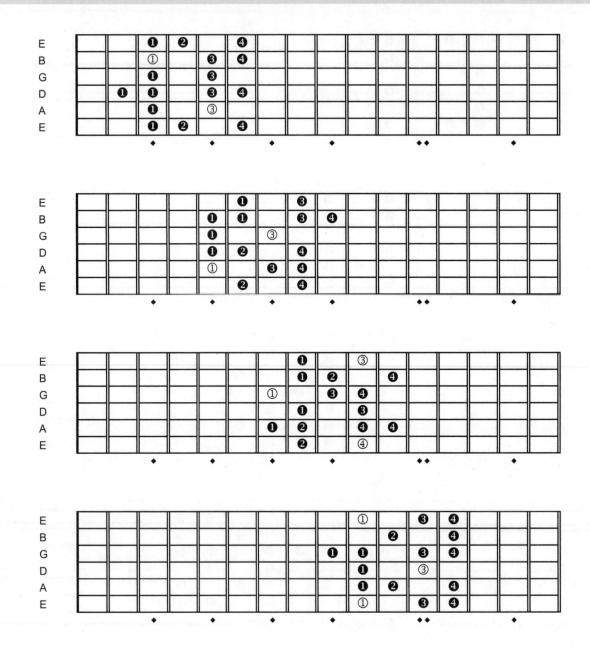

FIGURE 12-4: D♯/E♭ LOCRIAN #2

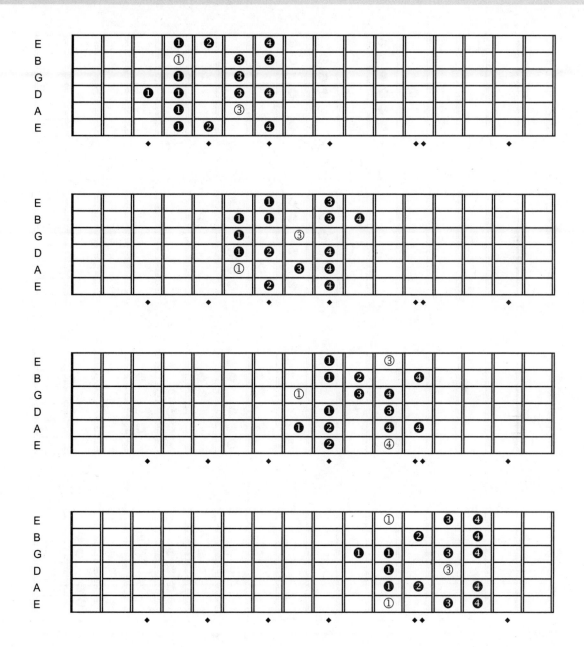

FIGURE 12-4: E LOCRIAN #2

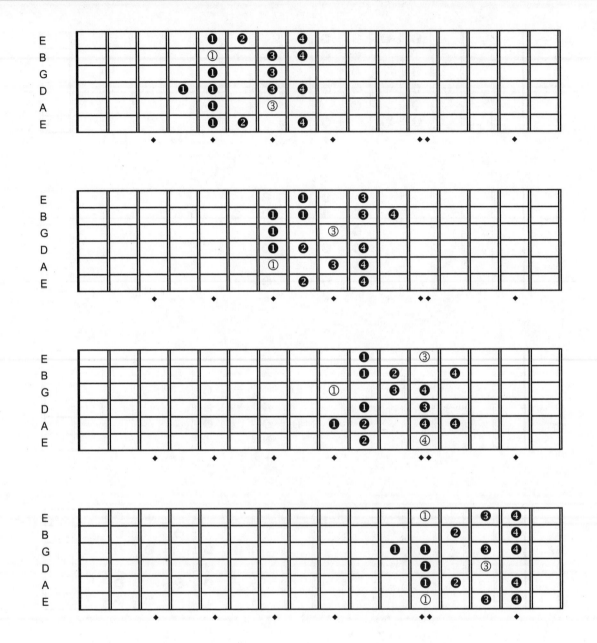

FIGURE 12-4: F LOCRIAN #2

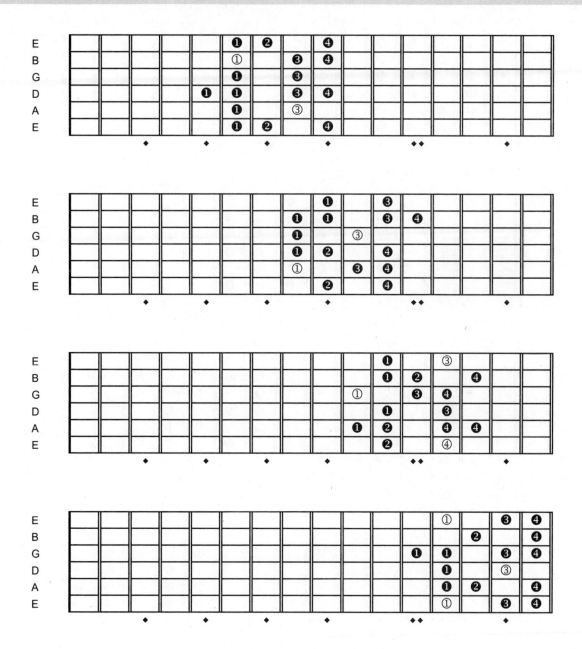

FIGURE 12-4: F#/G♭ LOCRIAN #2

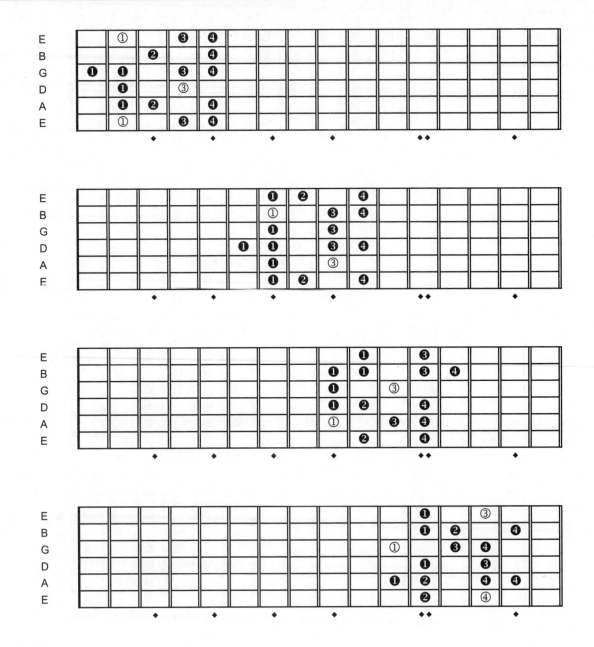

FIGURE 12-4: G LOCRIAN #2

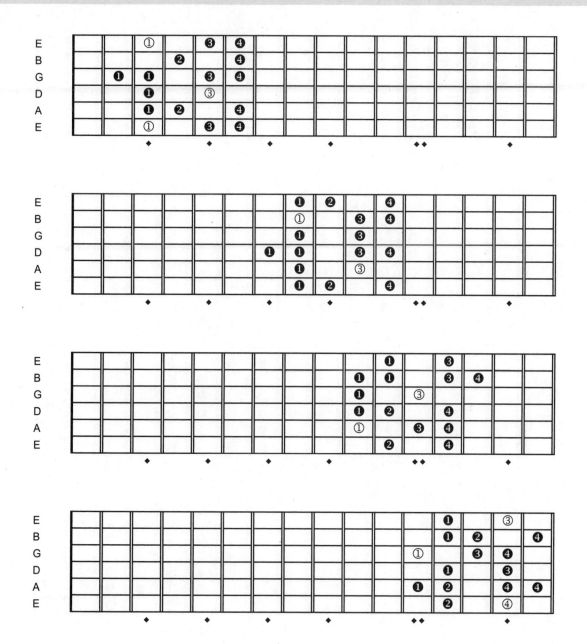

FIGURE 12-4: G#/A♭ LOCRIAN #2

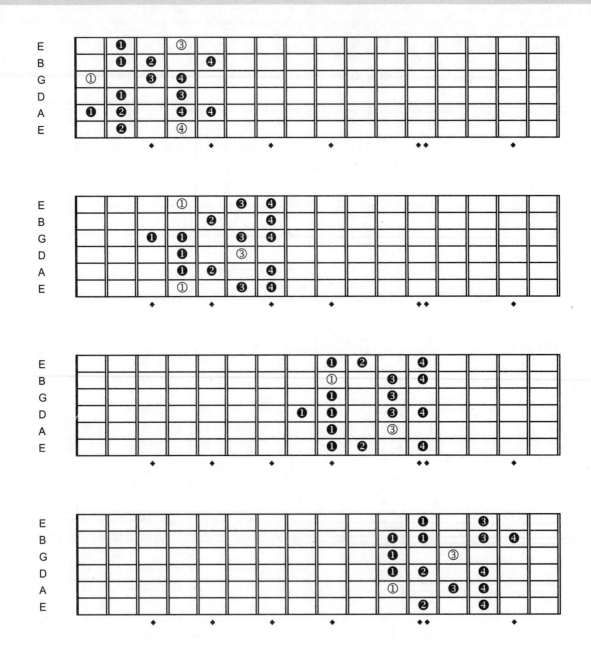

FIGURE 12-4: A LOCRIAN #2

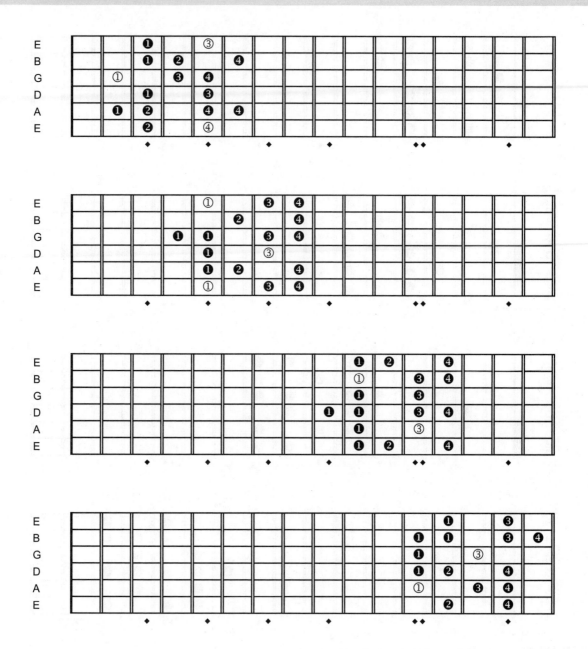

FIGURE 12-4: A♯/B♭ LOCRIAN #2

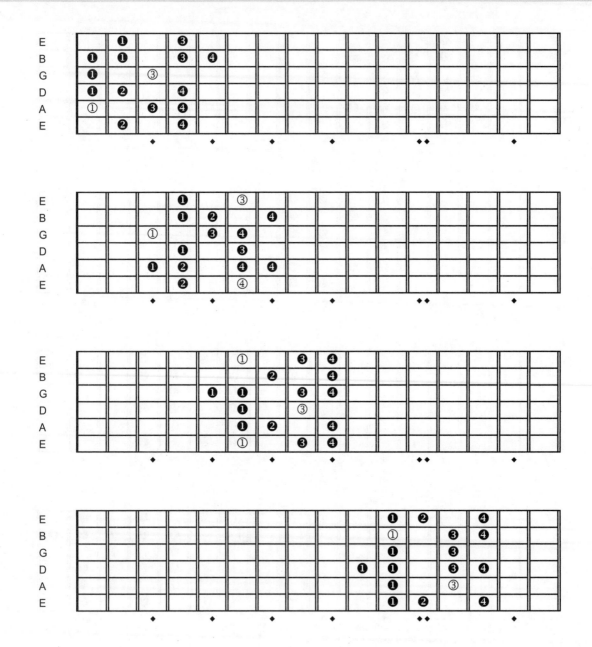

FIGURE 12-4: B LOCRIAN #2

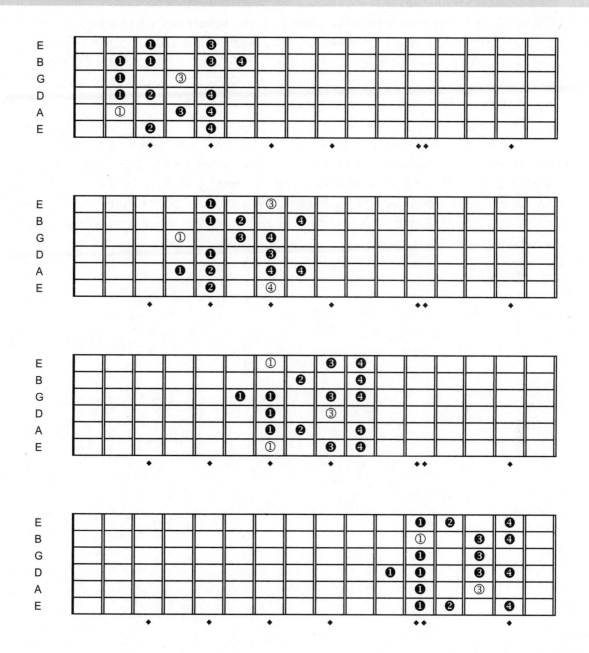

THE MIXOLYDIAN ♯4 SCALE IN ALL TWELVE KEYS

The last scale in this book is the Mixolydian ♯4 scale. Mixolydian scales are used over dominant chords, and in jazz, dominant chords are something special. Sometimes the chords are very plain while at other times they can be very altered. What's needed is an in-between sound, something not as plain as Mixolydian. Along comes the Mixolydian ♯4 scale (another mode of the melodic minor) to bridge the gap.

Many jazz players feel that when you play over a dominant 7th chord, the fourth note of the Mixolydian scale is dissonant. To fix that, you just raise it up half a step. You end up with the Mixolydian ♯4 scale (also called Lydian dominant by some), which spells in C as (C, D, E, F♯, G, A, B♭, C). Its interval pattern is (1, 2, 3, ♯4/♯11, 5, 6, ♭7). It's also the best scale to play over a dominant 7 ♯11 chord (C7 ♯11). It's a pretty-sounding scale—one that you won't use every day, but when the time is right, there's nothing better. See Figure 12-5.

FIGURE 12-5: C MIXOLYDIAN #4

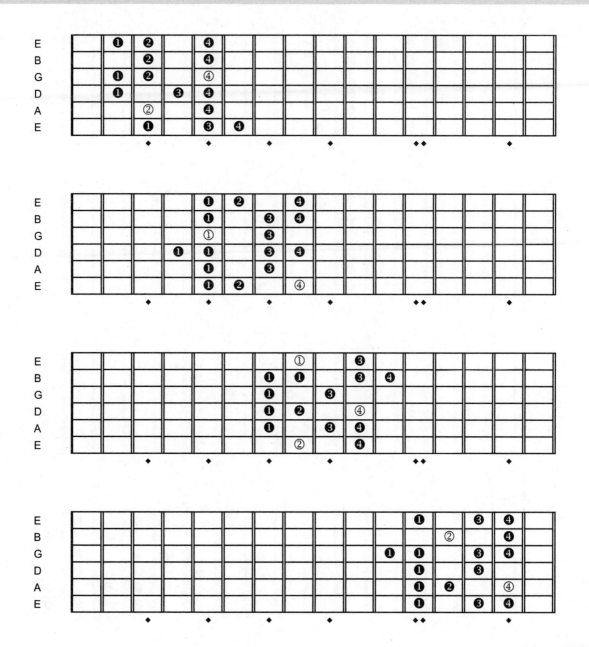

FIGURE 12-5: C♯/D♭ MIXOLYDIAN #4

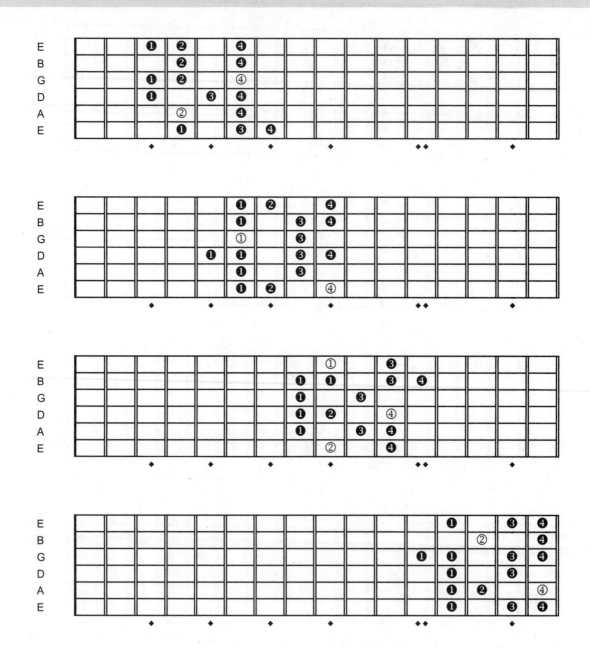

FIGURE 12-5: D MIXOLYDIAN #4

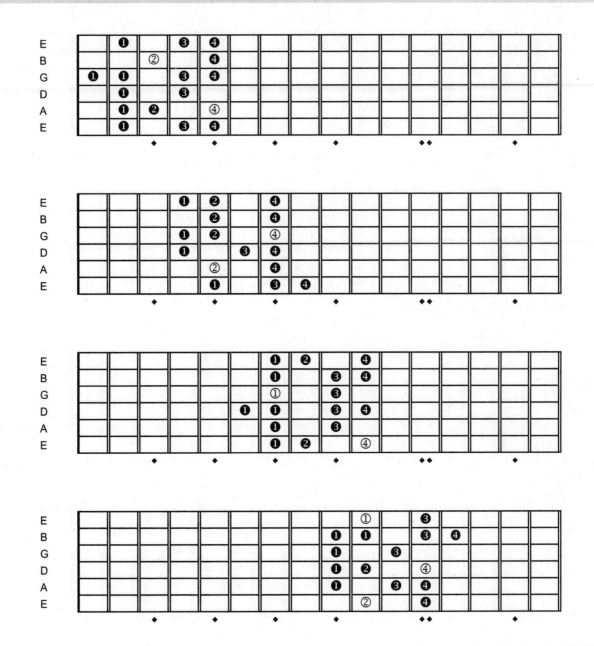

FIGURE 12-5: D#/E♭ MIXOLYDIAN #4

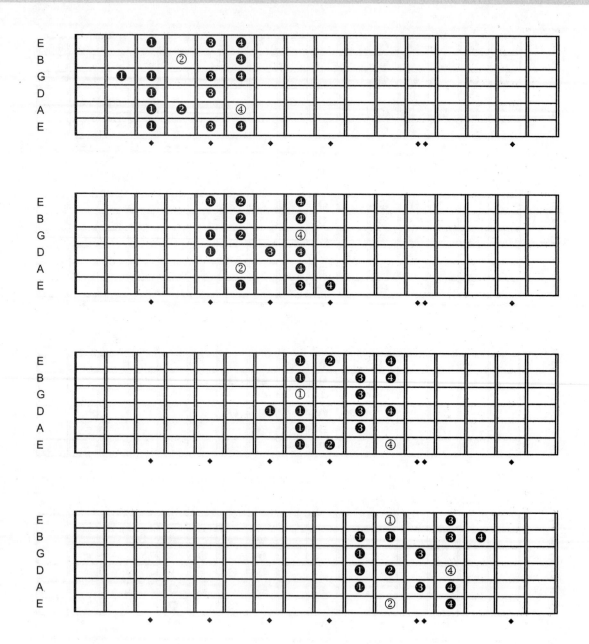

FIGURE 12-5: E MIXOLYDIAN #4

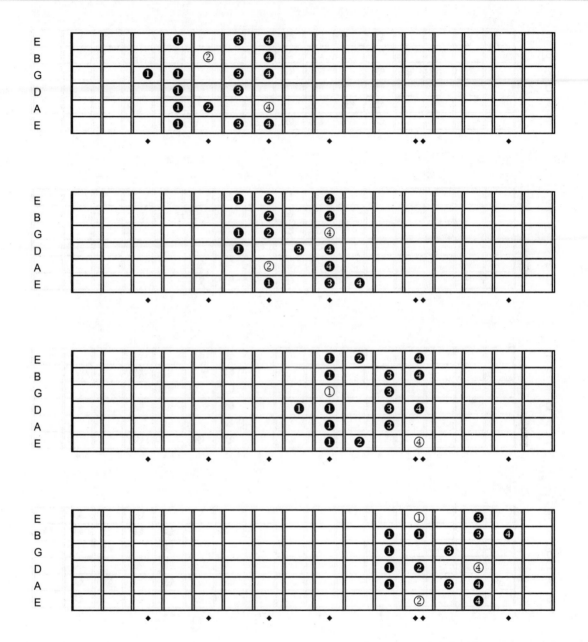

FIGURE 12-5: F MIXOLYDIAN #4

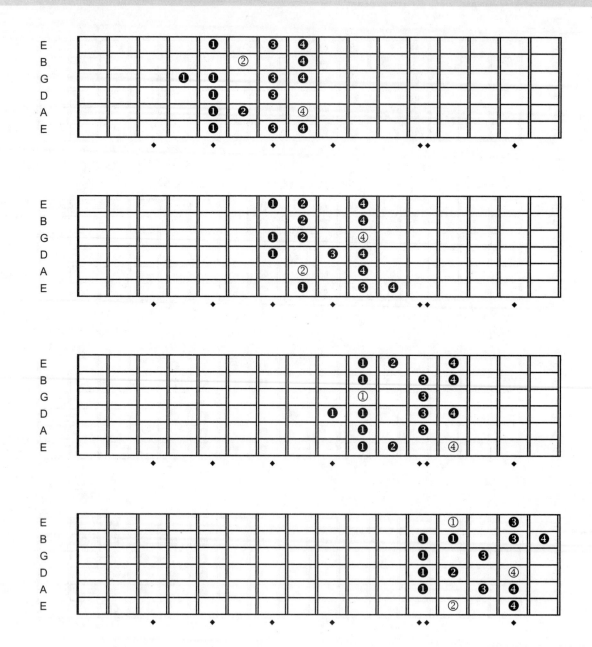

FIGURE 12-5: F#/Gb MIXOLYDIAN #4

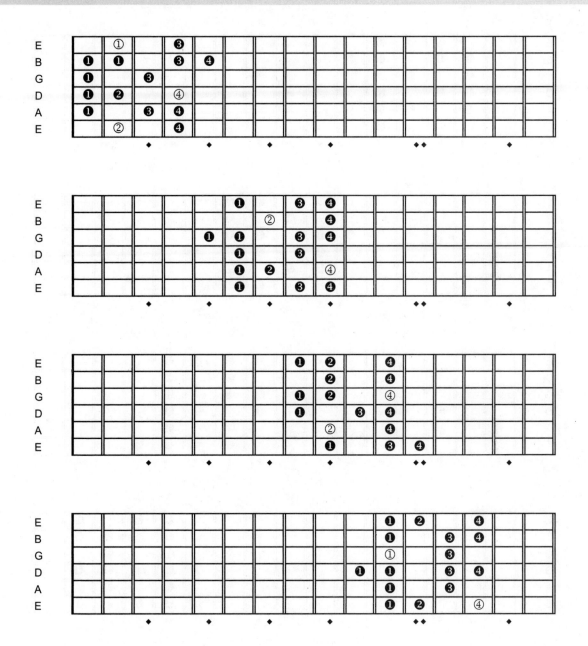

FIGURE 12-5: G MIXOLYDIAN #4

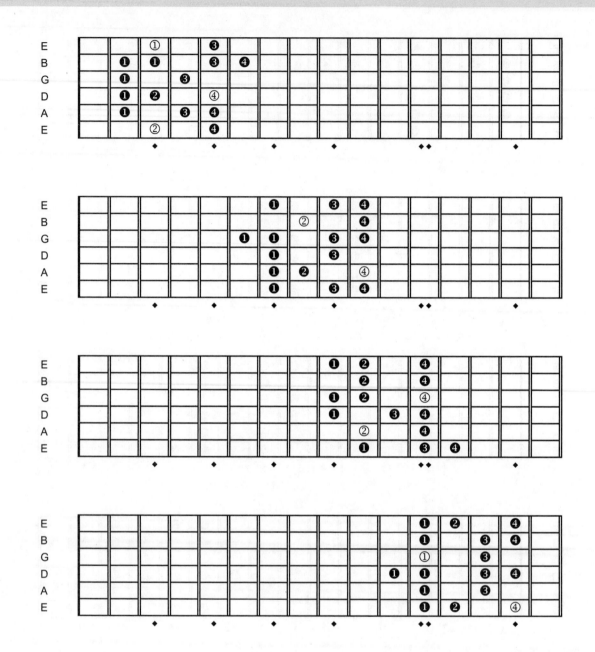

FIGURE 12-5: G♯/A♭ MIXOLYDIAN #4

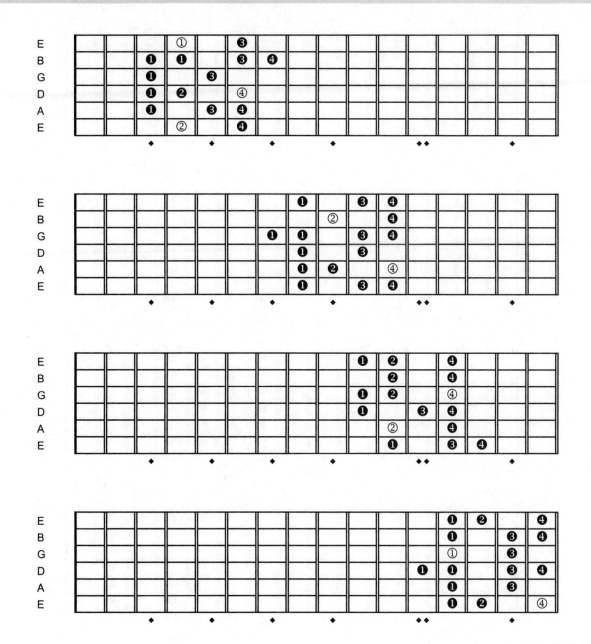

FIGURE 12-5: A MIXOLYDIAN #4

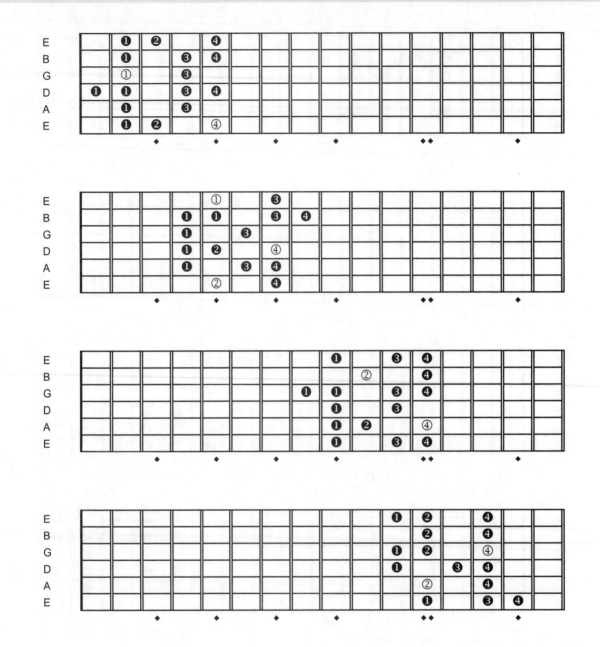

FIGURE 12-5: A#/B♭ MIXOLYDIAN #4

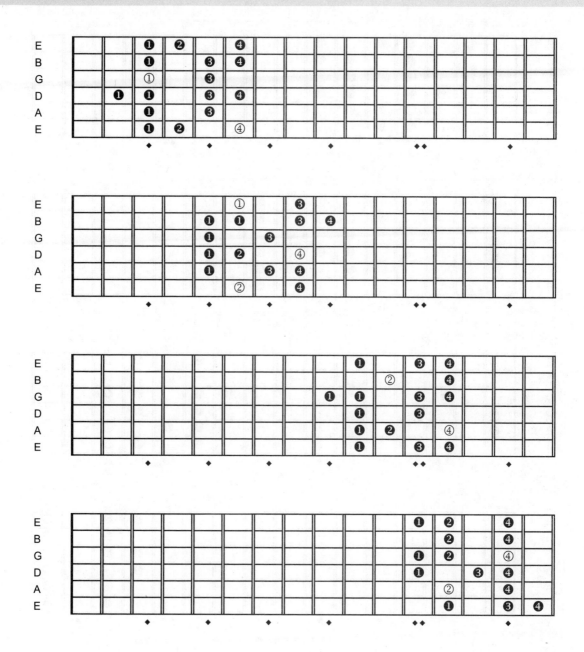

FIGURE 12-5: B MIXOLYDIAN #4

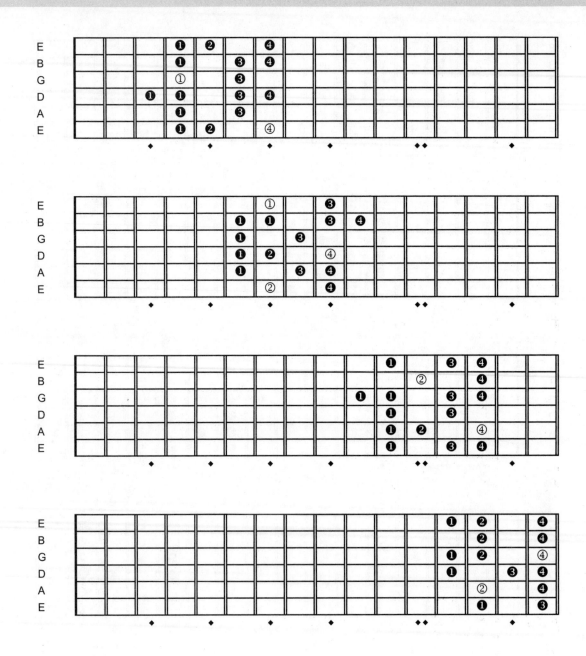

PART 3

Chords

What Is a Chord?

The combination of three or more notes is a chord. Three-note chords are called triads. Four-note chords are called seventh chords.

For many players, chord- and rhythm-playing is a good place to begin. Most students begin with a few open-position chords and move toward lead-playing as they get more comfortable. Since rhythm-playing is a great place to begin, let's discuss the open-position chords in detail.

OPEN-POSITION CHORDS

Open-position chords are chords that use the first four frets of the guitar in their formations. The term "open" is used because the chord is partly composed of open strings, meaning strings that your fingers don't press. Figure 13-1 shows you some common open-position chords.

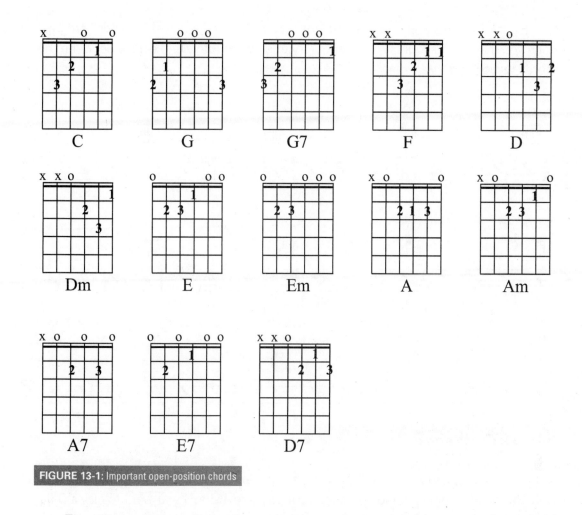

FIGURE 13-1: Important open-position chords

To really say that you know these chords, you have to be able to move from chord to chord with ease. You must memorize them because they are used in virtually every song you come across. Certain chord shifts can be very difficult to hit at first. Many students find the F chord a real problem—it's a tough chord—but the importance of chord-playing can't be overlooked.

The open-position chords are very common in rock and blues rhythm playing. There's a simple reason for this: open-position chords are easier to play. Open strings are like "free fingers" and allow us to play notes without fingering them. It can be strenuous to hold down all your fingers at once, and open strings give your fingers a break. Open-position chords tend to have five or six notes in them and have a larger range than other chords found on the guitar, which are normally, but not exclusively, limited to four notes—one per finger.

Figure 13-2 shows some examples of very common open-position chord progressions you may find in your favorite songs. Try to shift smoothly and evenly between the chords while you play.

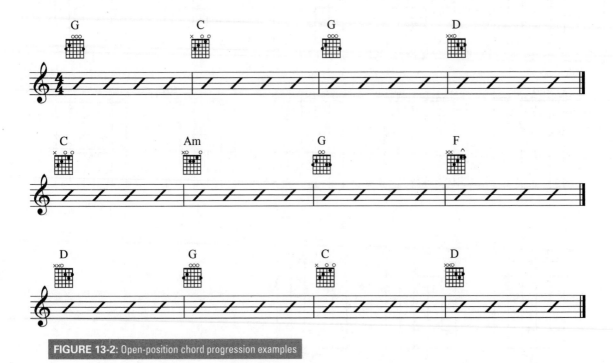

The limiting factor of open-position chords lies in the open strings themselves. Only chords that contain the open strings are possible. What if you want to play a B flat chord? A "B flat" chord doesn't have any open position; the open strings don't work with that chord. Same is true of many other chords, so you can see the open position won't help you gain full use of the guitar's chordal ability. The guitar is capable of playing wonderful and beautiful-sounding chords, but you will need to learn more than the open-position chords to get the full range of possibilities.

There aren't that many different chords. Couple this with the popularity of the guitar, and you can understand why so many songs sound similar: Many songs are based on exactly the same chords, just in a different order. The guitar's open position is limited; it takes a good player to get to the next step.

BARRE CHORDS

In order to play all the possible chords on the guitar, you must learn the concept of moveable chords. A moveable chord has a finger pattern than can be moved around the guitar without altering the shape of the chord. To achieve this, the guitar uses barre chords. The concept of a barre is very simple: one finger lies flat across the guitar neck and plays multiple notes. A barre is a technique that allows you to use the same finger for more than one string. Since you have only four fingers to fret chords with, and the guitar has six strings, you need to make efficient use of your fingers in order to play full chords. Barre chords allow you to make the most of your hands and play chords that contain five or six notes.

Look at Figure 13-3 to see what a G Major barre chord looks like.

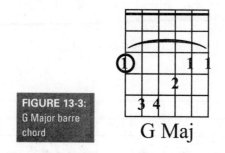

FIGURE 13-3:
G Major barre chord

G Maj

All of the notes that are played on the third fret are played with the first (index) finger. The finger lays flat across all the strings and clamps them down—this is what barre chords all do. Barre chords are difficult and require a lot of practice. It's normal to have trouble with them at first—keep practicing and you will get them. Barre chords enable you to play a five- or six-note chord with only four fingers. Without barre chords, guitar chords would be limited to only four notes—one per finger.

The beauty of barre chords is that they're moveable, meaning you can use the same shape as in Figure 13-3 and move it to another fret staying on the same string and change the name of the chord—without changing the fingering. This simplifies chords for guitar players. Instead of having to learn a different shape for each chord as in the open position, you can maintain the basic shapes and just move them to different frets.

The major chords and minor chords will probably be the most common chords you use as a guitar player. There are four different barre chord shapes to learn on the guitar to accomplish this task. There are two major barre chord forms, one on the sixth string, one on the fifth; and two minor barre chord forms, also on the sixth and fifth strings. The two forms result because the roots are placed on the sixth and fifth strings. Each string yields its own shape. Figure 13-4 is an example of the four different barre chord shapes broken down by string.

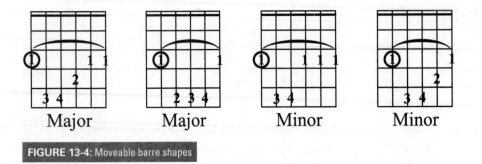

Major Major Minor Minor

FIGURE 13-4: Moveable barre shapes

To be able to move a chord, you have to know how chords get their names. All chords are named from the lowest note in the chord. With the moveable chord forms in Figure 13-4, the lowest note falls on either the sixth string or the fifth string. To move the chords, all you have to know is the name of the notes on the low strings. Then you can move the barre chord shapes to the appropriate location and play any chord you want. Figure 13-5 is a chart to help you find the chord names for moveable barre shapes.

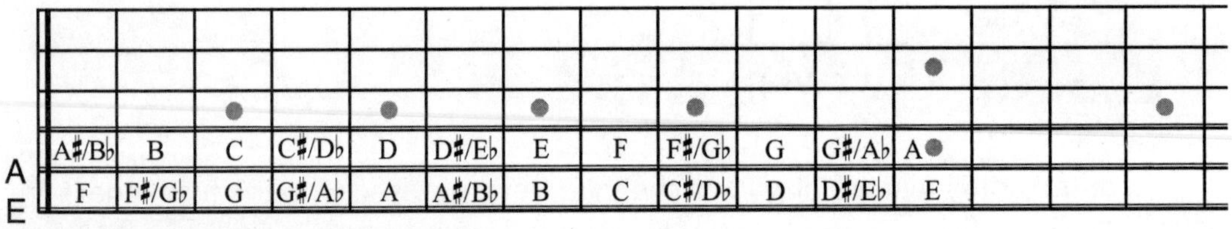

	A#/Bb	B	C	C#/Db	D	D#/Eb	E	F	F#/Gb	G	G#/Ab	A●			
A															
E	F	F#/Gb	G	G#/Ab	A	A#/Bb	B	C	C#/Db	D	D#/Eb	E			

FIGURE 13-5: String charts for E and A strings

Now that you have the concept down, let's apply this to a piece of music. Figure 13-6 uses barre chords in a standard rock chord progression.

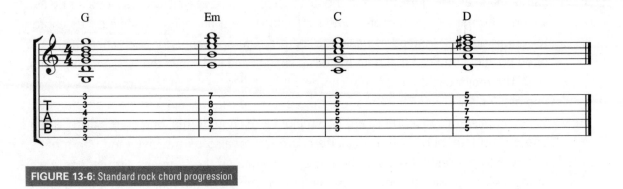

FIGURE 13-6: Standard rock chord progression

This example uses the same barre chord shapes from Figure 13-4 and applies them to some different chords. For a barre chord to work, you have to apply even pressure across the guitar neck. Otherwise, some strings will sound muted.

READING CHORD CHARTS

Once you've mastered the open-position chords and the moveable barre chords, you're ready to play almost anything that comes your way. Unlike music for the piano, guitar sheet music typically doesn't use standard notation for its chord playing. The ability to read standard notation is extremely important to being a good, well-rounded musician. As a guitarist, reading chord charts is a more common part of the job. Typically a chord chart consists of two elements: chord name and duration. Most chord charts won't show you exactly how to play the chords; you're expected to be able to play basic major and minor chords. Some charts will show a small chord box (like the ones in Figure 13-2) to aid you in playing the correct chord voicing.

Voicing refers to the way a chord is played. A simple C Major chord can be played many different ways on the guitar; each is a different voicing. For example, an open C Major chord and an eighth-fret barre chord are considered two different voicings of the same chord. If a guitar player is supposed to use an unusual chord voicing in place of a open chord, the chord charts will specify exactly how to play that chord.

The duration of the chord will be expressed in slash notation—one slash equals one strike of a chord with your pick or fingers. This simple way of notating guitar chords is common and acceptable. Chord charts are also used in jazz, country, blues, and commercial music styles. Many players find it faster to read the chord symbol C Major than to read the standard notation for the chord.

Figure 13-7 is a simple chord chart showing a D Major chord followed by an A-Major chord using open-position chords.

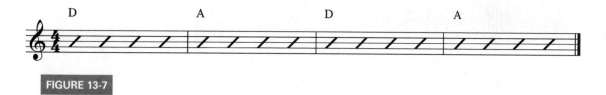

FIGURE 13-7

POWER CHORDS

Ah, the power chord. What a name for a chord. No one is sure who named it, but one thing is for sure—the title is fitting. A power chord, when played through a loud amplifier, especially in a rock setting, is one of the most powerful sounds you've ever heard. It is the standard chord of metal, rock, and punk music. There's no way to play guitar and never encounter a power chord. The real name for a power chord is a "fifth chord," as in C5.

Power chords are structurally different in that they contain only two notes: the root and the fifth of the chord. This breaks the traditional notion that chords contain three notes, but leave it to a guitar player to break the rules of music. Even though a power chord contains only the root and fifth, the root is usually doubled, so typically you play three notes anyway, just not three *different* notes. Power chords can be played anywhere on the neck of the guitar, but they sound best played as low as possible. Distortion is also a plus when dealing with power chords. Another neat thing about power chords is that they have a consistent finger shape that easily slides around the fingerboard.

After learning open-position and barre chords, mastering power chords is the next important step toward becoming a great player. Power chords are like barre chords because they are both movable chord shapes. Once you know the shape for a power chord, all you have to do is slide it around the guitar to make riffs. Figure 13-8 shows a power chord shape on the low E string and low A string.

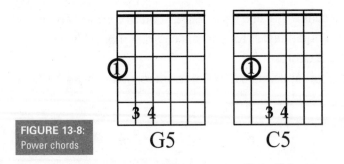

FIGURE 13-8:
Power chords

G5   C5

Notice how the shape is the same on both strings. This makes power chords very easy to move around: you end up locking your fingers into that shape and sliding your hand around the neck.

Power chords are commonly found on the low E and low A strings. Since they only use three fingers and don't have the complexity of barre chords, power chords can be moved around the guitar with ease. Power chord names follow the same rule other chords follow—the lowest note names the chord. In a power chord the lowest note will always fall on your first finger. Power chords are also called fifth chords. The standard symbol for a C power chord is C5. This type of notation helps distinguish it from the standard major and minor chord symbols. Power chords are neither major or minor; they are in a category all their own.

Some well-known songs that include power chords are:

- "Smells Like Teen Spirit" (Nirvana)
- "Welcome to Paradise" (Green Day)
- "Stairway to Heaven" before the solo (Led Zeppelin)
- "Purple Haze" (Jimi Hendrix)
- "Iron Man" (Black Sabbath)

STANDARD SHEET MUSIC

Now that you've learned a little bit about playing basic guitar chords, let's look at the nitty-gritty of reading sheet music so that you can expand your repertoire of chords. If you've ever looked at the sheet music to your favorite song, you probably noticed that standard sheet music usually doesn't include guitar tablature. Chords can be displayed as standard musical notation that every instrument can read, such as in Figure 13-9.

FIGURE 13-9

The only thing you'll find pertaining to the guitar are the chord boxes above the music. The chord boxes serve as a general suggestion of what you can play along with the song. Music publishers that include guitar chord boxes are not supplying the guitar parts exactly as played by your favorite artists. The chord boxes allow you to get the gist of how to play the song, but usually not exactly as the guitarist played it. Chord boxes typically rely on simple open-position chords. For exact versions of your songs, make sure the music includes guitar tablature and music staves. Look for versions that say "recorded guitar parts" printed on the sheet.

THE BASIC CHORD FRAME BOX

Because a picture is worth a thousand words, Figure 13-10 shows a sample chord frame box.

Let's break the box into its main elements:

- The first thing you need to see is the six strings of the guitar, represented vertically (as in Figure 13-11).
- The lowest string on the guitar is always on the left side, and the highest string is on the right side. This is standard. If you are a left-handed player, these will be backward to you. As unfair as this may sound, the guitar world has made little concession for southpaws, and you'll just have to learn to flip the diagram around in your head.
- On top of the vertical lines are horizontal lines that represent the frets of the guitar (as shown in Figure 13-12).

You now have a visual template for making chords. If you were to lay your guitar in your lap (strings up), you would be looking at a blank chord frame box. From here, you will learn the various elements that define the chords for you.

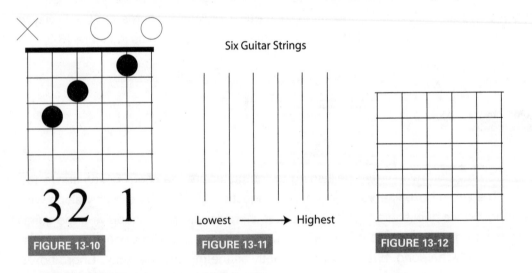

FIGURE 13-10

Six Guitar Strings

Lowest ⟶ Highest

FIGURE 13-11

FIGURE 13-12

Other Chord Frame Information

Once you have the blank template, you need to add information about which fingers to use to make these lifeless grids into music. We do so by adding black dots into the diagrams. The black dots sit right on the vertical strings they are played on, and in between the horizontal frets they are placed on. Figure 13-13 provides clarity.

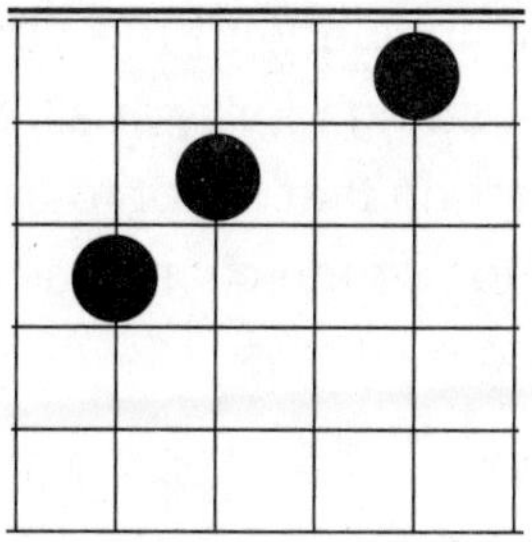

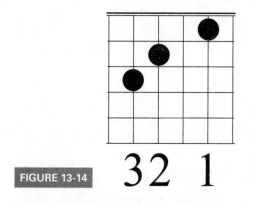

FIGURE 13-13

By assembling the chords this way, you can get a quick overview of where to put your fingers. If this is your first experience with chord frames, it may take a day or so to get used to them. Trust me, these boxes are very efficient and you'll be able to breeze through them in no time.

Using the Chord Frame Box

The chord frames now are infused with dots that show each chord's basic outline, but you still need a few more pieces of information in order to play the chords correctly. Once you learn how to read and interpret the chord frames, you will know where to place your fingers.

Fingering

First, you need to know which finger is responsible for which dot. Thankfully, this part is fairly obvious: Below each chord you will find a set of numbers. These numbers line up with the strings, and the dot markings tell you which finger to use to play each of the notes. This part is fairly simple (see Figure 13-14).

FIGURE 13-14

3 2 1

Open Strings and Dead Strings

In some chords, you play "open" strings—strings that contain no fretted fingers, but are part of the chords. To designate that a string is to be played open, a small open

"O" is placed above the chord frame, directly in line with the string. In the opposite sense, there are times when you don't want a string to play at all. This is designated in much the same way, using an "X" above the string that is not to be played. Just like an open-string indication, this will appear at the top of the chord frame diagram. See Figure 13-15 for the complete diagram with all the markings.

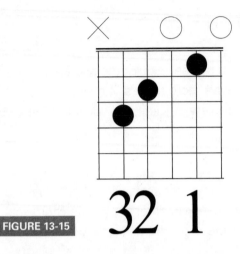

FIGURE 13-15

Location on the Fingerboard

You now have almost all the elements you need to play any chord in this book, but you still have to determine the exact location on the fingerboard. Each chord frame only displays five frets at a time. Most guitars have at least twenty or more frets, so how can this basic frame work for the whole guitar? That's simple—it's moveable. All you have to do is indicate where the chord frame sits. Let's look at Figure 13-16, a basic chord frame that sits in the open position (the first through fifth frets).

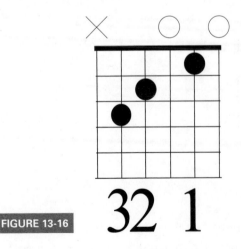

FIGURE 13-16

The big giveaway here is that the top horizontal line in the chord frame is a thick black line. This is to mimic the nut that your strings rest on, which is a thick piece of bone or plastic, depending on your guitar. If you see that thick black line, you know that you're in the open position.

For the chord frame to be moved, you have to be told where it's being moved. This is done with the marking "5 fr," meaning "fifth fret." What this tells you is that the first horizontal fret you see in the diagram is the fifth fret, and the five frets follow up from there (fifth through tenth frets). You'll also notice that the solid black line that indicated the open position is gone. This is another way to find out where you are if you happen to miss the fret marking. Take a look at Figure 13-17, which is a chord frame starting at the fifth fret.

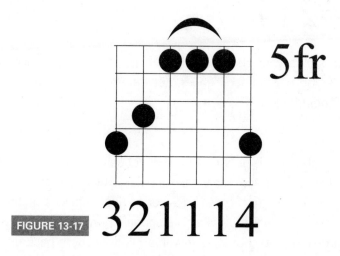

FIGURE 13-17

The marking is fairly prominent and easy to spot.

Barres

In the chord frame diagram you will see a barre indicated in two ways. The first is a curved line on top of the chord frame—this is the standard way to indicate a barre chord. The other way is to look at the fingering: If you see your first finger used three times in the same chord, you have a barre chord.

Just remember, your fingers are straight, and so are your frets. Though you will be playing multiple notes with the same finger, it will always be across the same frets. So if your hand is cramping up just thinking about this, have no fear; you simply flatten out your finger and lay it across the fret indicated. Figure 13-18 is an example of a barre chord.

Barre Indication

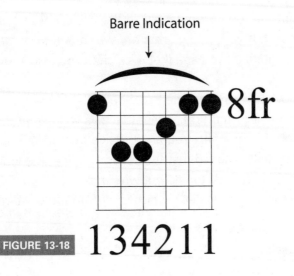

FIGURE 13-18 134211

Barre chords are common. As your chord vocabulary grows, you will encounter them often. Barres can happen on any left-hand finger, but the majority of barres occur on your first finger (your strongest finger).

Optional Notes

The last visual element to talk about is optional notes. Just because a chord can span five or six strings does not mean that it necessarily has to. Throughout this book you will notice that certain notes are gray. These gray notes can occur on fingers placed on the fingerboard, or on open strings themselves. Simply, if a note appears gray, you don't have to play it. Figure 13-19 is an example of two chords, one with an optional note occurring on a finger, and the other with an optional open string.

An optional fretted note   An optional open string

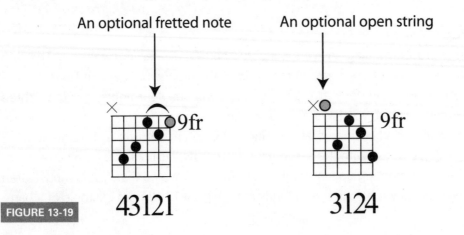

FIGURE 13-19   43121   3124

Now, let's talk about what constitutes an optional note. There are a few reasons that a note would be considered optional. Many times these "rules" go hand in hand and all are present at the same time. There isn't a way for you to know which rule is in place by simply looking at a chord grid. The gray note is optional for any of the reasons listed below; you'll see that certain optional note choices are more obvious than others.

Repeated Notes

Guitar chords typically have repeated notes within them. If the chord has a repeated note in it that isn't necessary to get the full sound of the chord, it can be considered optional. You can play the chord either way and you'll still be playing the exact same chord. The two chords will sound a bit different, but theoretically they are the same. This just leads to more variation in your chord playing!

Difficult Fingerings

If the optional note in question makes the chord really hard to play, either by introducing barre chords or unusual stretches, it is considered optional. Many times, difficult fingerings lead to exotic and interesting-sounding chords, so don't write them off totally. If you can slowly work up to playing all of the voicings in this section, you will get a greater picture of what's possible.

Dissonance

Dissonance is defined as a sound that is in conflict. At times, certain chords are voiced in such a way that certain notes, when played as part of the chord, cause a possible conflict. "Possible" because one man's meat is another man's poison, as the saying goes. You may not find the notes dissonant. The notes that may cause dissonance also are considered optional. Don't write them off if they don't sound beautiful to you yet. Give them time to grow on you. It's common for your ears to grow as you experience different sounds. In the end, you are given the choice; leave the note out if it doesn't suit your situation.

A Note on Fingering

This book is designed for all styles of guitar, including finger style, pick style, and any other style you can think of. You will be presented with chord shapes that seem impossible in your style (for example, muted notes in the middle of a chord). With a pick, muting notes inside of chords is very difficult, but for players who use their fingers, this is no big deal. The same goes for chords with wide spreads. Not every chord will be playable with a pick, though you can break the chord into two parts with a pick by playing the lowest note, skipping the muted string, and striking the rest of the chord a split second later. If you see a chord that you can't play, try switching to a different style.

WITHIN EACH CHAPTER

The first chord you will see in any chapter in this part is C, with all of its variations. Then you will see C♯ / D♭ and all its variations.

You will notice that C♯ and D♭ are listed on the same page. This is because these notes are considered "enharmonic": they are spelled differently but sound the same. All the enharmonic notes are listed together as "one" set of chord shapes, even though the music above each row of chords shows you two different note spellings. Here are the enharmonic notes in the book:

- C♯ / D♭
- D♯ / E♭
- F♯ / G♭
- G♯ / A♭
- A♯ / B♭

All twelve possible chord roots are listed chromatically. Once you get through all twelve of the chord roots, the chapter is complete.

Each individual chord is illustrated by five example shapes. Each of the five example shapes gives you real-world examples of how to play that particular chord at five different locations on the neck.

Why Five Shapes?

The five chords are set up in order from lowest-sounding chord to highest-sounding chord. This is done so you can have some sonic variety in your chord voicing. One of the neat things about chord voicing is that while any of the five chords in any set are all considered "the same chord," they will all sound just a bit different. This is due to the nature of chord building, which you will learn about in the next chapter. The goal here is to give you the five "best" shapes for any particular chord.

You may have seen books that advertise 35,000 chords for the guitar. No one knows that many chords. The chapters in this part are all about showing you the common, useful, and expected chord voicings. In some categories there are possibly hundreds of chords. For example, there are about eighty-eight possible C Major chords. How many do you think professional guitar players use? Certainly not eighty-eight. See the idea? These chapters are about giving you what you need to succeed as a chord player—and besides that, five chords fit nicely on a page!

THE COMPLEXITY OF THE GUITAR

The guitar is terribly complicated. Too many players never get out of the basic first position major and minor chords they are taught at early lessons or from friends. Why do so many players never reach beyond the "freshman fifteen"? (You will see this set of chords later in the book.) The reason for this is complicated and hard to explain. The truth is that the guitar is very logical in its layout. The strings and frets follow a predetermined order and if you study it well, you too may end up writing a book on guitar playing.

The guitar's true complexity, and for many its unique beauty, lies in what it can't do. It's not like a piano, which is an instrument with almost unlimited chordal possibilities. The guitar is hampered by the design of the instrument, the fact that you have only four fingers to form chords, and the fact that the instrument itself has only six strings (it could have more, but then you'd be playing the lute, and not reading a guitar book). Those factors limit the way you can play chords on the guitar. It also yields some unique and unusual ways to play chords that other instruments, such as piano, cannot approach.

ENDLESS POSSIBILITIES OF CHORDS

The briefest possible definition of a chord is that it is three notes played at one time. Chords can extend to much greater numbers than three notes; some chords have six or eight notes. When you couple this with the fact that the guitar has a range close to that of a grand piano, the possibilities of what you can consider a chord and name as a chord get absurd.

The complexity of music theory and the rules for how you name chords also make life a bit difficult. You can look at a certain guitar chord one way and call it "x" one day and then call it "y" the next. All these factors combine to make chord playing on guitar a bottomless well.

14

Chord Theory

Since this is a part about chords, it might not be the worst thing in the world to explain what a chord actually is. To the vast majority of guitar players, chords are "finger shapes" or "boxes" or "grips." Whatever you call them, few players think of them as groupings of notes that have order and structure. This very fact makes most guitar players look at a book that contains more than 2,000 chords and wonder how any player could possibly know that many shapes. The answer is that few players know that many individual shapes. The shapes are nothing more than combinations of notes. A simple three-note combination can yield many shapes—as many as eighty-eight shapes from the same three notes. The trick is to ignore the grandeur of "eighty-eight shapes" and remember that they all come from one thing: a pattern of notes. The best place to start is the triad.

THE TRIAD

A chord is any grouping of three or more notes played simultaneously. Disregard the "three or more" statement, and focus on the basic chord: the triad. You Latin scholars know that "tri" means "three"; therefore, a triad is a three-note chord. The "tri" also has another meaning: Each of the notes are three notes apart from each other. So, a triad is a three-note chord based on notes that are three notes apart from each other. The musician's term for distance is an "interval," so a triad has intervals of thirds between the notes.

Let's look at a very basic triad, the C Major triad, which is composed of the notes C, E, and G (see Figure 14-1).

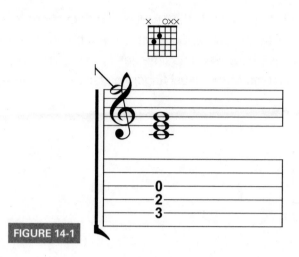

FIGURE 14-1

The triad is displayed three ways: in a chord grid, on a music staff, and in tablature. It's amazing how these visual systems look so different from each other, though each displays the exact same set of information.

CHORD VOICINGS

In truth, the basic C E G triad is more of a model than anything else. Have you ever played that particular C Major chord shown in Figure 14-1? No, most likely you don't encounter that exact triad. However, some of you may have noted an alarming similarity to the regular C Major chord that all guitar players play. The C Major triad appears to be part of the "full" C chord. Let's look at both side-by-side in chord frames (Figure 14-2).

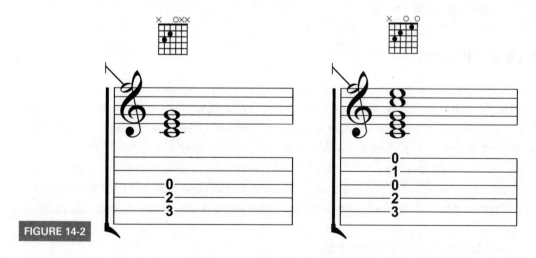

FIGURE 14-2

The chord on the left is the triad; on the right is the "typical" C Major chord. You can see that the first three notes are exactly the same. So what is the difference between the two? Let's look at Figure 14-2 again. However, this time, let's provide the names of the notes below the chord frames, instead of the usual fingerings (see Figure 14-3).

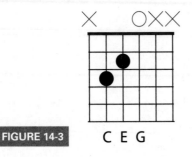

FIGURE 14-3   C E G

As you can see, the only difference between the two chords is that the traditional C Major chord simply "doubles" or "repeats" notes that are already in the chord. An extra C and an extra E fill out the chord more, and give you five contiguous strings to play, which is convenient for strumming chords. What you've just witnessed is the birth of a chord "voicing."

Triads will always be the perfect model of what a chord should be. Chord voicings are adaptations of those perfect models to fit within the framework of what the guitar can do. Now do you see how three notes can spawn eighty-eight or more chords?

The bottom line, in the case of a C Major chord, is that as long as it has C, E, and G in it, no matter where on the neck, and no matter what the order is, it's still a C Major chord. The only difference is that the chords are different voicings of each other, and will sound subtly different.

BASIC TRIADS

The most basic chords in the world are triads, just like the ones discussed earlier in the chapter. A triad is simply a group of three notes, with third intervals between the notes. The two most used triads are major and minor. They are used far more commonly than are the other two triads. Simply speaking, major chords have a "happy" feeling to them, while minor triads feel "sad" or "dark." It may seem like a silly explanation, but chords can conjure up emotions, and major and minor are often used to paint sonic pictures.

There are four different types of triads that make up the whole musical universe:

- Major triads (root, third, fifth)
- Minor triads (root, ♭third, fifth)

- Diminished triads (root, ♭third, ♭fifth)
- Augmented triads (root, third, ♯fifth)

The four triads above are the four basic building blocks of western music. The words in parentheses show the theoretical blueprint for how each chord is formed. The numbers correspond to the intervals away from the root. A third is three notes away from the root, and so on.

SEVENTH CHORDS

Once you start from the basic categories of triads, the next step is to make them more advanced. Simply take any of the triads and add another third interval. That takes you to what are called "seventh" chords. The theoretical blueprint for a C Major 7 chord would be root, third, fifth, and seventh, or C E G B in pitch.

Chords like C Major 7, F7, and G Diminished 7 are all examples of seventh chords. A seventh chord is a four-note chord, built in thirds. Because there are so many different combinations of triads and sevenths, there are a lot of seventh chords! One more hint: they are also called seventh chords because the root of the chord is seven notes away from the highest note of the chord. Chord naming is very literal; more on this in a minute.

Dominants

There are a ton of seventh chords. Every triad can have a seventh of some sort. There are major sevenths, minor sevenths, augmented sevenths, diminished sevenths, and so on. There are subvarieties of those chords as well. However, there is an area of confusion to clear up right away: There is one extremely common type of seventh chord that musicians refer to as "dominant seventh" chords. These are the most typical and common seventh chords. If you've only been playing guitar a little bit, these are the first seventh chords that you will come into contact with. Here is what a dominant seventh chord looks like when you write it out: D7. The formula for this construction is: chord root (in this case, D), directly followed by the number 7.

All of these chords are dominant seventh chords: C7, D7, E7, F7, G7, A7, B7.

So many people think that these are the *only* seventh chords in the universe! They are very common, so they come up often. Remember that while there are many different types of seventh chords, most guitar players commonly refer to the dominant seventh chord simply as *the* seventh chord, so be aware of this to avoid confusion.

To signify one of the "other" seventh chords, you'd need to add more information, such as the "major" and "minor" in C Major 7 and C Minor 7. As long as you can spot the distinction and not get confused, you will be in good shape.

SIXTH CHORDS

This may seem out of order, considering that we just talked about seventh chords and now we're onto sixth chords, but there is a reason! Seventh chords follow the nice triad pattern of thirds and are the next logical step from the triads. Sixth chords are in their own little family.

Jumping back to dominant seventh chords for a second, you just learned that when you see a letter and number combination, it indicates a dominant chord; for example, C7. Unfortunately, music is full of inconsistencies, and here is one of them: A chord such as C6 belongs in the family of major chords, not in the family of dominant chords. This is an exception you need to learn. Sixth chords are major or minor and do not belong with dominant chords even though they follow the same "rule" for written expression that dominants do: a letter directly followed by a number. As to what a sixth chord is, chord names are literal, so take a guess. What makes sense? How about a triad, with a sixth note attached? C6 = C E G A, with A being six notes higher than the root of C. See, chord naming isn't that hard at all! C6 is a major chord; sixth chords also exist in the minor section, but thankfully, they are easy to spot: "C Minor 6." Just don't get them confused with dominant chords! Tip: sixth chords are some of the prettiest-sounding chords out there. Go find some to play!

TALL CHORDS

The next step after seventh chords is to make your chords taller. They're called "taller" because as you stack the chords on the music staff, they reach vertically higher on the page. Making taller chords is as simple as adding additional third intervals. Remember, chords are made up almost completely of third intervals. This is called "tertian" (based on three) harmony, and is the foundation of the western system of harmony.

Here is how the next group of chords stacks up. After seventh chords, there are:

- Ninth chords (root, third, fifth, seventh, ninth)
- Eleventh chords (root, third, fifth, seventh, ninth, eleventh)
- Thirteenth chords (root, third, fifth, seventh, ninth, eleventh, thirteenth)

You can't go any higher than thirteenth chords because adding one more third will loop you back around to where you started by adding another root. Also realize that a thirteenth chord has seven notes in it, and you have six strings and four fingers. Part of the art of guitar chord voicing is compromising on these tall chords in order to make them playable.

Tall chords aren't exclusively a "jazz" thing, but they are used most commonly in jazz. They have a truly unique sound that's worth checking out, even if you don't play jazz. You never know when you'll want to use them to spice up your music.

Finger Limits

Tall chords can sometimes lead to problems. The guitar is a limited harmonic instrument. This may seem hard to believe, considering the number of chords you can play, but compared to the piano, the guitar is extremely limited. If you look at the chord pages themselves, you will see that each page has five chords, with the music staff on top spelling out the chord as it appears in written music. The guitar is rarely, if ever, capable of playing the exact written chord specified in each section. This is an important point to touch on. The music staff at the top of each set of chords is there for theoretical display only. It is never represented *exactly* that same way in the chords below. What the chords below show are voicings of the music at the top of the page. Basically, they are different versions of the chord, working within the confines of the tuning of the guitar and the number of fingers you have to play with. Remember, a thirteenth chord has seven notes in it, so you'd never be able to play that chord with four fingers and six strings; the five voicings shown are five of the ways that the guitar can play a thirteenth chord. Don't feel that this is a limitation! What the guitar can do, and what a great guitarist can do, is play the essence of the chord, the notes that best define the harmony. The beauty of the guitar is overcoming this limitation and finding some unique chord voicings. The written music is the model, and the five resulting voicings are the best-case scenarios for reproducing that chord. If only there were more strings and you had more fingers—well, just more fingers; they make guitars with thirteen strings.

ODD-LOOKING DOMINANT CHORDS

Dominant chords are broken into two categories, unaltered and altered. The unaltered chords are easy to spot: In the key of C they are C 7, C 9, and C 13. Looking at the rest of the chapter, you will see some very unusual-looking chords. For example, take a look at C 7 ♯ 11 or C 7 ♯ 5. These chords are called "altered" dominant chords. Altered dominant chords are a staple of jazz. Basically, you alter one or more of the pitches in the chord, up or down one fret, to create a new and unusual sound. If you are reading a jazz chart, you will see these chords. They are not just here for fun; they are commonly used in jazz music.

There are many varieties of altered dominant chords. This part of the book gives you the garden-variety chords, which will get you through most any situation. When in doubt, please look at the chord simplification section found later in this chapter. It will get you through anything that might come your way.

OTHER CHORDS

You now have progressed through most of the chords that you will encounter in music. There are a few "rogue" categories of chords that you also need to handle as a guitar player. Here is the lowdown on what those chords are.

Suspended Chords

A suspended chord is a fairly common chord in all styles of music. The basic chord is still the triad. The triad, as you learned earlier, is composed of the root, third, and fifth (C E G for C Major triad). In any chord, the third (in this case, E) is the defining member of the chord. The third of *any* chord is very important. When you take the third away completely you get a power chord, which yields a unique sound. In the case of a suspended chord, you take the third of the chord away and replace it with another tone: either the second or the fourth note above the root. This yields **two possible** suspended, or "sus" chords: sus 2 and sus 4. The name "suspended" is literal; these chords seem to be frozen and suspended in motion and sound. Taking away the most important tone of the chord and replacing it with something else produces a sound that isn't dissonant, just *unresolved.* Typically, suspended chords are momentary chords. You often see C Major, Csus2, and then C Major, as the suspension serves as a temporary "pass-through." Suspended chords are neither major nor minor chords. They are harmonically ambiguous because the third is missing. The third of the chord is the defining element. Without it, it's not really much of a "chord" in the traditional sense. Sus chords do have intriguing sounds and are used as chords that don't ever resolve. They are simply another color in your palette.

In your music, you will usually see exactly which suspension is called for, either the sus 2 or the sus 4. If the chord just says "C sus," it's up to you to choose one or the other. There is no right or wrong choice in that case. Most likely, the composer wanted an ambiguous sound, and both the sus 2 and sus 4 will suffice in that regard.

Triads over Bass Notes (Slash Chords)

There is one last chord type to explain before you can get the most out of this book. Slash chords, which also are called triads over bass notes, are another subset of chords. A slash chord is presented like this: C/E or C min/Ab. A slash chord is composed of two elements: On the left side is the basic chord, and on the right side is the note that should be the lowest-sounding note. Usually, slash chords are used to show specific chord motions and specific voicings.

The beauty of slash chords is that typically, the right side of the slash chord (the bass note), is not played by the guitar player. Typically, the job of playing the lowest note is left up to the bass player. When encountering a slash chord, you simply play the left side of the slash and the bass player plays the right side. Together, you get the correct sound. Since theoretically any chord can be played over any bass note, these have been left out altogether, because they would muddy up this book with chords that truly may never come into play. It's enough to know that all of the chords on the left side of the slash chords are covered in this book.

If you are playing guitar alone, without a bass player, it isn't too hard to create a slash chord. Simply take a chord voicing you know, and try to place the appropriate bass note on your lowest string. Sometimes this is easy. Sometimes this is hard. It's really great when the bass note is an open string! A great example is A/E, which is telling you to play an A Major chord with an E in the bass. Because E is an open string, you can play this chord (shown in Figure 14-4).

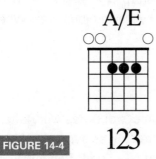

FIGURE 14-4

This is nothing more than a simple open A chord with an open E added to the chord. When in doubt, just play the triads on the left side of the slash. You won't be wrong.

CHORD SIMPLIFICATION

Jazz and pop music make use of "extensions" on chords. Extensions are notes added to the top of the chords. Typically these extensions are intervals of a ninth, eleventh, and thirteenth. You learned earlier that these are called tall chords. Extensions can also be any combination, and in the case of altered dominants, they can be very messy chords. The good news about extensions is that you don't have to play them. Extensions provide a more colorful harmony, one that is more jazz-like. However, the basic chord still stays the same. For example, if you see C Major 13, you will know that it's in the family of C Major 7, and you can play that instead. The same holds true for any extended chord:

- C m 13, C m 11, C m 9 = C m 7 (C Minor 7)
- C 9, C 11, C 13 = C 7 (C Dominant 7)

This is the case no matter how elaborate the chord is. Here is a scary example: E 7 ♯ 9♭ 9♭ 5♯ 13.

That's an actual chord! Disregard everything after the E7 and simply play an E7 chord. Even though the chord asks for more, by playing less you're not playing anything wrong—you're just playing a simpler harmony.

The one alteration that you need to watch out for is an alteration to the fifth note: ♯5 or ♭5. The fifth is considered a core note of the chord and not an extension as a ninth or an eleventh is. When the fifth is altered, if at all possible you should try to play it, even if it means excluding the extensions (just playing E 7♭ 5) in the example above.

Alterations and extensions are there for a reason, so whenever possible try to play the chord as best as you can. Often, the altered notes are part of melodies that other instruments are playing, so you end up supporting them by playing the notes. When you can't do that, simplify.

CHORDS WRITTEN AS SYMBOLS

Guitar chords don't usually appear in written music as stacks of notes. Very often, and especially in jazz and show music, you'll find chords written out as symbols of text. The player is responsible for knowing how to play that chord in a comfortable way on the guitar. Unfortunately, no one standard exists. Over the years, several conventions for writing out chords have been used:

- A major chord can appear as one of the following symbols: C, C Maj, C M, C △.
- A minor chord can appear as one of the following symbols: C min, C m, C -.
- Diminished chords are written the following way: C °, C dim.
- Augmented chords are written this way: C +, C aug.
- Dominant seventh chords are written this way: C 7.
- Major seventh chords are written this way: C Maj 7, C M 7, C △ 7.
- Minor seventh chords are written this way: C min 7, C m 7, C - 7.
- Diminished seventh chords are written this way: C dim 7, C ° 7.
- Half diminished seventh chords are written this way: C min 7♭ 5, C ø 7, C − 7♭ 5.

THE FRESHMAN FIFTEEN

Here are the first chords you should know by heart before going any further in this book. These are your "freshman fifteen."

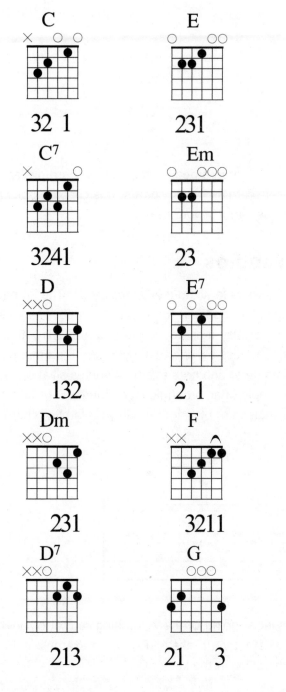

C
32 1

E
231

G⁷
32   1

C⁷
3241

Em
23

A
123

D
132

E⁷
2 1

Am
231

Dm
231

F
3211

A⁷
2 3

D⁷
213

G
21   3

B⁷
213 4

15

Arpeggios

The name may sound grandiose, but an arpeggio is simply a chord played one note at a time. Arpeggios are also referred to as frozen chords. This chapter looks at what you need to know to master them as a tool in your repertoire.

THE THEORY OF ARPEGGIOS

You've heard many arpeggios in your life without even realizing it. The intro to "Stairway to Heaven"? That's an arpeggio. The opening to "Freebird" is all arpeggios. Any time you finger-pick through a chord or play a chord slowly, you're playing an arpeggio. An arpeggio shares the exact same notes as a chord, but you vary the timing of each note. It's the presentation that differs here: one note at a time versus all at once.

Let's look at a simple example of an arpeggio (see Figure 15-1). Take the notes of a C Major chord (C, E, G) and instead of playing them in your familiar chord shape, play them one note at a time.

FIGURE 15-1: C Major arpeggio

There's really nothing special going on here, nothing radical or new. But when done right, you won't know what hit you! Take a look at the example in Figure 15-2 of arpeggios over a I-vi-IV-V progression in the key of C.

FIGURE 15-2: Arpeggios over a I-vi-IV-V progression

The example is laid out with one measure per chord (four measures in total). For each measure, you've taken the notes of the chords and spelled them out one by one.

One of the greatest examples of arpeggios is in the Eagles' song "Hotel California." The famous two-guitars lead at the end of the solo is comprised entirely of arpeggios. The arpeggios are taken from the same repeating chord progression that is used throughout the song.

Becoming Aware

It happens to every guitar player at a certain point—you become aware. You become aware of chords, you become aware of scales, and, in general, you become aware of how other guitar players create solos and riffs. This is akin to finding out that there's a secret camera on you at all times; all of a sudden it really matters what you say and do.

For players early in their guitar-playing experiences, it's okay to just crank away at the blues scale, riffing endlessly without knowing or caring too much about the smaller details. But for guitar students, a real cathartic moment comes when they become aware of chords and their relationship to everything else in music. Simply put, chords rule everything. Chords dictate what notes can be in the melody, what notes are in the bass lines, and what tones sound good in a solo. Chords have a lot of power. Once you become aware of them, it's hard to ignore them.

Chord Dictatorship

Chords are like questions. When you play a C Major chord you expect a certain answer—notes from that chord or scale. When a chord is played, the notes from that chord become the strongest notes to improvise melodies with. For any given chord you play over, the notes in those chords are the best and most direct choices. If you play a C Major chord, the notes C, E, and G sound the best. They sound good because they're played in the chord, and you are merely reiterating them.

The Big Picture

As you can see, the relationship between chords and music is undeniable. When most singers create a melody, they do so over preexisting chords. If you went back and compared any melody line to the chords, you'd find that the melody line utilizes notes from those chords. If music ignored the chords totally, it wouldn't sound very good. This interaction between chords and melodies is vital to tonal music.

Arpeggios are usually played in order, meaning that the notes follow their usual order, unlike normal guitar chords that shuffle the notes around for convenience. Basic arpeggios are only three or four notes long, and unless you repeated them in different octaves, any examples would be very short. Since arpeggios correlate with the chords, we will look at major, minor, and diminished arpeggio fingerings. Augmented arpeggios will be left out because they're used so seldom, but don't let that stop you from trying them on your own!

FINGERINGS FOR MAJOR ARPEGGIOS

To form major arpeggio fingerings, all you need to do is identify the notes of a major chord and play them one after another. Let's use G Major this time for variety. The notes of a G Major chord are G, B, D. Look at the notes G, B, D over the entire fingerboard in the full neck diagram in Figure 15-3 of a G Major arpeggio.

FIGURE 15-3: G Major arpeggio full neck diagram

Again, looking at the whole neck like this can be a little intimidating, but we can distill this information into some moveable shapes. In Figure 15-4, the first shape starts with a root on the sixth string. Just as in the major scales, this shape begins on a second finger.

FIGURE 15-4: G Major arpeggio root on sixth string

There is an alternate fingering for this arpeggio that starts with the second finger. See Figure 15-5.

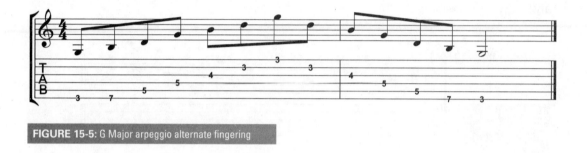

FIGURE 15-5: G Major arpeggio alternate fingering

While there may be common fingerings for these arpeggios, choose the fingering that is the most comfortable for you. As you move to the fifth string, there are two arpeggio shapes, one from the pinky finger and one from the first finger. Figures 15-6 and 15-7 share the same notes, but finger shapes change; we've seen this happen often in scales and chords.

FIGURE 15-6: G Major arpeggio root on the fifth string

These four shapes constitute the most typical and comfortable shapes on the guitar, but don't let this stop you from exploring the neck. Any combination of G, B, D will make a G Major arpeggio. Figure 15-8 is an unorthodox fingering that spans many frets and traverses the neck.

FIGURE 15-8:
G Major arpeggio,
long fingering

FINGERINGS FOR MINOR ARPEGGIOS

Minor arpeggios get their tones from minor chords. To turn a G Major chord into a G minor chord, all you have to do is lower the third note from B to B♭. The same holds true for arpeggios: To transform the major arpeggios to minor arpeggios, you lower B to B♭. Doing so changes the shapes completely, but that's okay—only one note changes, so they don't look that different. For the sixth string, you get only one fingering shape; this one starts with the first finger. See Figure 15-9.

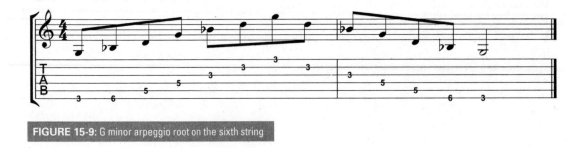

FIGURE 15-9: G minor arpeggio root on the sixth string

For the fifth string, there are two fingerings, and like major arpeggios they start with the first and fourth fingers, and both contain the exact same notes. Choose the shape that feels more comfortable to play. See Figures 15-10 and 15-11.

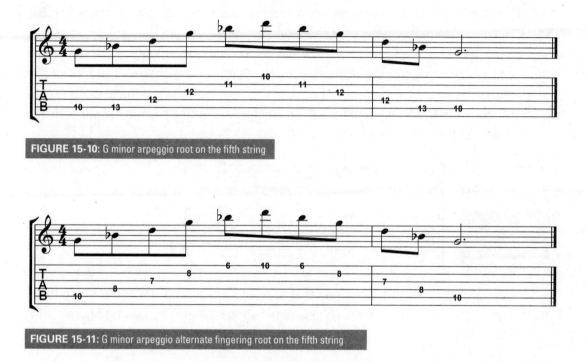

FIGURE 15-10: G minor arpeggio root on the fifth string

FIGURE 15-11: G minor arpeggio alternate fingering root on the fifth string

You can also do a long arching lick (as shown in figure 15-8) in minor, by simply changing the Bs to B♭s. Figure 15-12 shows the long arpeggio fingering for minor.

FIGURE 15-12: G minor arpeggio, long fingering

FINGERINGS FOR DIMINISHED ARPEGGIOS

Approaching the diminished arpeggio requires a little bit different tack than with major and minor. The diminished triad is not used much; therefore, the examples here are based on the diminished seventh chord. A G diminished seventh triad is spelled G, B♭, D♭, E. All diminished seventh chords share one very special trait: They are symmetrical. The distance between each of the notes is a minor third; no arpeggios we've studied thus far have had this symmetrical relationship. Symmetrical shapes are a lot of fun on guitar, because their fingerings repeat. Let's look at what symmetrical looks like on guitar. Here is the basic fingering for a G diminished seventh arpeggio in Figure 15-13.

FIGURE 15-13:
G diminished
seven arpeggio

Now you can take this exact finger shape, and move it up the same string three frets higher, and you will still be playing G diminished seventh. Try playing figure 15-14.

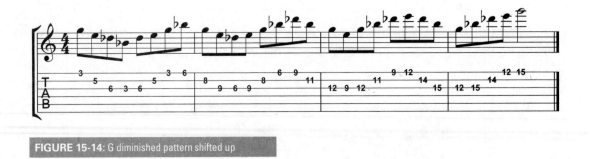

FIGURE 15-14: G diminished pattern shifted up

You can keep moving this pattern up three frets, and you will always be playing G diminished seventh. It's extremely easy to play diminished, because the fingerings across the neck are all the same. If you need to move this into other keys, just look where the circled finger is to find the root. You can move that finger to any root you need and repeat the process up every three frets.

There's another shape that utilizes some lower strings that you can move the same way. Figure 15-15 utilizes a G diminished shape on the second, third, and fourth strings.

FIGURE 15-15: G diminished seven arpeggio on inside strings

You can shift this shape up the neck as well; just move up three frets and the pattern repeats.

There are some shapes that utilize simpler fingerings. Look at Figure 15-16 that starts on the sixth string and moves across the neck all the way up to the high string.

FIGURE 15-16: G diminished seventh arpeggio across all strings

To hear diminished arpeggios in rock music, listen to Richie Blackmore of Deep Purple and Yngwie Malmsteen. If you'd like to go to the source, J.S. Bach is a great place to start. Check out his sonatas and partitas for solo violin.

APPLYING ARPEGGIOS

Enough talk about shapes and such! You're ready to apply this to music. Let's invent a chord progression using simple open-position chords to play arpeggios over. Let's use this simple chord progression in the key of C Major: C Major, A minor, F Major, G Major, E minor, D minor, C Major. Play through that cycle of chords and get the sound in your head. To make an arpeggio solo, all we have to do is move the shapes we learned earlier to the correct roots. For the example in Figure 15-17, let's use only shapes with roots on the fifth strings.

FIGURE 15-17: Arpeggio, example one

It's amazing what you can do with these shapes, and they sound so good! Figure 15-18 shows another example utilizing just two chords, A minor and B diminished seventh.

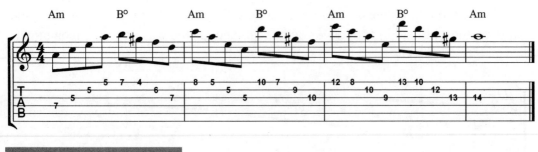

FIGURE 15-18: Arpeggio, example two

As you can see from these two examples, making your own fingerings isn't that difficult, but it does mean that you have to know what chords you're playing over. Until you have a lot of experience, you probably won't be whipping these out on the spur of the moment; many of your arpeggio solos will be planned, and that's just fine! There's nothing wrong with working things out in advance; you have to crawl before you walk.

Other Arpeggios

Since an arpeggio is nothing more than a chord frozen, do you have to limit your arpeggio options to just simple triads? Of course not! Some of the most beautiful chords on the guitar have extra notes in them. Figure 15-19 is a great chord progression using added-ninth chords.

FIGURE 15-19: Chord progression using added ninths

How would you create an arpeggio pattern for C Major added ninth and A minor added ninth? Simple, figure out what the extra note is and fit it into your arpeggio shape. For C Major, the ninth is D. Add that into your arpeggio shape, and you come up with figure 15-20.

FIGURE 15-20: C Major added-ninth arpeggio

For the A minor ninth chord, the ninth is B. You can also add that into the shape to come up with Figure 15-21.

FIGURE 15-21: A minor added-ninth arpeggio

You can combine these shapes into a run and come up with a very cool lick. Again, a little brainpower goes a long way here. See Figure 15-22.

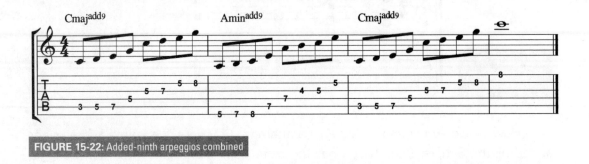

FIGURE 15-22: Added-ninth arpeggios combined

Musical Notes

Players who use arpeggios include Steve Vai, Joe Satriani, Yngwie Malmsteen, Joe Walsh, Don Felder, Trey Anastasio, and John Petrucci.

ARPEGGIOS IN THE BLUES PROGRESSION

The blues isn't just the blues scale. True blues playing is a conglomeration of scales and arpeggios used freely. Trying to talk about the elements separately is difficult, because when you hear a great player you hear the finished product, not the process the player learned. Since you know that the blues progression is built from three chords, you can take those chords and make them into arpeggios. Figure 15-23 shows an example of the twelve-bar blues progression in F using nothing but triads for the chords.

FIGURE 15-23: Twelve-bar F blues using arpeggios

All of these notes sound great over the chords. But in reality no blues player plays just arpeggios; he or she incorporates many different things to make solos. Use this as a guide to what's available to play, and try mixing scales and arpeggios into great blues solos.

The best way to practice this material is to apply it to real music. Take sample chord progressions from songs and try to create arpeggio lines with them. Make up your own chord progressions as exercises and work them out. For you blues players, work through the blues progression in different keys—especially A and E. The more work you do on this the better you will know the material. And most important, study solos you like. You may not "get" what arpeggios are really about until you hear an experienced player use them. If you like the more modern technical players like Vai, Satriani, and Malmsteen, then you've heard arpeggios a lot of the time. Blues players use arpeggios all the time, but they're harder to spot; they may use one or two notes from an arpeggio and then move on to something else. But in the end the result is music, and to speak the language of music well you have to be versed in all aspects of musical vocabulary. Arpeggios are just one more trick in your bag.

16

Major Chords

Much of today's music is made up of major chords. In our society, these chords make up the "happy" sounds in music. In popular music, they are a staple with many possibilities.

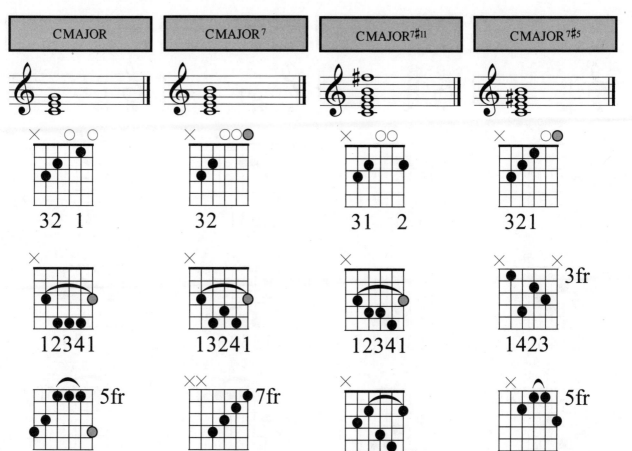

CMAJOR	CMAJOR⁷	CMAJOR⁷#¹¹	CMAJOR⁷#⁵

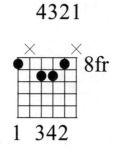
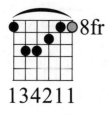
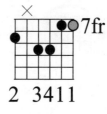
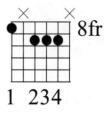
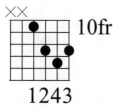
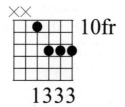
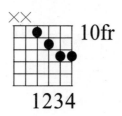
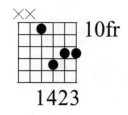

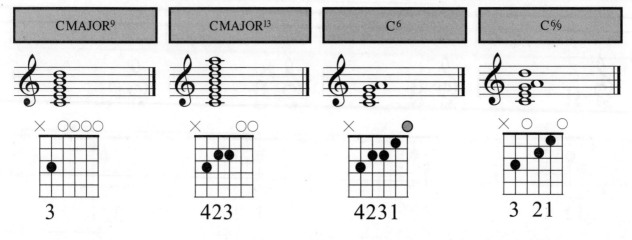

CMAJOR⁹	CMAJOR¹³	C⁶	C⁶⁄₉

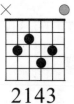
3

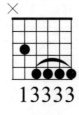
423

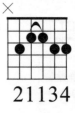
4231

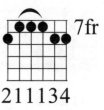
3 21

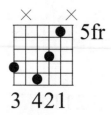
2143

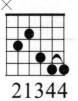
13244

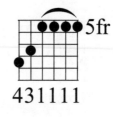
13333

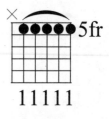
21134

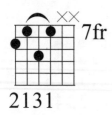
3 421

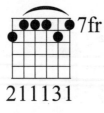
21344

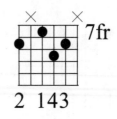
431111 5fr

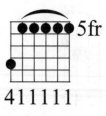
11111 5fr

2131 7fr

211131 7fr

2 143 7fr

411111 5fr

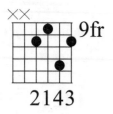
2143 9fr

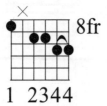
1 2344 8fr

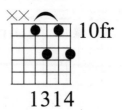
1314 10fr

211134 7fr

C MAJOR add9	C#/Db MAJOR	C#/Db MAJOR7	C#/Db MAJOR7#11

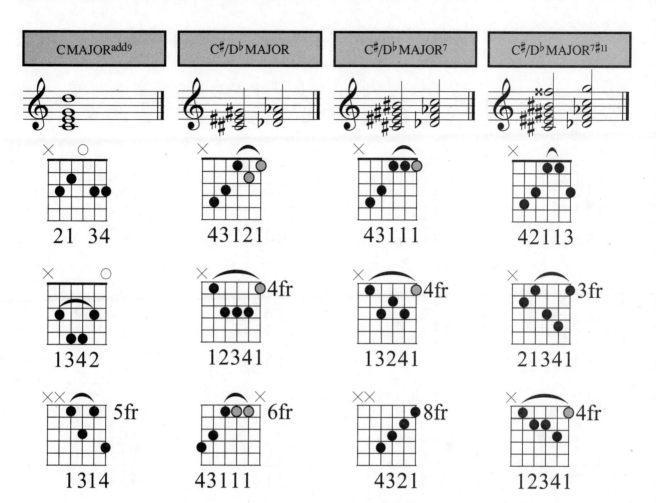

21 34   43121   43111   42113

1342   12341 4fr   13241 4fr   21341 3fr

1314 5fr   43111 6fr   4321 8fr   12341 4fr

3214 8fr   134211 9fr   1 342 9fr   2 3411 8fr

1341 10fr   1243 11fr   1333 11fr   34111 6fr

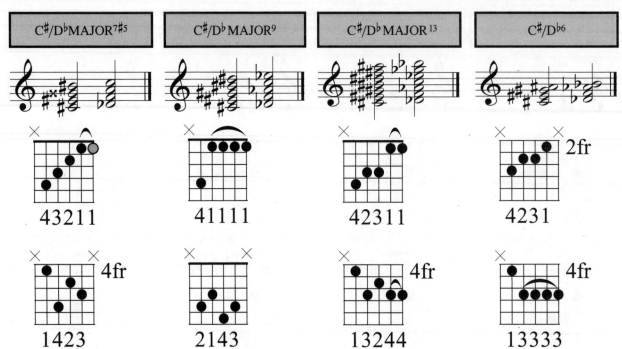

C#/Db MAJOR7#5	C#/Db MAJOR9	C#/Db MAJOR13	C#/Db6
43211	41111	42311	4231 (2fr)
1423 (4fr)	2143 (4fr)	13244 (4fr)	13333 (4fr)
2114 (6fr)	3 421 (6fr)	21344 (3fr)	431111 (6fr)
1 234 (9fr)	2131 (8fr)	211131 (8fr)	1 243 (8fr)
1423 (11fr)	2143 (10fr)	1 2344 (9fr)	1314 (11fr)

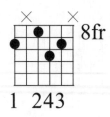
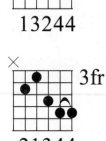
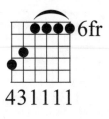

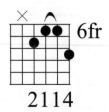
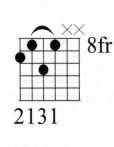
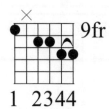
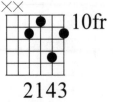
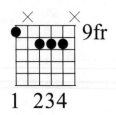
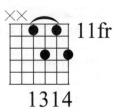
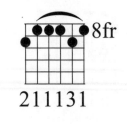

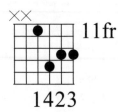

| C♯/D♭6/9 | C♯/D♭add9 | D MAJOR | D MAJOR⁷ |

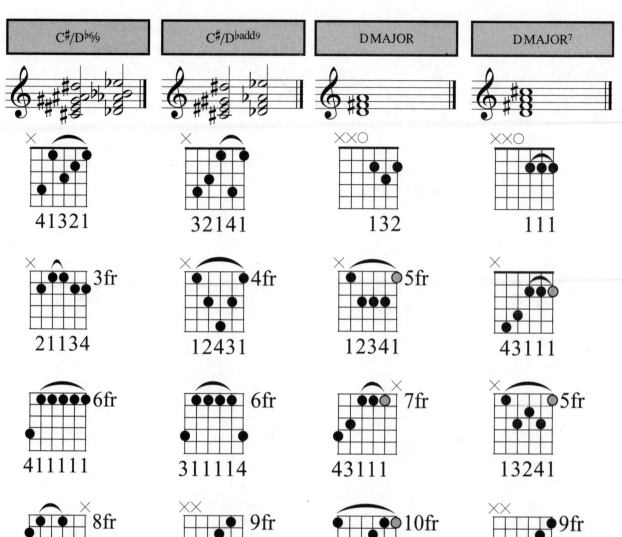

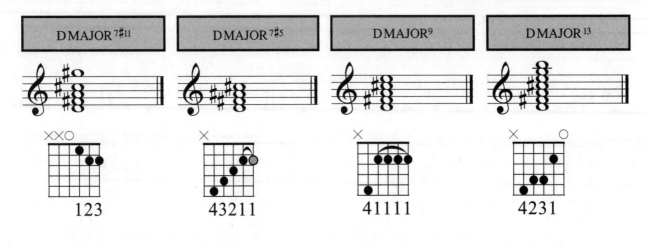

DMAJOR 7#11	DMAJOR 7#5	DMAJOR 9	DMAJOR 13

123 | **43211** | **41111** | **4231**

 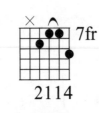 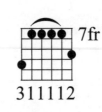 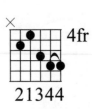

21341 | **1423** | **2143** | **13244**

   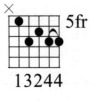

1234 | **2114** | **311112** | **21344**

 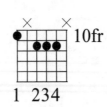 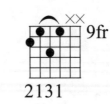 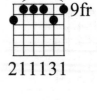

2 341 | **1 234** | **2131** | **211131**

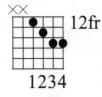 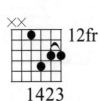 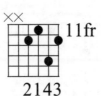 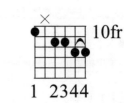

1234 | **1423** | **2143** | **1 2344**

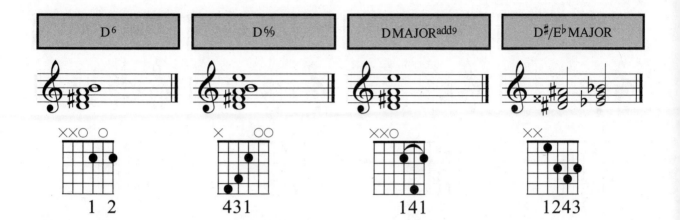

D^6	D$^{6}_{9}$	D MAJOR^{add9}	D$^\sharp$/E$^\flat$ MAJOR

 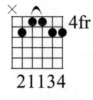 

| 1 2 | 431 | 141 | 1243 |

 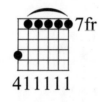 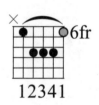

| 4231 3fr | 21134 4fr | 32141 | 43121 3fr |

 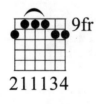 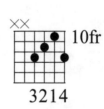 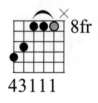

| 13333 5fr | 411111 7fr | 311214 7fr | 12341 6fr |

| 431111 7fr | 211134 9fr | 3214 10fr | 43111 8fr |

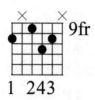 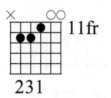 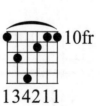 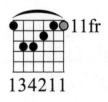

| 1 243 9fr | 231 11fr | 134211 10fr | 134211 11fr |

D#/E♭ MAJOR⁷	D#/E♭ MAJOR⁷♯¹¹	D#/E♭ MAJOR⁷♯⁵	D#/E♭ MAJOR⁹

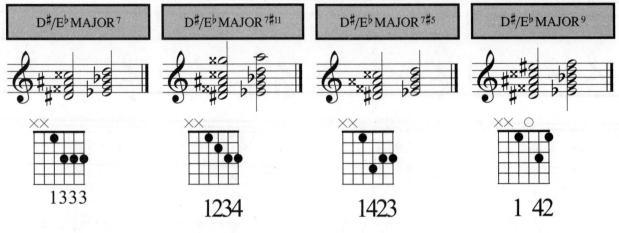

1333 · 1234 · 1423 · 1 42

43111 · 21341 · 43211 · 41111

13241 · 1234 · 1423 · 2143

4321 · 4311 · 2114 · 311112

1 342 · 2 341 · 1 234 · 2131

D#/E♭ MAJOR 13	D#/E♭ 6	D#/E♭ 6/9	D#/E♭ add9

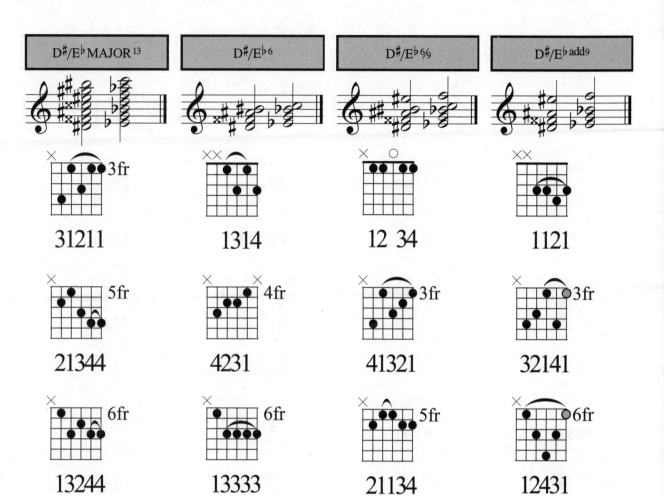

31211	1314	12 34	1121
21344	4231	41321	32141
13244	13333	21134	12431
211131	431111	411111	3214
1 2344	2 143	211134	134211

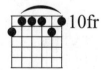
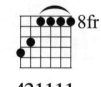
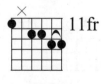
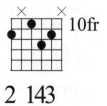
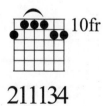
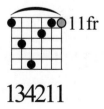

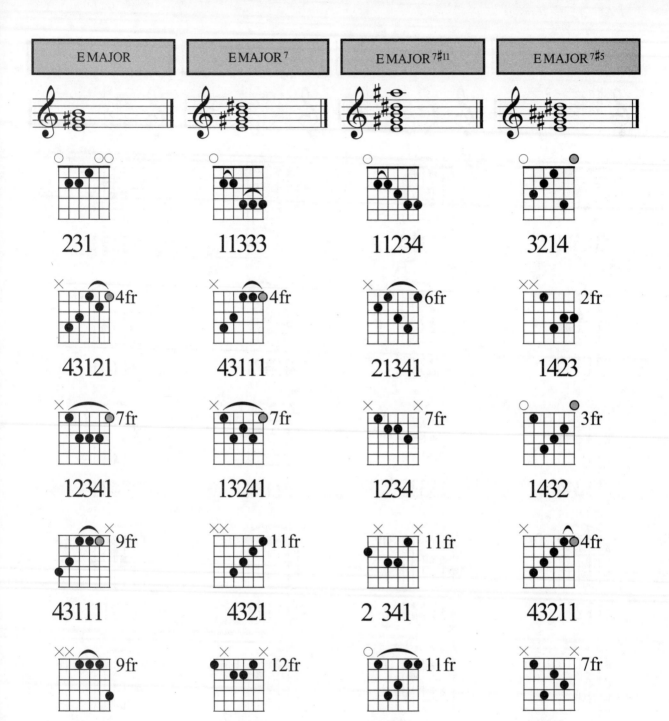

E MAJOR

E MAJOR⁷

E MAJOR⁷#11

E MAJOR⁷#5

231   11333   11234   3214

43121   43111   21341   1423

12341   13241   1234   1432

43111   4321   2 341   43211

1114   1 342   14311   1423

E MAJOR⁹	E MAJOR¹³	E⁶	E⁶⁄₉

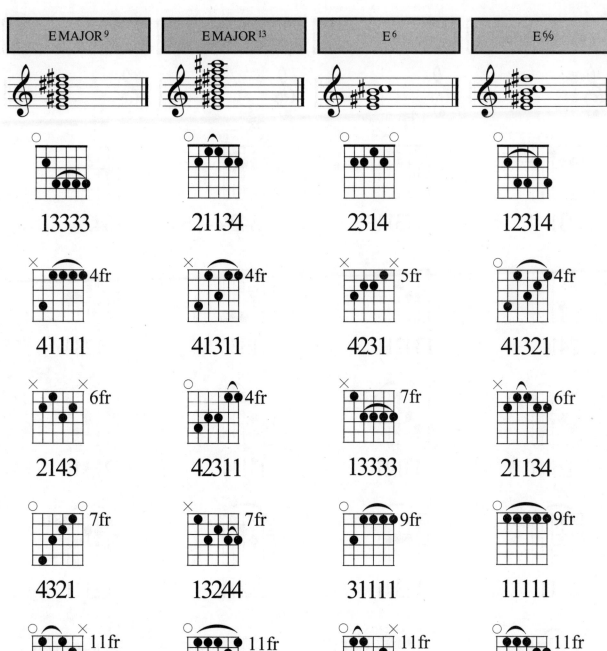

13333   21134   2314   12314

41111   41311   4231   41321

2143   42311   13333   21134

4321   13244   31111   11111

1312   11121   1132   11123

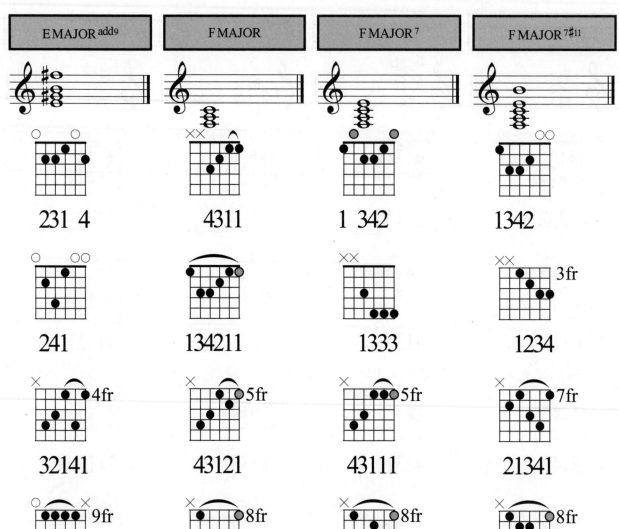

E MAJOR add9	F MAJOR	F MAJOR 7	F MAJOR 7#11
231 4	4311	1 342	1342
241	134211	1333	1234
32141 (4fr)	43121 (5fr)	43111 (5fr)	21341 (7fr)
1111 (9fr)	12341 (8fr)	13241 (8fr)	12341 (8fr)
21314 (9fr)	1114 (10fr)	4321 (12fr)	2 341 (12fr)

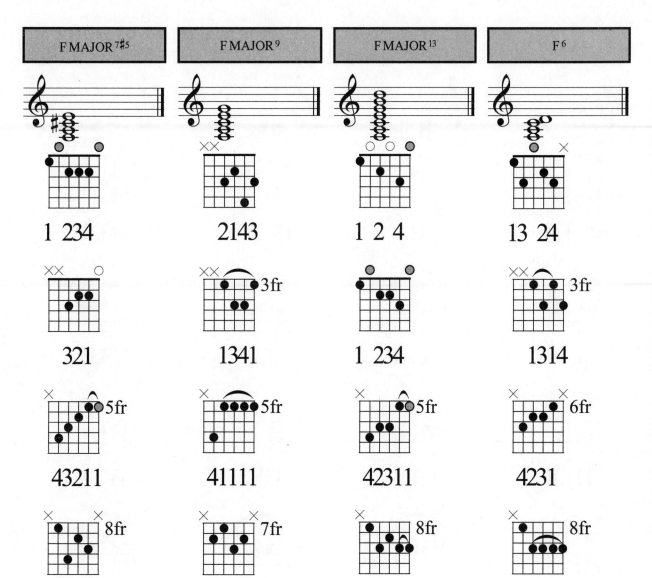

F MAJOR 7#5	F MAJOR 9	F MAJOR 13	F 6
1 234	2143	1 2 4	13 24
321	1341	1 234	1314
43211	41111	42311	4231
1423	2143	13244	13333
4321	2131	211131	431111

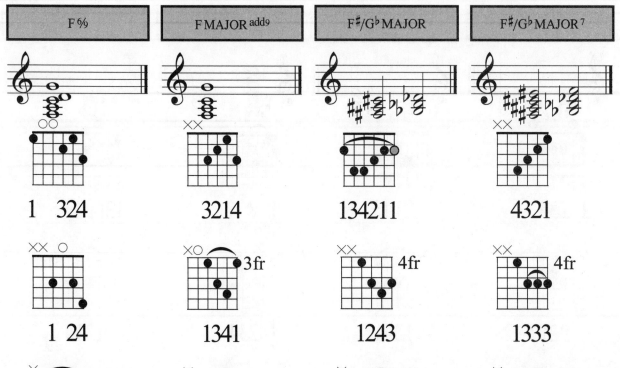

F 6/9	F MAJOR add9	F#/Gb MAJOR	F#/Gb MAJOR 7
1 324	3214	134211	4321
1 24	1341	1243	1333
11121	32141	43121	43111
21134	13411	12341	13241
211134	21314	1114	1113

F#/Gb MAJOR 7#11	F#/Gb MAJOR 7#5	F#/Gb MAJOR 9	F#/Gb MAJOR 13

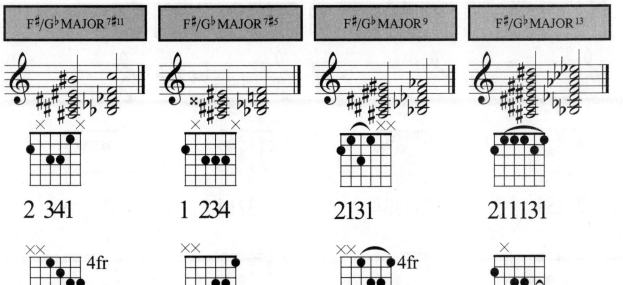

2 341	1 234	2131	211131

1234	4231	1341	1 2344
4fr	4fr	4fr	

21341	1423	2143	3241
8fr	4fr	3fr	

12341	43211	41111	42311
9fr	6fr	6fr	6fr

1134	1423	2143	13244
11fr	9fr	8fr	9fr

F#/G♭ 6	F#/G♭ 6/9	F#/G♭ MAJOR add9	G MAJOR

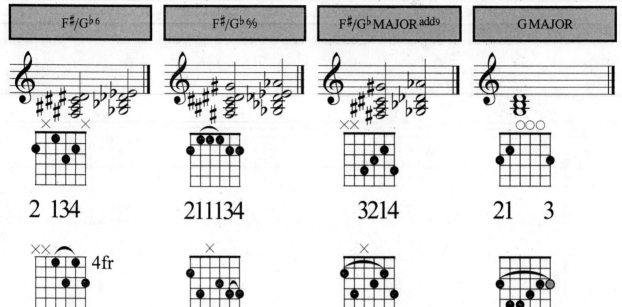

| 2 134 | 211134 | 3214 | 21 3 |

| 1314 | 13 244 | 13 214 | 134211 |

| 4231 | 11121 | 32141 | 1243 |

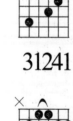

| 2314 | 31241 | 2143 | 43121 |

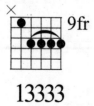

| 13333 | 21134 | 1111 | 12341 |

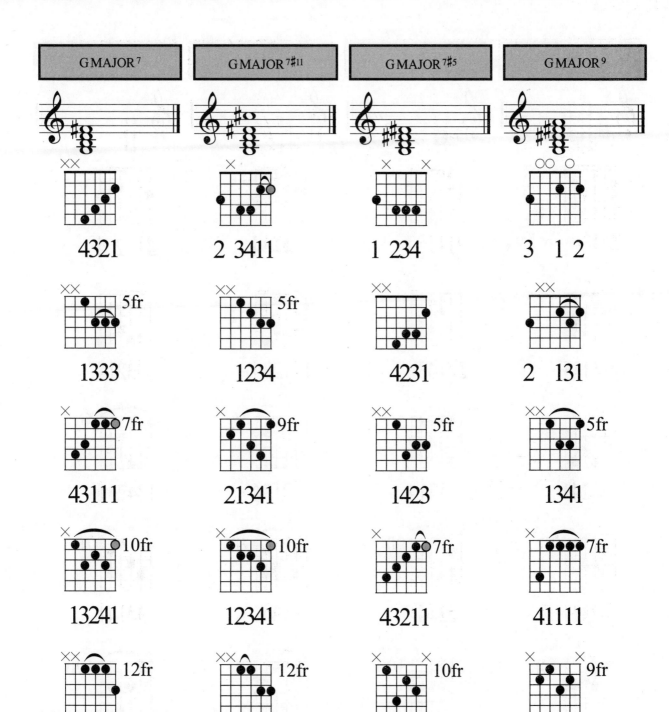

G MAJOR¹³	G⁶	G⁶⁄₉	G MAJOR ᵃᵈᵈ⁹

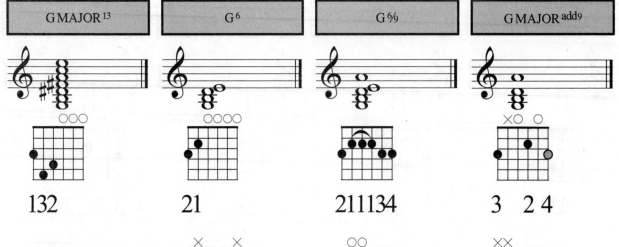

132   **21**   **211134**   **3 2 4**

 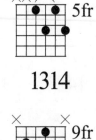 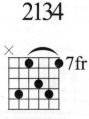 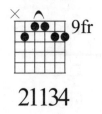

211131   **2 143**   **1 234**   **3214**

 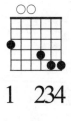

3241   **1314**   **2134**   **134211**

42311   **2314**   **31241**   **32141**

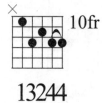 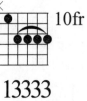

13244   **13333**   **21134**   **12431**

G#/A♭ MAJOR	G#/A♭ MAJOR 7	G#/A♭ MAJOR 7#11	G#/A♭ MAJOR 7#5

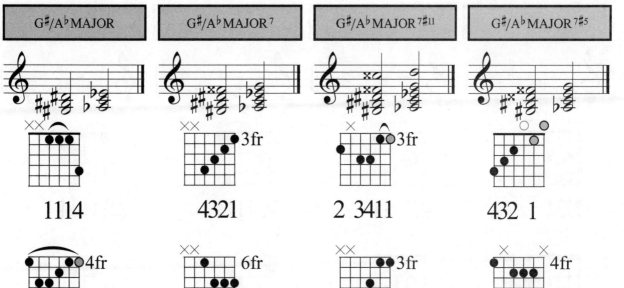

1114   4321   2 3411   432 1

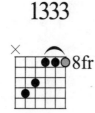

134211   1333   4311   1 234

1243   43111   1234   1423

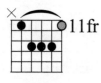
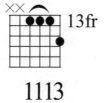
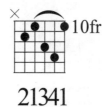
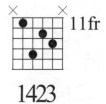

43121   13241   21341   43211

12341   1113   12341   1423

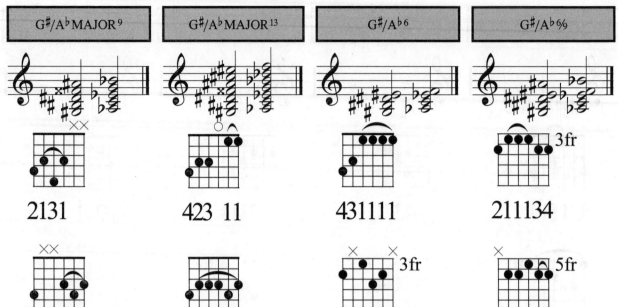

G#/Ab MAJOR 9	G#/Ab MAJOR 13	G#/Ab 6	G#/Ab 6/9
2131	423 11	431111	211134 3fr

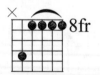

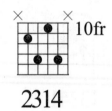

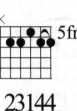

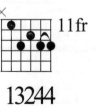

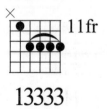

2 131	211131	2 143 3fr	23144 5fr
1341 6fr	3241 3fr	1314 6fr	11121 8fr
41111 8fr	42311 8fr	2314 10fr	31241 8fr
2143 10fr	13244 11fr	13333 11fr	21134 10fr

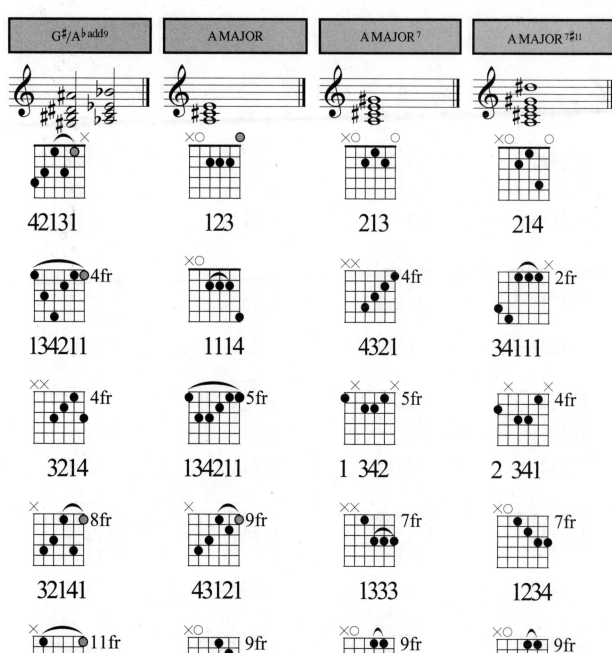

G#/Ab add9	A MAJOR	A MAJOR 7	A MAJOR 7#11
42131	123	213	214
134211	1114	4321	34111
3214	134211	1 342	2 341
32141	43121	1333	1234
12431	3124	3114	3114

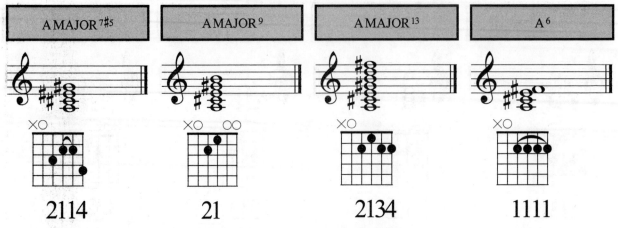

A MAJOR⁷#5	A MAJOR⁹	A MAJOR¹³	A⁶
2114	21	2134	1111
4231	1314	2314	2 143
1 234	2314	211131	3241
1423	1111	2344	1314
43211	2143	3411	231

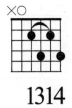

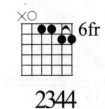

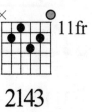
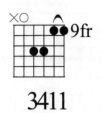

A $^6_9$	A MAJOR ^{add9}	A$^\sharp$/B$^\flat$ MAJOR	A$^\sharp$/B$^\flat$ MAJOR ^{7}

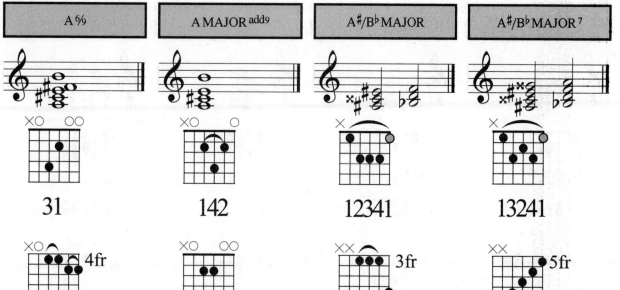

31	142	12341	13241
1122	23	1114	4321
211134	1314	134211	1 342
2134	3214	1243	1333
23	3141	43121	3241

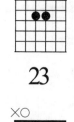

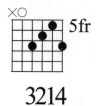
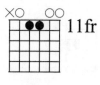
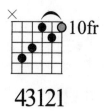
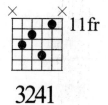

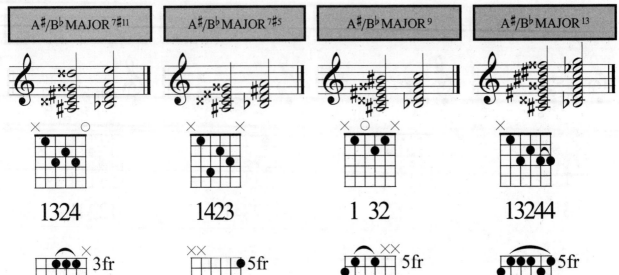

A#/Bb MAJOR 7#11	A#/Bb MAJOR 7#5	A#/Bb MAJOR 9	A#/Bb MAJOR 13
1324	1423	1 32	13244

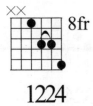

34111

2 341

1234

1224

4231

1 234

1423

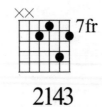

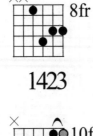

43211

2131

1 2314

2143

41111

211131

3241

1 2344

42311

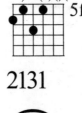

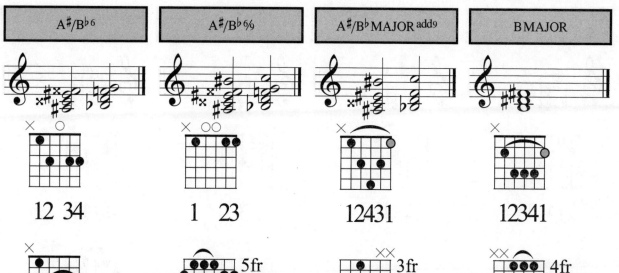

A#/Bb 6	A#/Bb 6/9	A#/Bb MAJOR add9	B MAJOR

12 34

1 23

12431

12341

13333

211134

4312

1114

1 243

21314

134211

43111

1314

2134

3214

134211

4231

11121

32141

1243

BMAJOR⁷	BMAJOR⁷♯11	BMAJOR⁷♯5	BMAJOR⁹

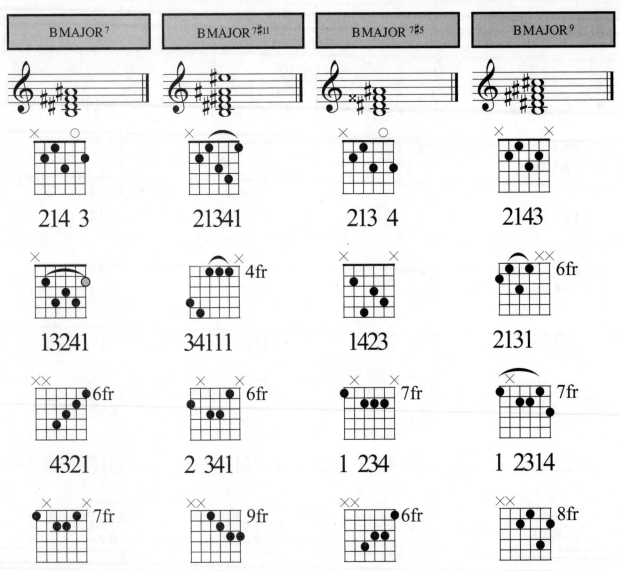

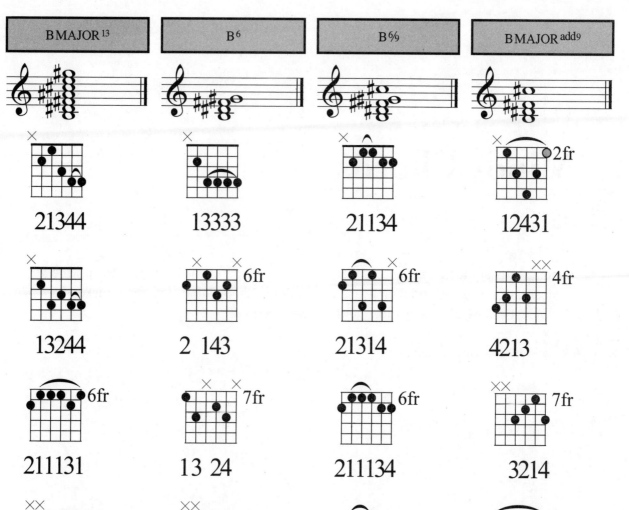

B MAJOR¹³	B⁶	B⁶⁄₉	B MAJOR add9
21344	13333	21134	12431
13244	2 143	21314	4213
211131	13 24	211134	3214
3241	3241	211134	134211
1 2344	1314	2134	42 1

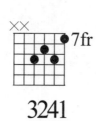
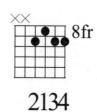
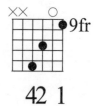

16: MAJOR CHORDS **285**

17

Minor Chords

Minor chords are the darker and sadder cousins to the perky major chords. Their place in music is long settled and their use is widespread. Along with major, minor makes up the widest variety of sounds most guitar players explore.

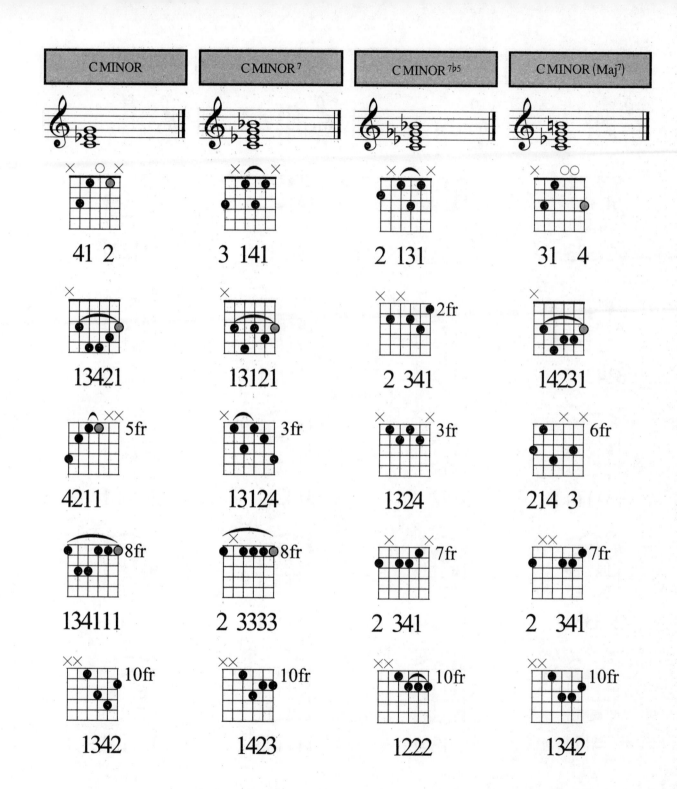

C MINOR⁹	C MINOR⁹ (Maj⁷)	C MINOR¹¹	C MINOR¹³

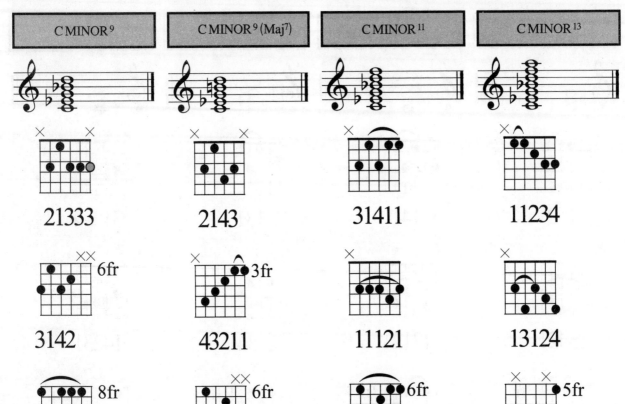

21333	2143	31411	11234
3142	43211	11121	13124
131114	3142	314211	2 34 1
2 3334	132114	111111	312411
4111	1341	111143	131141

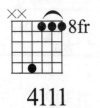
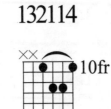

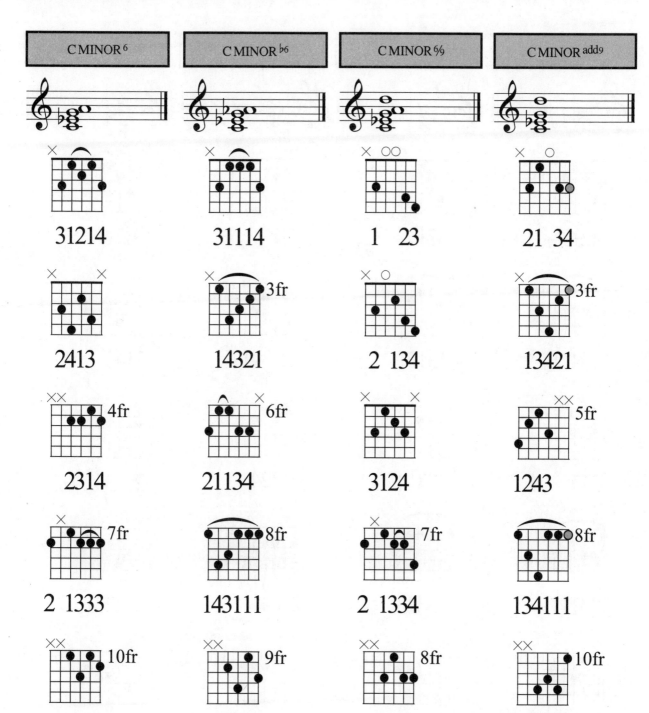

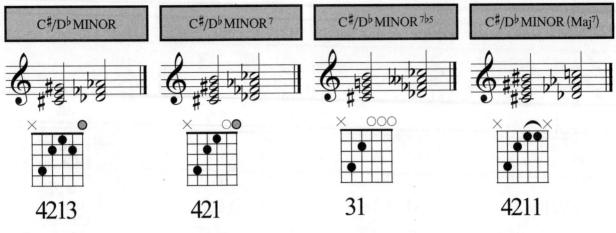

C#/Db MINOR	C#/Db MINOR 7	C#/Db MINOR 7b5	C#/Db MINOR (Maj7)

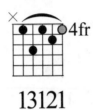

4213

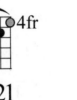

421

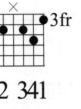

31

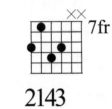

4211

13421

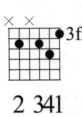

13121

2 341

2143

4211

2314

1324

2   341

134111

2 3333

2 341

4231

1342

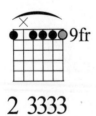

1423

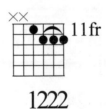

1222

1342

C#/Db MINOR 9	C#/Db MINOR 9 (Maj7)	C#/Db MINOR 11	C#/Db MINOR 13

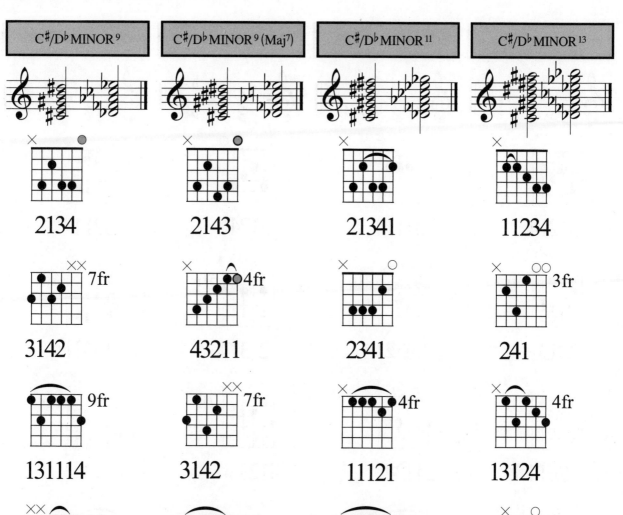

2134	2143	21341	11234
3142	43211	2341	241
131114	3142	11121	13124
1113	132114	111111	2 34 1
4111	1341	111143	131141

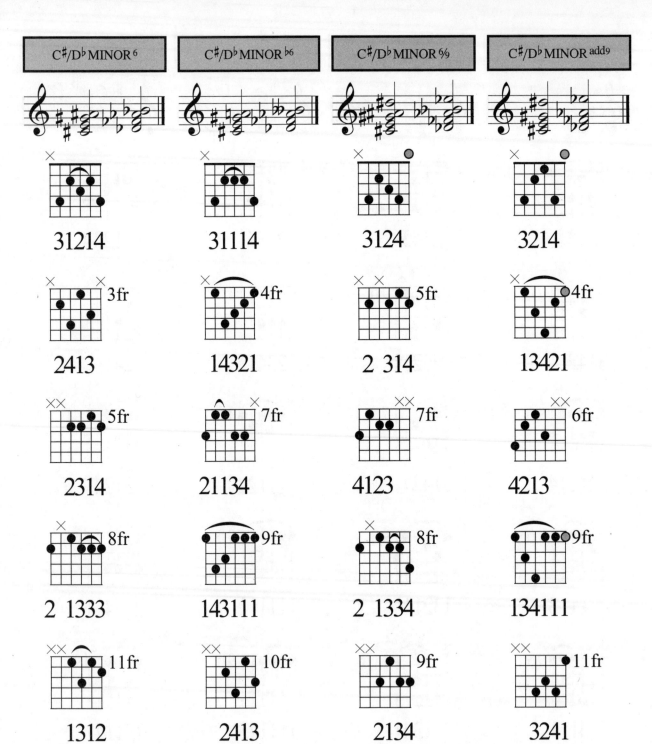

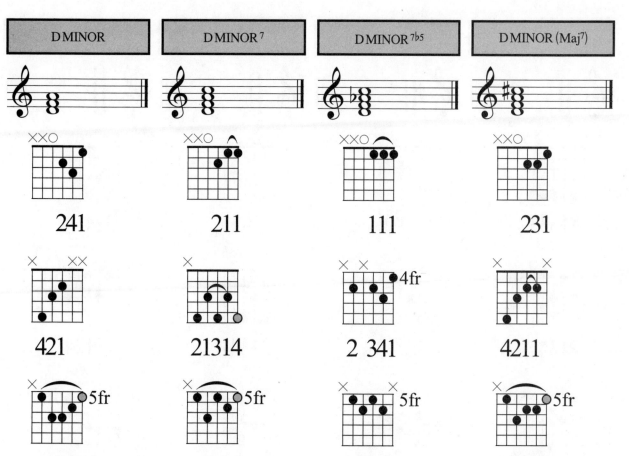

D MINOR	D MINOR⁷	D MINOR⁷ᵇ⁵	D MINOR (Maj⁷)
241	211	111	231
421	21314	2 341	4211
13421	13121	1324	14231
4211	2314	3 421	2143
134111	2 3333	2 341	341

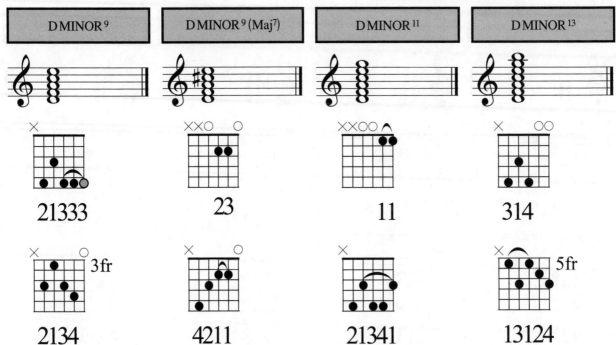

D MINOR⁹	D MINOR⁹ (Maj⁷)	D MINOR¹¹	D MINOR¹³
21333	23	11	314
2134	4211	21341	13124
3142	2143	231	2 34 1
131114	43211	11121	312411
4321	132114	111111	131141

D MINOR⁶	D MINOR^{♭6}	D MINOR^{6/9}	D MINOR^{add9}

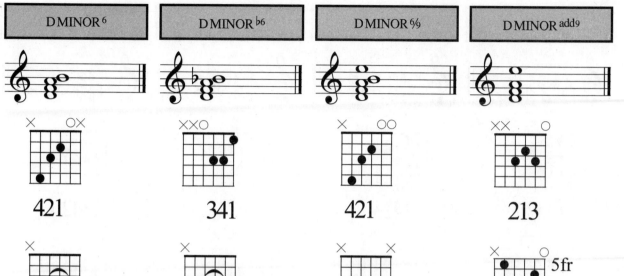

421	341	421	213
31214	31114	3124	1342
2413	14321	3124	13421
2314	21134	4123	1243
2 1333	143111	2134	134111

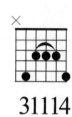

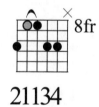

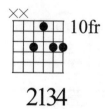
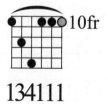

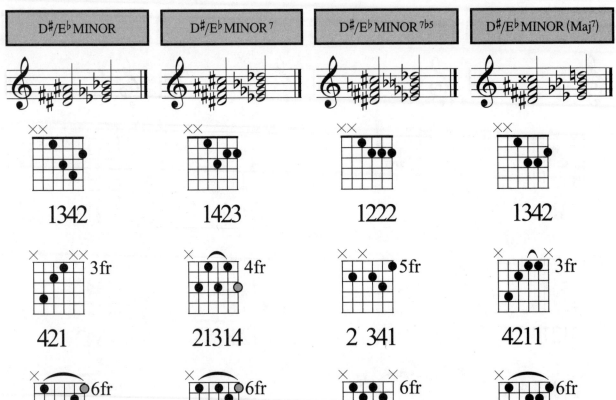

D#/Eb MINOR	D#/Eb MINOR 7	D#/Eb MINOR 7b5	D#/Eb MINOR (Maj7)

1342   1423   1222   1342

421   21314   2 341   4211

13421   13121   1324   14231

4211   2314   3   421   2143

134111   2 3333   2 341   2   341

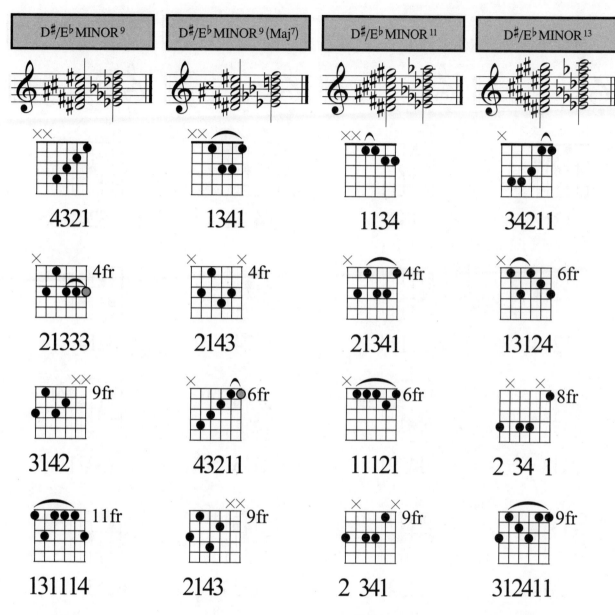

D#/Eb MINOR 9	D#/Eb MINOR 9 (Maj7)	D#/Eb MINOR 11	D#/Eb MINOR 13
4321	1341	1134	34211
21333	2143	21341	13124
3142	43211	11121	2 34 1
131114	2143	2 341	312411
1113	132114	111111	131141

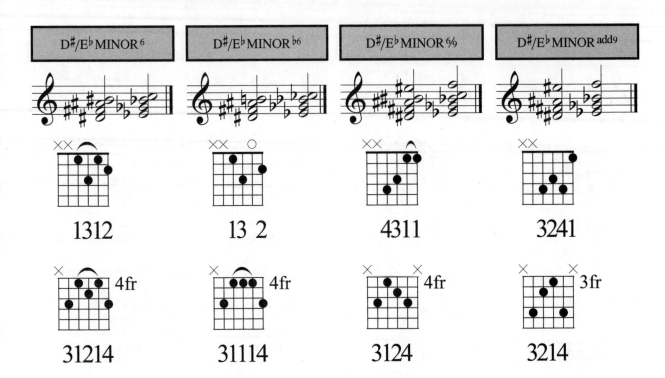

D♯/E♭ MINOR⁶	D♯/E♭ MINOR♭⁶	D♯/E♭ MINOR⁶⁄₉	D♯/E♭ MINORadd9
1312	13 2	4311	3241
31214 (4fr)	31114 (4fr)	3124 (4fr)	3214 (3fr)

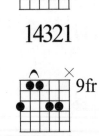

2413 (5fr)   14321 (6fr)   2413 (5fr)   13421 (6fr)

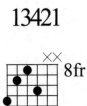

2314 (7fr)   21134 (9fr)   2 1334 (10fr)   4213 (8fr)

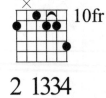

2 1333 (10fr)   143111 (11fr)   2134 (11fr)   134111 (11fr)

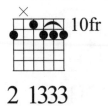
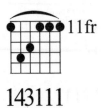
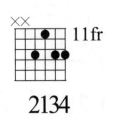

E MINOR	E MINOR⁷	E MINOR⁷ᵇ⁵	E MINOR (Maj⁷)

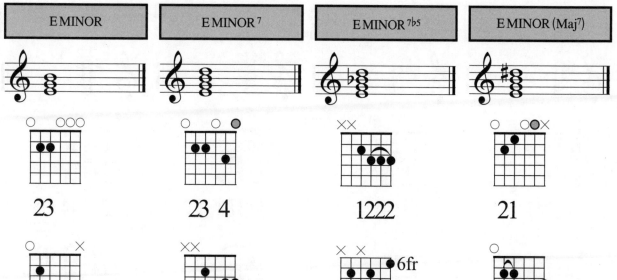

23

23 4

1222

21

1324

1423

2 341

11342

11342

21314

1324

4211

421

13121

31214

21413

13421

2314

3421

14231

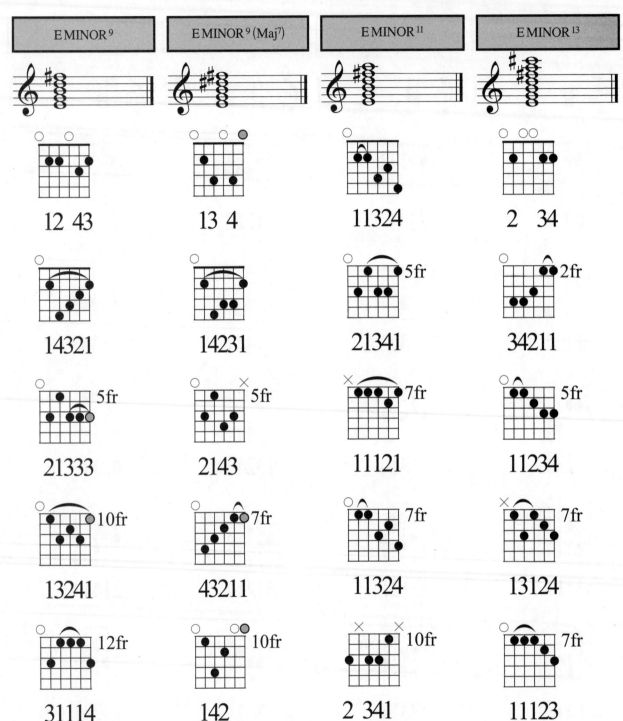

E MINOR 9   E MINOR 9 (Maj7)   E MINOR 11   E MINOR 13

12 43   13 4   11324   2 34

14321   14231   21341 5fr   34211 2fr

21333 5fr   2143 5fr   11121 7fr   11234 5fr

13241 10fr   43211 7fr   11324 7fr   13124 7fr

31114 12fr   142 10fr   2 341 10fr   11123 7fr

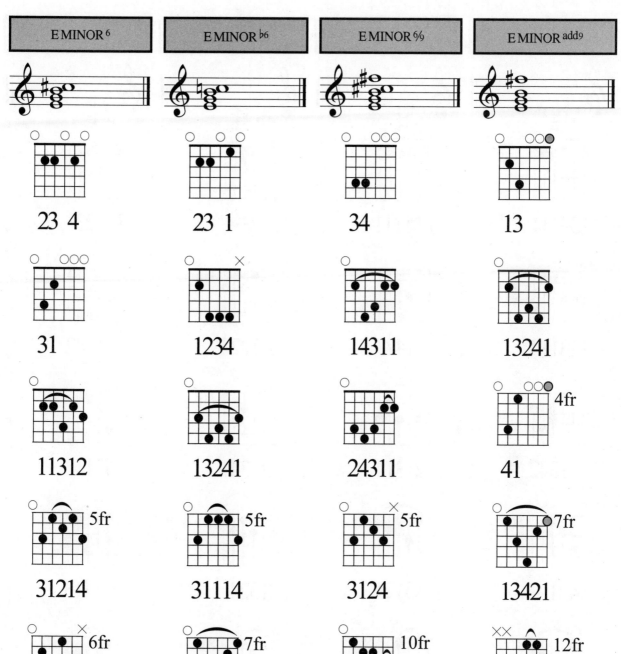

E MINOR 6	E MINOR ♭6	E MINOR 6/9	E MINOR add9
23 4	23 1	34	13
31	1234	14311	13241
11312	13241	24311	41 4fr
31214 5fr	31114 5fr	3124 5fr	13421 7fr
2413 6fr	14321 7fr	12344 10fr	3114 12fr

F MINOR	F MINOR⁷	F MINOR⁷ᵇ⁵	F MINOR (Maj⁷)

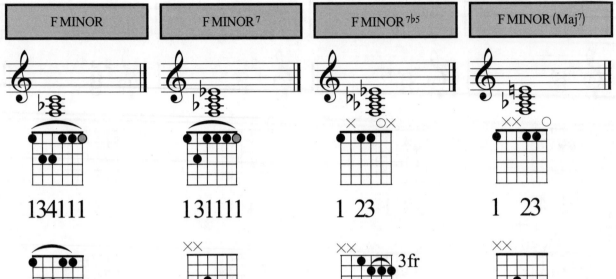

134111	131111	1 23	1 23
123114	1423	1222	1342
1342	21314	2 341	4211
421	13121	1324	21413
13421	13124	12134	14231

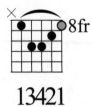

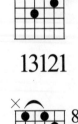

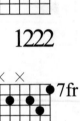
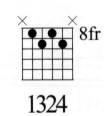
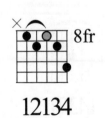
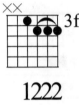

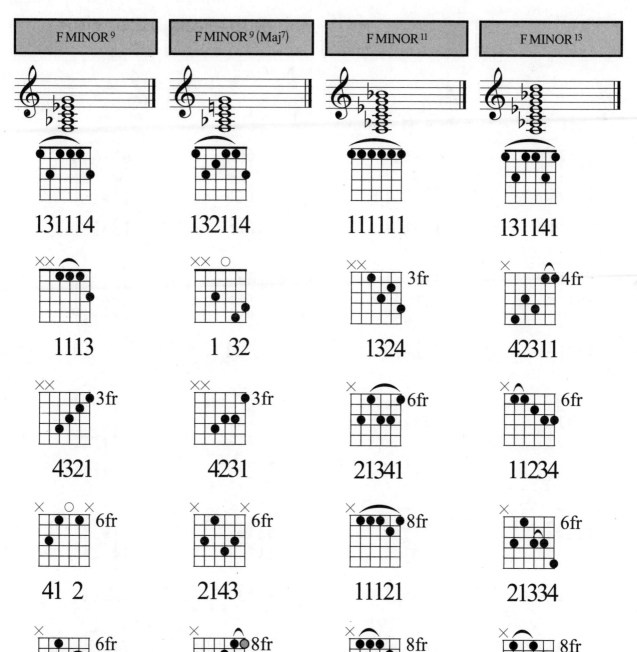

F MINOR 9	F MINOR 9 (Maj7)	F MINOR 11	F MINOR 13
131114	132114	111111	131141
1113	1 32	1324	42311
4321	4231	21341	11234
41 2	2143	11121	21334
21333	43211	11124	13124

F MINOR 6	F MINOR b6	F MINOR 6/9	F MINOR add9

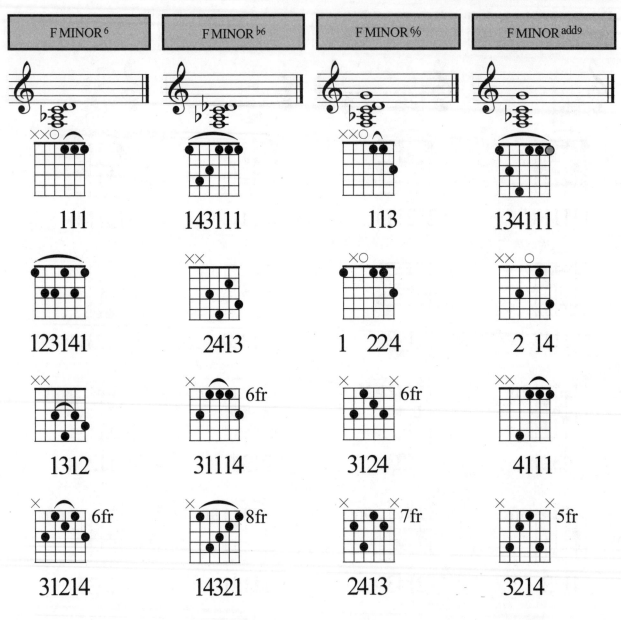

111	143111	113	134111
123141	2413	1 224	2 14
1312	31114	3124	4111
31214	14321	2413	3214
2413	13422	2 1334	13421

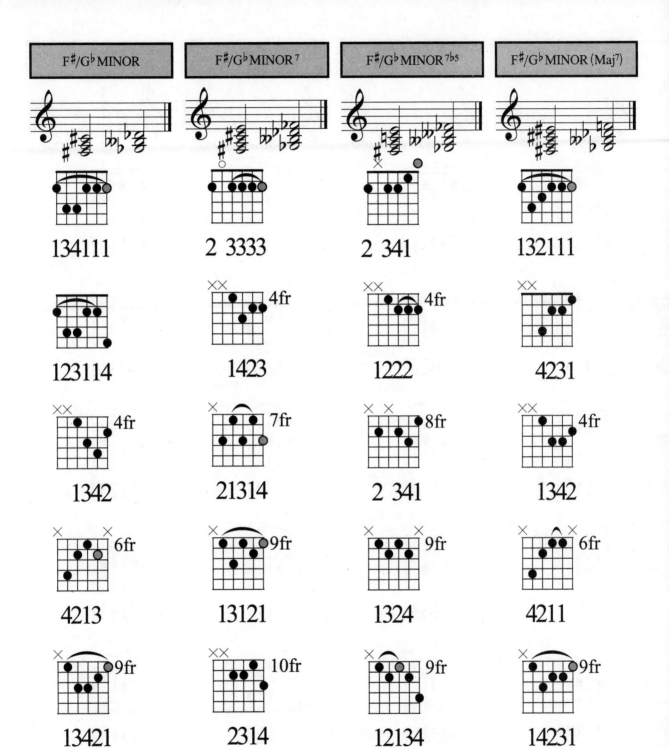

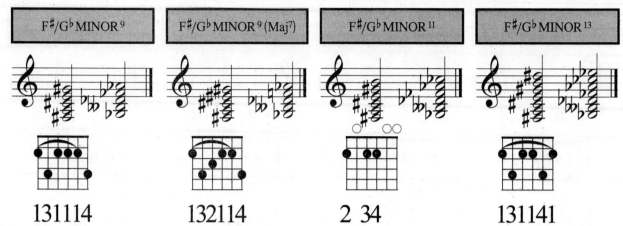

131114   132114   2 34   131141

2 314   4231   1324   42311

 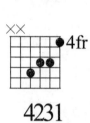 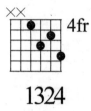

1114   1341   21341   11234

  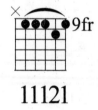

4321   2143   11121   21334

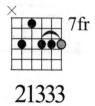 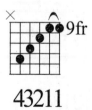 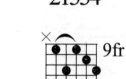

21333   43211   11124   13124

F#/Gb MINOR 6	F#/Gb MINOR b6	F#/Gb MINOR 6/9	F#/Gb MINOR add9

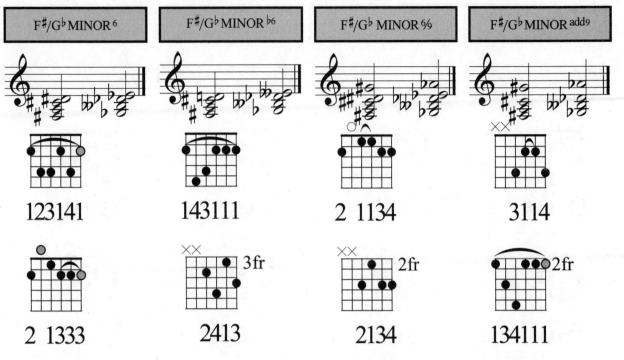

123141

143111

2 1134

3114

2 1333

2413 (3fr)

2134 (2fr)

134111 (2fr)

1312 (4fr)

31114 (7fr)

34211 (4fr)

4111 (2fr)

31214 (7fr)

14321 (9fr)

3124 (7fr)

3214 (6fr)

2413 (8fr)

13422 (9fr)

2413 (8fr)

13421 (9fr)

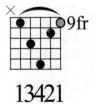

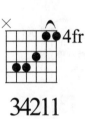

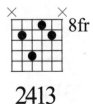
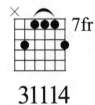

G MINOR	G MINOR⁷	G MINOR⁷ᵇ⁵	G MINOR (Maj⁷)

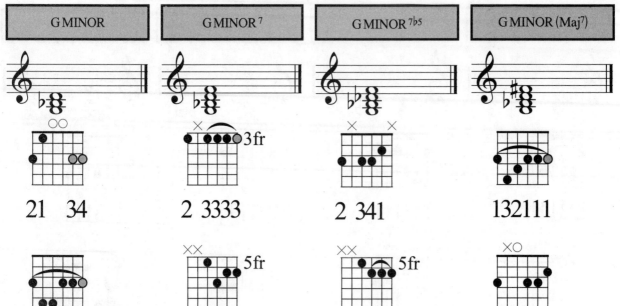

21　34	2 3333	2 341	132111
134111	1423	1222	2　341
1342	21314	2 341	1342
4213	13121	1324	4211
13421	2314	12134	14231

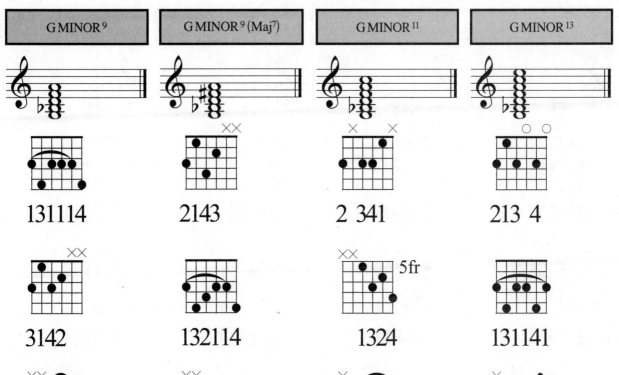

G MINOR⁹	G MINOR⁹ (Maj⁷)	G MINOR¹¹	G MINOR¹³
131114	2143	2 341	213 4
3142	132114	1324	131141
1113	4231	21341	42311
4321	1341	11121	21334
21333	2143	11124	13124

G MINOR ^{6}	G MINOR $^{♭6}$	G MINOR $^{6/9}$	G MINOR ^{add9}

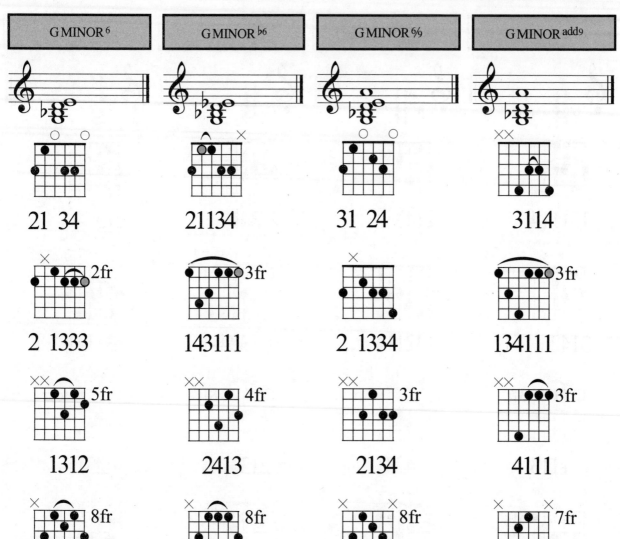

21 34	21134	31 24	3114
2 1333	143111	2 1334	134111
1312	2413	2134	4111
31214	31114	3124	3214
2413	14231	2413	13421

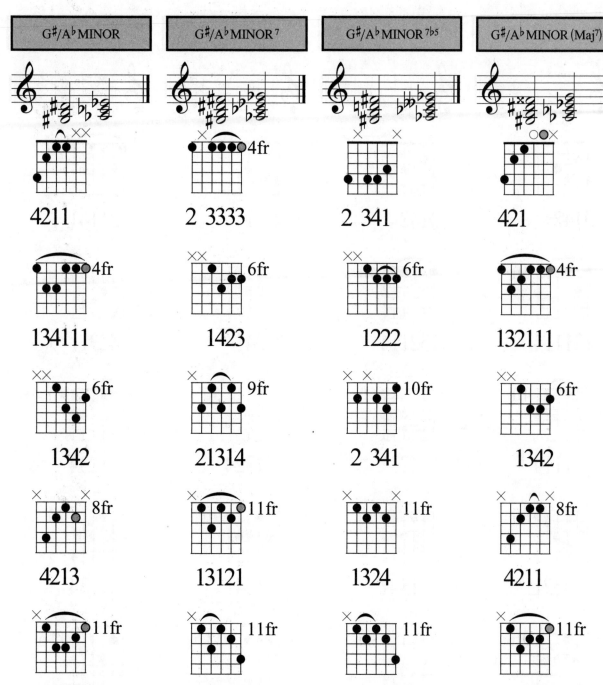

G#/Ab MINOR	G#/Ab MINOR 7	G#/Ab MINOR 7b5	G#/Ab MINOR (Maj7)
4211	2 3333	2 341	421
134111	1423	1222	132111
1342	21314	2 341	1342
4213	13121	1324	4211
13421	13124	12134	14231

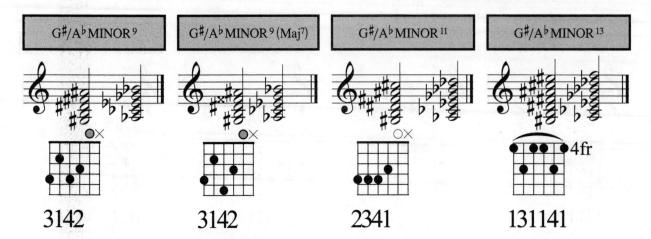

G#/A♭ MINOR 9	G#/A♭ MINOR 9 (Maj7)	G#/A♭ MINOR 11	G#/A♭ MINOR 13

  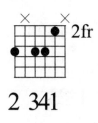 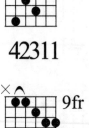

| 3142 | 3142 | 2341 | 131141 |

| 131114 | 132114 | 2 341 | 42311 |

| 1114 | 4231 | 1324 | 11234 |

 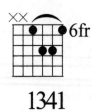

| 4321 | 1341 | 21341 | 21334 |

 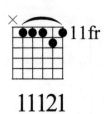

| 21333 | 2143 | 11121 | 13124 |

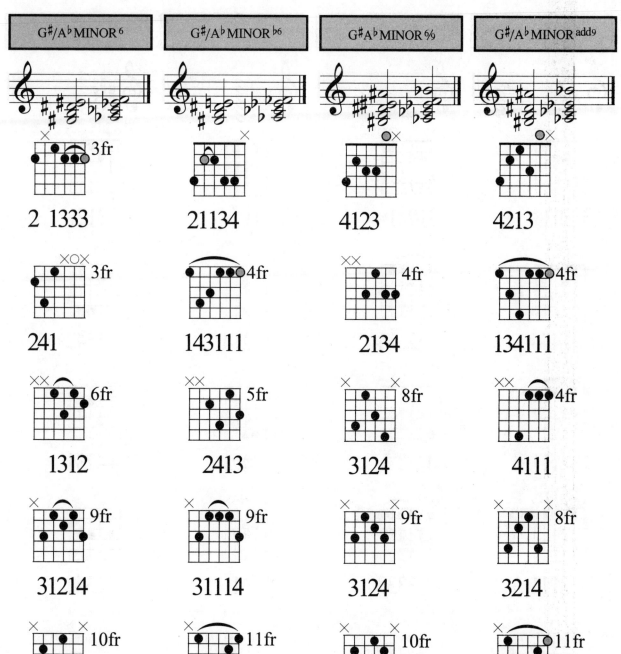

G#/A♭ MINOR 6	G#/A♭ MINOR ♭6	G#/A♭ MINOR 6⁄9	G#/A♭ MINOR add9
3fr 2 1333	21134	4123	4213
3fr 241	4fr 143111	4fr 2134	4fr 134111
6fr 1312	5fr 2413	8fr 3124	4fr 4111
9fr 31214	9fr 31114	9fr 3124	8fr 3214
10fr 2413	11fr 14231	10fr 2413	11fr 13432

A MINOR	A MINOR⁷	A MINOR⁷ᵇ⁵	A MINOR (Maj⁷)

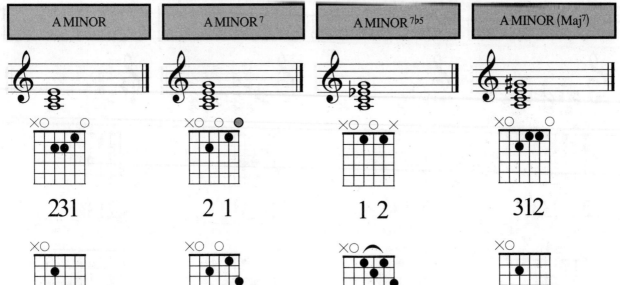

231 | 2 1 | 1 2 | 312

1444 | 2 14 | 1214 | 1342

134111 | 421 | 3421 | 4231

3111 | 2 3333 | 2 341 | 1342

1342 | 1423 | 1222 | 4211

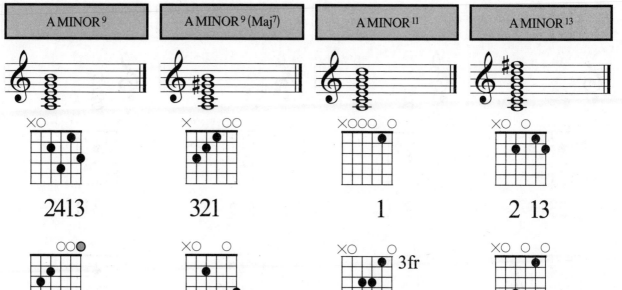

A MINOR⁹	A MINOR⁹(Maj⁷)	A MINOR¹¹	A MINOR¹³

2413   321   1   2 13

421   14 3   341   4 1

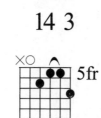

131114   2113   314211   2341

1321   4231   111114   3241

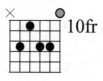 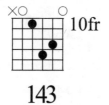 

2134   143   3214   131141

A MINOR ⁶	A MINOR ^{b6}	A MINOR ^{6/9}	A MINOR ^{add9}

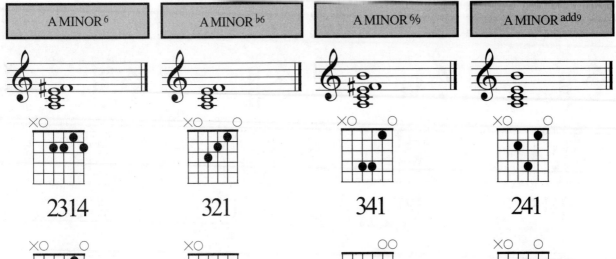

2314   321   341   241

421   1333   3124   13 4

123141   134   1224   3114

1312   143111   2134   31

132   2413   3124   21

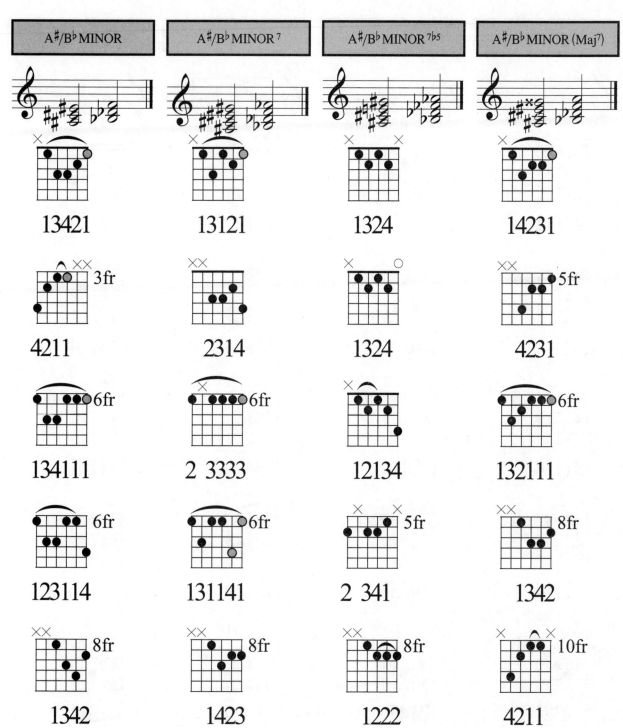

A#/B♭ MINOR 9	A#/B♭ MINOR 9 (Maj7)	A#/B♭ MINOR 11	A#/B♭ MINOR 13

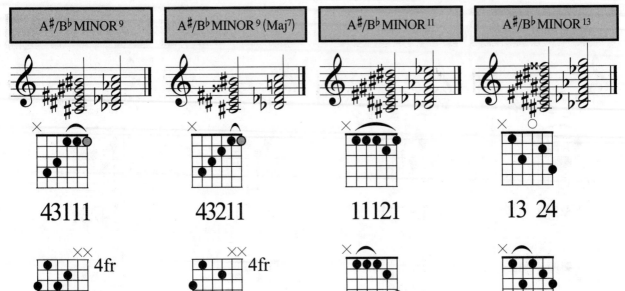

43111   43211   11121   13 24

 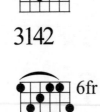 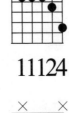

2143   3142   11124   13124

4fr   4fr

131114   132114   2 341   131141

6fr   6fr   4fr   6fr

1114   4231   111114   121134

6fr   8fr   6fr   6fr

 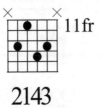

4321   2143   1324   42311

8fr   11fr   8fr   9fr

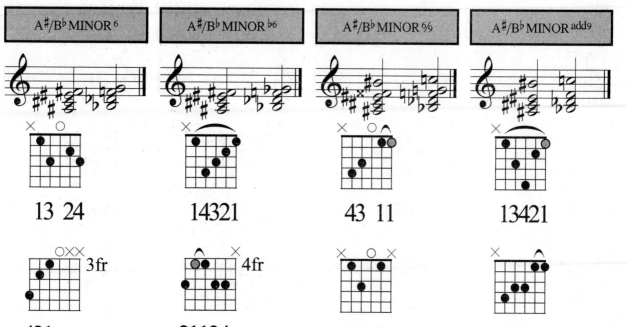

A#/Bb MINOR 6	A#/Bb MINOR b6	A#/Bb MINOR 6/9	A#/Bb MINOR add9
13 24	14321	43 11	13421
421 (3fr)	21134 (4fr)	13 2	42311
2 1333 (5fr)	143111 (6fr)	2 1334 (5fr)	4213 (3fr)
123141 (6fr)	132114 (6fr)	2134 (6fr)	134111 (6fr)
1312 (8fr)	2413 (7fr)	3124 (11fr)	4111 (6fr)

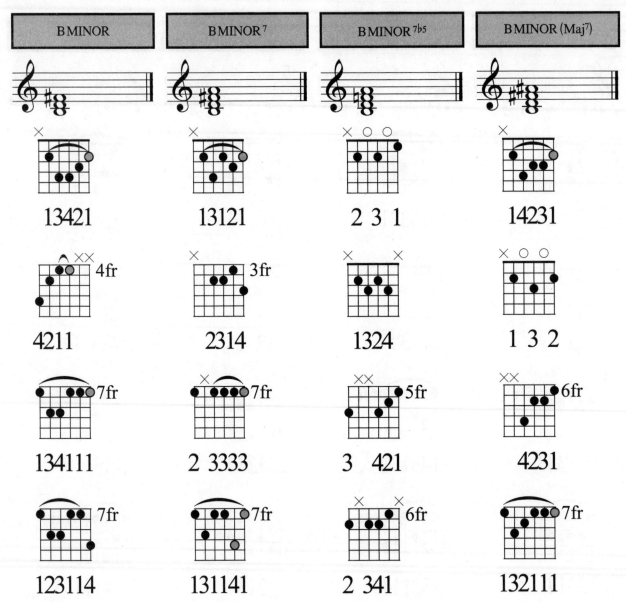

B MINOR	B MINOR⁷	B MINOR⁷ᵇ⁵	B MINOR (Maj⁷)
13421	13121	2 3 1	14231
4211	2314	1324	1 3 2
134111	2 3333	3 421	4231
123114	131141	2 341	132111
1342	1423	1222	1342

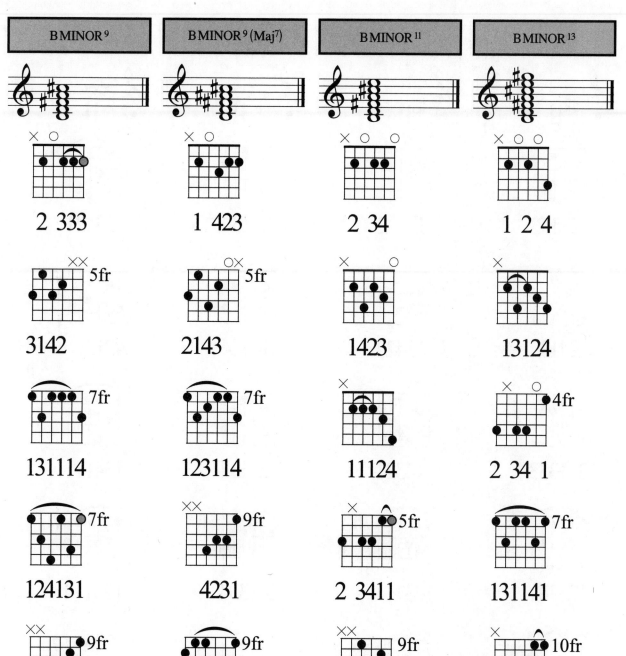

B MINOR 9	B MINOR 9 (Maj7)	B MINOR 11	B MINOR 13
2 333	1 423	2 34	1 2 4
3142	2143	1423	13124
131114	123114	11124	2 34 1
124131	4231	2 3411	131141
4321	211341	1324	42311

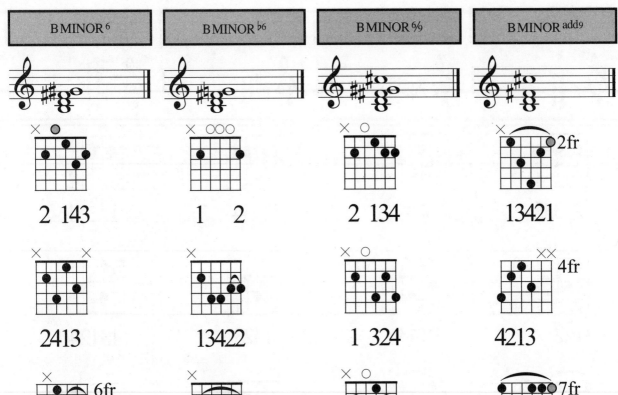

B MINOR 6	B MINOR b6	B MINOR 6/9	B MINOR add9
2 143	1 2	2 134	13421
2413	13422	1 324	4213
2 1333	14321	2 134	134111
123141	143111	2 1334	123114
1312	2413	2134	3114

18

Common Chord Progressions

Let's put your chords to work. Here you will find five styles of music: blues, rock, jazz, folk/country, and classical. The chord progressions here demonstrate typical ways to use the chords in sequence—typical ways for the chords to group together. Some will be simple, and some will highlight the lesser-known voicings scattered throughout this book, which are worth integrating into your music. No matter what style you play, this chapter will give you a clearer picture of how to use the information provided in this book.

BLUES PROGRESSIONS

Figure 18-1 is a very standard blues progression using open chords.

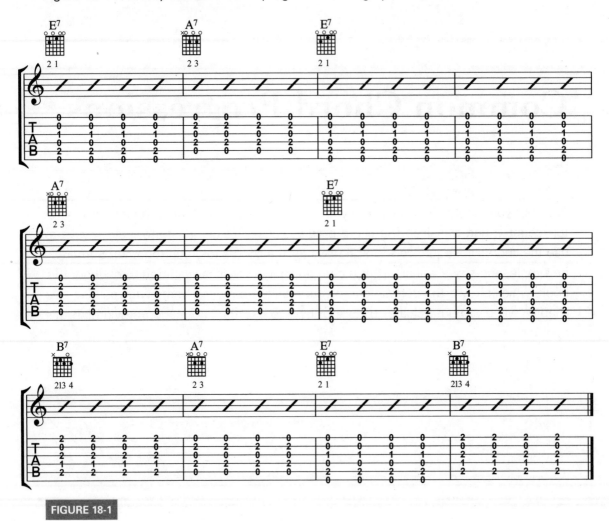

FIGURE 18-1

The next thing you'll want to do when playing blues is to stop using open chords. The example in Figure 18-2 uses barre chord shapes across the neck. Notice how different they sound.

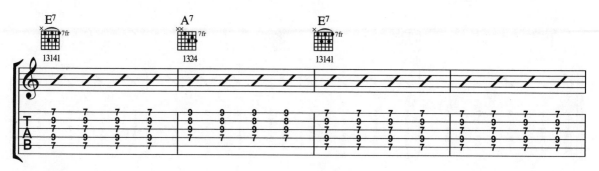

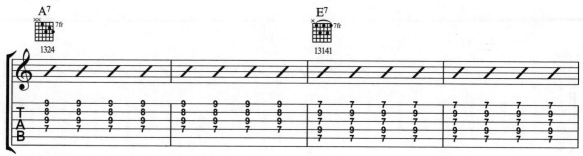

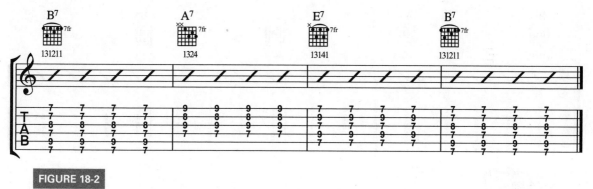

FIGURE 18-2

The next step in your evolution is to try some substitute chords. These are some ninth and thirteenth chords. This is still the same basic progression, but see how much "fancier" it sounds (Figure 18-3).

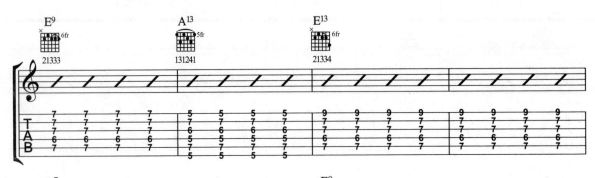

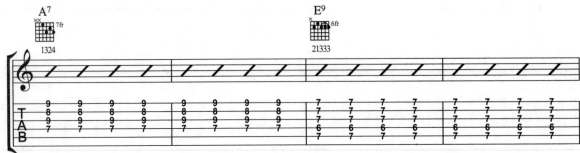

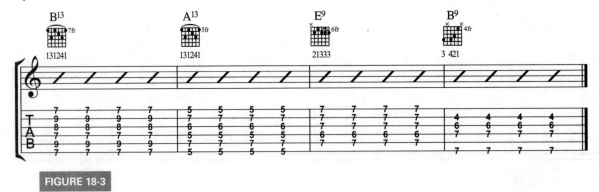

FIGURE 18-3

Now it's time to really go to town and use some of the more obscure chords found in the book. Again, notice everything is the same but altered the types of chords used. It's amazing how much variation you can achieve from this basic foundation (see Figure 18-4).

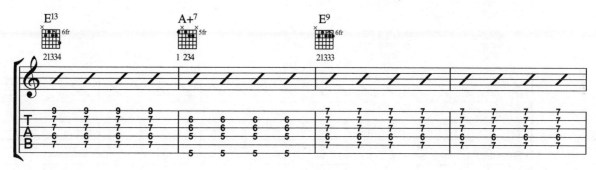

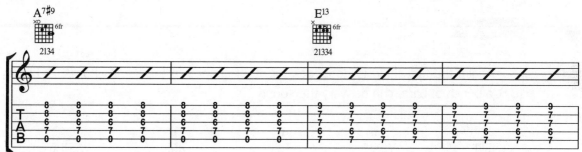

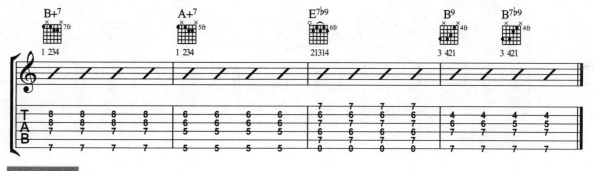

FIGURE 18-4

BASIC ROCK PROGRESSIONS

Figure 18-5 shows the basic rock progression, which you've probably played a few million times by now.

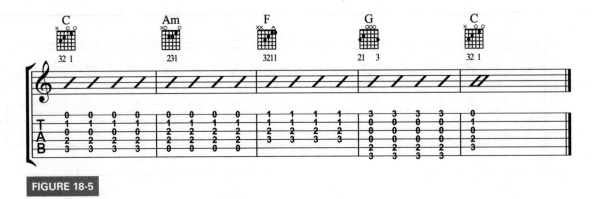

FIGURE 18-5

Again, the first thing to do is look for other shapes of the same chords. In Figure 18-6, a bunch of barre chords vary the sound.

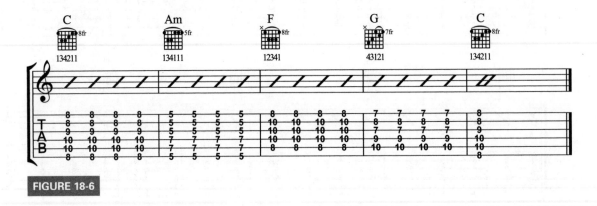

FIGURE 18-6

In Figure 18-7, the chords contain open strings. The basic chords are the same, but contain more creative options. Since every chord has the same open strings, the sound is very smooth and flowing.

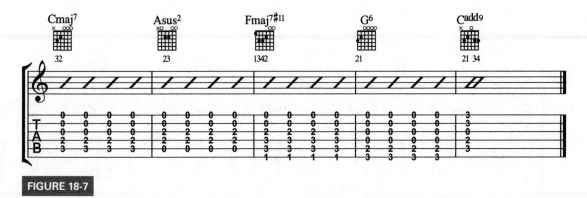

This last one (Figure 18-8) explores different types of the basic chords. Simple chords can transform into more colorful choices simply by looking in the same section and choosing other chords. Listen to how this progression has elevated from mundane to ethereal.

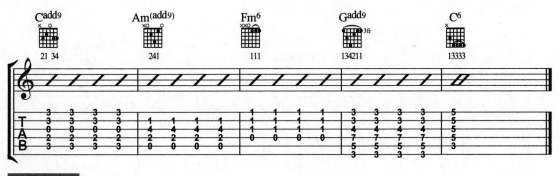

BASIC JAZZ PROGRESSIONS

Here is a very basic jazz progression (Figure 18-9). These simple jazz voicings are all pretty low on the neck. Though this is more than "passable" as a jazz chord example, it is easy to do even more.

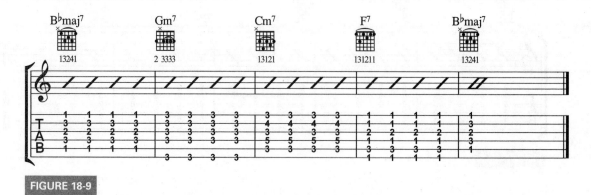

FIGURE 18-9

Simply choosing other voicings for the chords that are present and making sure that you keep the chords relatively close to one another yields another interesting sound. It's amazing how different your music can sound simply by choosing alternate locations for the chords you already know (see Figure 18-10).

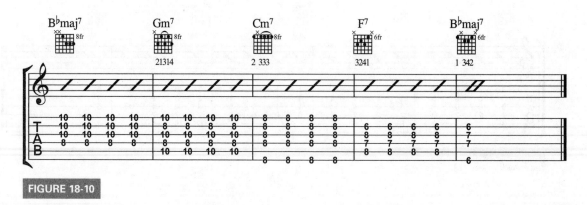

FIGURE 18-10

In the example in Figure 18-11, the G minor chord has been changed to G7 and a new set of voicings has been used. Changing the "quality" of a chord is a common occurrence in jazz music. Listen to how different this example sounds from the others!

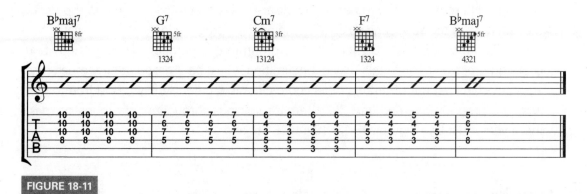

FIGURE 18-11

Of course, the most advanced chord progressions are last. These extended and altered chords are based on the original progressions. By doing this, you get a sound that is more closely associated with modern jazz (see Figure 18-12).

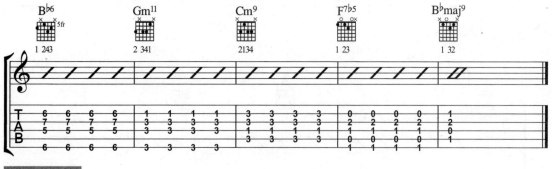

FIGURE 18-12

BASIC FOLK/COUNTRY PROGRESSIONS

This set of chords shows you the kinds of chords you find in folk and country: open chords. The examples follow the same harmonic configuration in each example (I, IV, V, I) but do so in four different keys. The roman numerals are a way that musicians name chords. I is the first note of the scale, and so on. A sample I, IV, V progression in C major would be a C chord, an F chord, and a G chord. It is common to use numbers when talking about chord progressions. While this may seem limiting, you'd be amazed at how much mileage musicians get out of three simple chords in a few different keys. Feel free to start with the progressions and look for alternate voicings throughout the book to make them your own. See Figures 18-13, 18-14, 18-15, and 18-16.

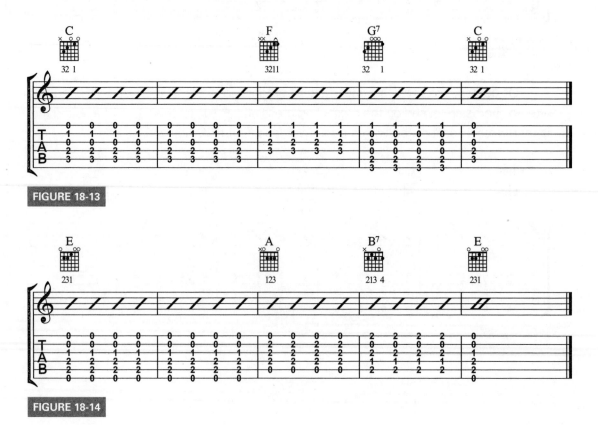

FIGURE 18-13

FIGURE 18-14

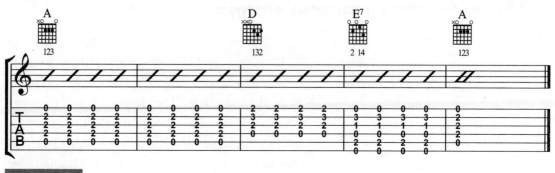

FIGURE 18-15

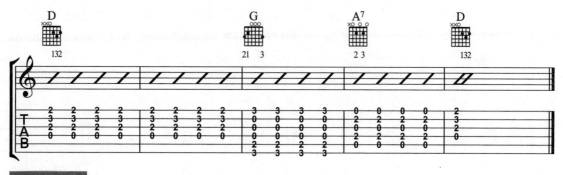

FIGURE 18-16

CLASSICAL STYLE PROGRESSIONS

The next sets of progressions are in classical style. Not only is "classical" a style of music; it's also a way of playing the guitar with your right-hand fingers. What you'll notice is that the chords in the next examples have no chord boxes, but only music and tablature. (See Figures 18-17 through 18-20) Pay attention to the chord symbols and compare them with how you normally play those chords. It's amazing to see the difference in how these chords look from what you are used to. Because classical guitar is played entirely with your fingers, without a pick, the types of chords you can play will sound quite different from the standard "freshman fifteen" chords that you learn at first.

Of course, classical guitar is too big of a topic to cover in four examples! Just notice how the chords are used and how they sound in comparison to the folk/country progressions. Both use simple triads. The four progressions are standard classical style progressions found all over classical guitar literature. You can enjoy them even if you've never played classical guitar.

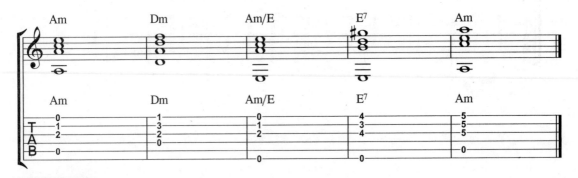

FIGURE 18-17

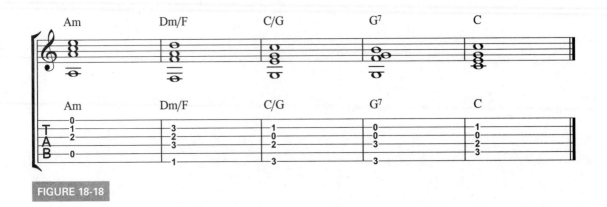

FIGURE 18-18

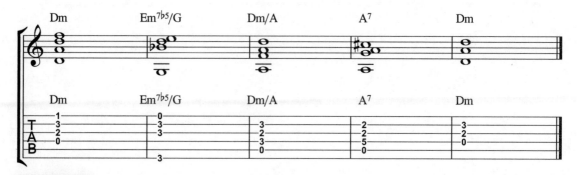

FIGURE 18-19

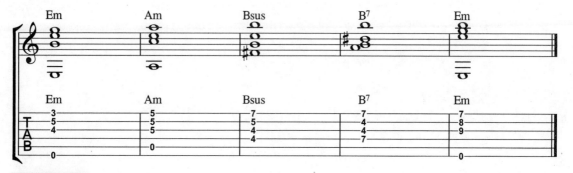

FIGURE 18-20

PART 4

Sound, Gear, and Technology

Using Amplifiers to Get Good Sound

Now that you have reached a comfort level with strumming, playing chords, and single-note playing, you should start to think about the kind of sound you want to get out of your instrument. Sound is a personal thing and is heard in a different way by every musician. To get the best sound out of your guitar, you may want to consider getting an amplifier. You may feel that an amp is an unneeded expense but its impressive effect on the quality of your guitar's sound will (hopefully) change your mind.

THE HISTORY OF AMPLIFIERS

By 1930, anyone familiar with electricity knew that the movement of metal through a magnetic field caused a disturbance that could be translated into an electric current by a nearby coil of wire. Electrical generators and phonograph (record player) pickups already used this principle. The problem in building a guitar pickup was creating a practical way of turning a string's vibration into a current.

After months of trial and error, Hawaiian steel-guitar player George Beauchamp—who, with Adolph Rickenbacker, formed the Electro String Company in the early 1930s—developed a pickup that consisted of two horseshoe magnets. The strings passed through these and over a coil, which had six pole pieces concentrating the magnetic field under each string.

When the pickup seemed to work, Beauchamp enlisted Harry Watson, a skilled guitar maker for National Guitars, to make an electric Hawaiian guitar. It was nicknamed the Frying Pan.

Electro String had to overcome several obstacles, however. To begin with, 1931 was the worst year of the Great Depression, and no one had money to spend on newfangled guitars. Furthermore, only the most farsighted of musicians saw the potential, and the U.S. Patent Office did not know if the Frying Pan was an electrical device or a musical instrument.

From the very beginning, Electro String developed and sold amplifiers. This is an obvious first step, really, because without an amplifier the new electric guitar would have been useless. The first production-model amp was designed and built by a Mr. Van Nest at his Los Angeles radio shop.

Soon after, Beauchamp and Rickenbacker hired design engineer Ralph Robertson to work on amplifiers. He developed the new circuitry for a line that by 1941 included at least four models. Early Rickenbacker amps influenced, among others, Leo Fender, who by the early 1940s was repairing them at his radio shop in nearby Fullerton, California.

By today's standards, the amps were pretty meek. Their output was about 10 watts, which is pretty low, and they used radio technology, vacuum tubes, and small loudspeakers. However, as the popularity of the electric guitar grew, there was a corresponding demand for louder amps.

The breach was filled by Leo Fender. In 1949 he worked with his engineer, Don Randall, to produce the first Super Amp model amplifier. With the Fender solid-bodied guitars (the Telecaster and Stratocaster) in general production, and the introduction of the Gibson Les Paul in 1952, the demand for amps went through the roof as the popularity of the solid body grew. Output rose to a reasonable 50 watts, with twelve-inch speakers, still the norm for guitar amps.

By the late 1950s, the British company Vox had produced the AC30, which is as much a classic amp today as the Fender Twin Reverb. The Vox was particularly popular with blues and rock musicians because it produced a warm tone, which musicians such as Jimi Hendrix, Jeff Beck, and other heavy-metal rockers discovered could be overdriven to create the fuzzy, distorted effect that has come to define the early 1960s rock guitar sound.

Splitting up a combo amp into individual components came about during the rock era of the 1960s. The amp became known as the head, and the speakers became known as the stack. You could get more powerful amps and much bigger speakers this way, and by combining various amps and speaker combinations, musicians could produce more volume.

As the 1960s wore on, and rock bands played bigger and bigger venues, power and volume once more became a problem. This was solved when the British engineer Jim Marshall produced a 100-watt amp connected to a stack of four twelve-inch speakers. Pretty soon the Marshall stack was the norm for rock concerts.

By the 1970s, the vacuum-tube technology of the 1930s was finally being replaced by cheaper and more predictable solid-state transistors, although musicians complained about the coldness of the sound as compared to the warmth of the tube amp. It was popular among those who liked a thinner, cleaner sound.

The transistors' brittle sound was offset by the wider frequency range and the ability to play cleanly (without distorting) at higher volumes. Different tubes could produce different sounds, but they needed to be replaced periodically because they came loose or burned out.

By the 1980s, amplifier makers went back to creating a valve sound, often creating hybrid models that featured tube pre-amps and solid-state power amplifiers, getting the best of both worlds. Today, a traditional guitar amp combines an amplifier and a loudspeaker in one unit, called a combo. They are compact and relatively easy to transport.

UNDERSTANDING AMPLIFIERS

Combo amps (and amps in general) come in a variety of sizes and shapes, but certain functions are common to most models. These are input sockets, individual channel volume controls, and tone controls, plus a master volume control.

There are two basic stages in producing a sound through a combo amp: the pre-amp, which controls the input volume and tone, and the power amp, which controls the overall volume. Most of the tone colors are created during the pre-amp stage.

Input Socket

The input socket takes the signal from the guitar and sends it through the cord that connects the guitar to the amp via a jack socket. If there is more than one input socket, other instruments, such as a second guitar, or a microphone can be fed into the amp at the same time through these other input sockets.

Volume and Tone Controls

Channel input volume controls allows the player to adjust the volume on the amp. It usually boosts the signal from the guitar and passes that signal along to the tone controls.

Channel tone controls can often be as simple as bass and treble controls. More sophisticated models such as the Mesa Boogie can feature a full-blown graphic equalizer. Basically, the controls split the signal into two or more bands, allowing for precise programming of the sound.

Output volume is the final stage of the process. The signal from the pre-amp passes through the power amplifier and is controlled by a master volume knob that controls the signal to the loudspeaker. The master volume controls the volume of the total output to the speaker, regardless of how many input channels are being used.

Other Controls

More sophisticated models have controls that affect distortion, reverb, and tremolo. Speakers come in a wide range of sizes and can be linked together to produce different kinds and volume of sound. Basically, a loudspeaker is the opposite of a microphone. When a string creates a disturbance in the magnetic field around the pickup, the final adjusted signal (having passed through pre-amp and power amp) is passed to a voice coil, connected to a large diaphragm, often made out of cardboard or some other responsive and flexible material. The coil receives the signal, transmutes that into a magnetic field of its own, and causes the diaphragm and cone to vibrate. The vibration disturbs the surrounding air, and recreates the sound waves that were originally generated by striking the guitar string.

Most guitar amp loudspeakers are rated by their impedance factor, which varies from 8 ohms to 16 ohms. (Impedance is an electrical term. Measured in ohms, it is the total opposition to the flow of the alternating current in a circuit.) It's important that amp output and speaker impedance are matched up. Too high a rating and the overall volume of the combo will be reduced. Standard twelve-inch speakers can be connected together in pairs or quads (though ten-inch and fifteen-inch are also common now), although the way they are connected will affect the overall sound output.

GETTING STARTED

It's a good idea to begin with a small practice amp that can deliver a good signal at 6 or 12 watts. In general, what you pay for in an amp is power, not features, so practice amps can be quite cheap, less than a hundred dollars.

FIGURE 19-1: Tech 21 Trademark 30 combo amp

It's also worth bearing in mind that you can often plug your guitar into the auxiliary or tape jack of a home stereo unit. If the unit doesn't have a suitable jack plug socket, go to a local electronics store and tell the salespeople what you want to do. They can usually find you an adapter plug that will allow you to plug the guitar jack into a phono plug that will work on the stereo unit.

Before you plug in, however, make sure the volume is way down on the stereo unit, or you'll risk blowing out the speakers. You can even connect small practice amps, with no speakers, to headphones. That way, you can get a range of effects—such as distortion, EQs, and compression—without disturbing anyone else.

EFFECTS

Electronic effects allow you to produce quite a range of tones and colors. Some new combo amps have effects built into them, but most of the time nearly all of the effects you want to produce will have to be created by interposing an effects unit of some sort between the guitar and the amp. The jack plug that would normally be inserted into the amp is inserted in the "in" socket of the effects unit, and another chord connects the "out" socket of the effects unit to the amp. Most effects units are powered by nine-volt batteries, although they also have a wall-socket transformer. A transformer that's not created for the unit can hum, damage the foot pedal, or not even work.

Reverb

This is a natural effect that gives the impression that the sound is bouncing off walls and ceilings. Modern units allow you to program the parameters of the sound, such as the size and shape of the imaginary room. Reverb is often used to breathe life into dead sound and is perhaps the most common effect used in a recording studio.

Delay

Like reverb, delay gives the sense of sound bounced off a faraway object. You can create different effects depending on the length of the delay, which is measured in milliseconds (500 milliseconds = half a second).

Echo

When the delay is long enough that the repeated signal can be heard as a distinct sound in its own right, then you have an echo. You can control the speed of the echo and get sounds that range from the early days of 1950s rock-and-roll to the experiments of Robert Fripp or Queen's Brian May.

Phase and Flange

Phasing takes place when the same signal sounds as though it is being played back from two different sources at the same time. When the two signals are slightly out of sync—that is, when the peaks of the sound wave of one signal are overlaid on the valleys of the second signal—you get a sweeping sound called phase cancellation that sounds a little like a revolving Leslie speaker for a Hammond organ, popular in the 1970s. If the delay is more dramatic, then the sweeping sound becomes known as flanging.

Chorus

By adding variations in pitch to a delayed signal, it's possible to create the sound of a doubled signal, as if a six-string guitar has become a twelve-string, in a crude analogy.

Pitch Shifting

With pitch shifting, the signal is digitally sampled—that is, a piece of a recorded track is digitally copied and then fed into a loop to be played endlessly. Then it is replayed at a different speed, which changes the original pitch to a new pitch. Units often have a range of an octave above and an octave below the original note. If, for example, you set the unit to play sixths, then every sound that goes into the unit will be played a major sixth higher.

Distortion

The best known of all effects, distorted sound can be created in a number of different ways. The volume of the signal is boosted to the point of distortion in a pre-amp, and then that distorted signal is amplified by the power amp.

Compression

Often used in conjunction with other effects, compression makes the guitar notes sustain for a longer period, giving them more body, although it smoothes out the overall dynamics of a note.

Wah-Wah

Wah-wah is a sound popularized in the 1960s and 1970s by Frank Zappa and Jimi Hendrix. A foot pedal controls a filter similar to a guitar's tone control, causing an almost vocal-like quality on occasion. The rhythm guitar sound in the original version of the movie *Shaft*, for instance, is a typical wah-wah funk sound.

Tremolo

Tremolo is another effect that has a dated 1950s retro sound. Solid-body guitars used to have tremolo arms that could be manually activated. Now it primarily comes in a pedal unit, and it sounds as though you're playing through a slowly moving fan. However, tremolo arms are standard equipment on Fender Stratocasters even today.

Volume Pedal

The volume pedal can be set so that you can alternate, at the dip of a switch, between playing lead guitar and rhythm guitar. The pedal instantly raises or lowers the volume of the amplifier.

COMBINING EFFECTS

Effects pedals can be combined, linking them together. However, the exact sequence of effects used can change the sound, depending on whether a particular effect is placed before or after another. If you use more than one effect, it's probably worthwhile considering buying a switching foot pedal unit that will help you control which effect you want to have dominate your sound, and in what order you want the effects to be.

A modern solution to this problem has been the development of a multiple-effects pedal, which can be programmed to remember a particular sound, or sequence of sounds, and also does away with a suitcase full of effects pedals littering the floor before you like mouse traps.

A word of caution: effects will not make you play better, or help you disguise mistakes. If you can't play well acoustically, you won't play better with a bunch of tricks loaded onto your guitar.

Choose your effects with some taste. They can date you, and they can interfere with the tracking of the guitar signal, making it seem as though you are constantly playing out of sequence—that is, with "bad" time—from the other members of the group.

Always carry a good supply of batteries if you don't have a transformer, and really practice with the effect at home before you decide to use it on a gig or recording.

BRINGING TECHNIQUE, AMPLIFICATION, AND EFFECTS TOGETHER

Try these following effects. You'll be very pleased!

Delayed Eighth Notes

The delayed eighth note is a lot of fun to play with. Commonly used by guitarist The Edge of U2, this effect is simple to set. First you get a delay unit and set the feedback (how many repeats you want) on "1." Figure 19-2 shows a C scale to a D minor sounding scale played as eighth notes. The result of using an eighth note delay is seen below with the notes in parenthesis.

Wah-Wah Style

This is simply fun. Using a wah-wah pedal (popularized by Jimi Hendrix), play the example shown in Figure 19-3. The fun comes in when you play the first chord, then you mute the remaining chords while moving the wah-wah pedal up and down. You'll notice your mouth moving along as well. No worries, it's not habit-forming.

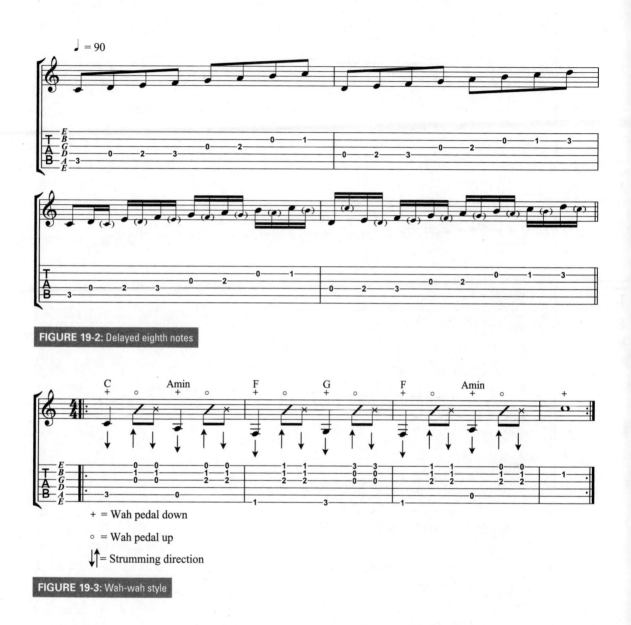

FIGURE 19-2: Delayed eighth notes

+ = Wah pedal down

○ = Wah pedal up

↓↑ = Strumming direction

FIGURE 19-3: Wah-wah style

INTERMEDIATE TO ADVANCED PLAYING TECHNIQUES

Now we'll look at all the scale shape techniques you have mastered and apply effects to them. These scale shapes are called sequences. To make them more fun to play, use the effect listed on each scale shown in 19-4 through 19-7. As you get more proficient, you can also increase your speed. You are going for accuracy, but remember to enjoy the sound of the effect as well.

C Major scale sequence - open strings

Chorus effect

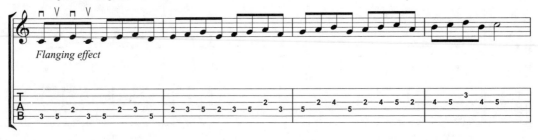

C Major scale sequence - closed

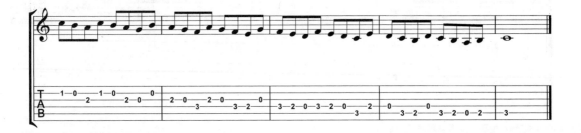

Flanging effect

FIGURE 19-4: C Major sequence with effects

FIGURE 19-5: G Major sequence with effects

C Major scale sequence - open strings

Delay effect

C Major scale sequence - closed

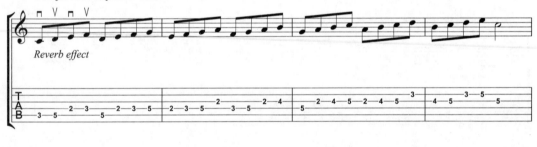

Reverb effect

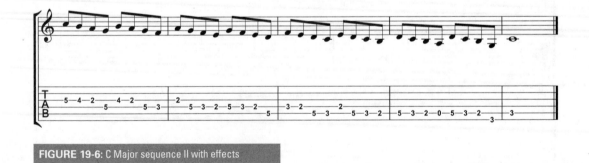

FIGURE 19-6: C Major sequence II with effects

G Major scale sequence - open strings

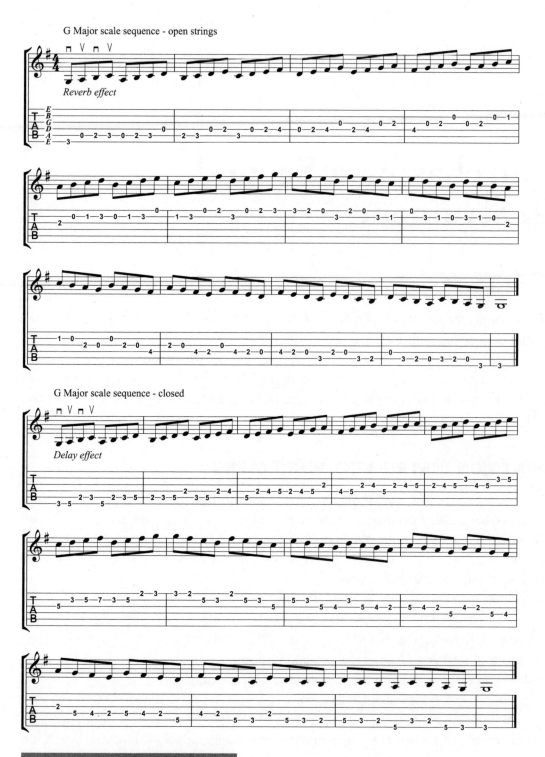

G Major scale sequence - closed

FIGURE 19-7: G Major sequence II with effects

Purchasing a Second Instrument

You have purchased your first guitar and because of this book, you have begun to get better acquainted with the inner workings of the instrument and you're feeling like a future guitar hero. Now you're ready to get a second guitar! Maybe you started off with an acoustic guitar and now the electric is talking in your ear. Or, maybe you started with an electric and the idea of playing acoustic guitar in coffee bars has become an interesting future prospect.

HINTS ON INSTRUMENT PURCHASES

You know that choosing and buying a guitar is a fairly important step in learning how to play. The absolutely best thing you can do is to read more magazines, like *Guitar Player*, *Acoustic Guitar*, and *Guitar World*, to name a few. Reading these magazines over a period of a few months will give you a better overall look at what's out there before you purchase your second instrument. Take along a friend or ask a teacher to help you. While this won't always be possible, it's worth considering.

Regardless of how well you've done your homework, you should never buy a new instrument (whether it's your first, second, or third) on your first visit to a music store. Test lots of different types of guitars and visit lots of music stores more than once before you make a decision on your second instrument. Coming up with a plan now that defines your ideas about music doesn't mean you can't change your mind later on. This isn't do or die, here. It's just a place to start. To begin, you'll want to consider issues such as type, expense, appearance, construction, neck, and action, which are discussed later in this chapter.

HOW TO DO RESEARCH

Doing research is really the key to buying any instrument. Research includes doing price comparisons between different types of guitars and then comparing store prices. You may take the time to go guitar-store hopping—always more fun with a buddy. You will also want to consider some online shopping comparisons. Once again, the music magazines are always your best starting line for your research. They have product reviews in every issue, and these reviews are always very informative when it comes to details, playability, and price value.

You can also use the old tried-and-true method of simply asking people you know and see how they pick their instruments and why they chose a certain manufacturer. Sometimes, people who are asked kindly about their choice of musical instrument will be more than pleased to share information on their pride and joy.

BUYING FROM A STORE

When you go to a music store, be very clear and focused on your objective. Sometimes salespeople can be pushy and overbearing, which can be a turn-off. Bring your research materials—books, price comparisons, and product reviews with you. (You know the old expression, "Forewarned is forearmed.") Often, salespeople in music stores work on commission, meaning that they make their salary based on the dollar amount of products they sell. So they may tend to be pushier than a salesperson who has no direct profit from your purchase. Sometimes a commissioned salesperson can make shopping uncomfortable, but don't let it bother you. Kindly let them know you are looking to purchase a second instrument, and that you are interested in a certain type of guitar, and that you are "just looking."

It is also possible to get distracted by the show-off players who come in all the time and play the guitars all day without buying anything. This frustrates salespeople as well, so be alert to the vibe in the store. Now that you are playing guitar a little more regularly, be prepared to test the different types of instruments and their sounds. As you become a more experienced player, physical differences and tonalities are going to be more apparent to you.

Musical Notes

Many people have difficulties bringing up the subject of getting a discount with a salesperson. Ask the salesperson to give you the price, including tax and case, for the guitar. When he gives you the final quote ask, "Now what can you do for me to get that price a little lower?" You might have to use a little bit of pressure, but it's something you'll get used to doing.

BUYING ON THE INTERNET

One word: eBay! What eBay has done for guitar buying is amazing. eBay has allowed stores to sell guitars online to people around the world that their local clientele wouldn't necessarily be interested in. This is a great deal for you, the second-guitar purchaser. When a store is clearing out its inventory, you have the opportunity to get a great deal on an instrument you really want to purchase with limited funds. In addition to eBay, many of the larger store chains have websites. Even some guitar manufacturers allow you to buy directly from them online. For example, Carvin, a musical instrument and pro audio company that has been around for over sixty years, only sells direct to the consumer and continues to do it successfully.

But is it a good idea to buy a guitar through a mail order or over the Internet? Some people may say "not really." If you are someone who needs to test-drive the instrument and make sure that you're comfortable with it and that it works, then continue to do so. Everyone has a different way of doing things. The main objective is to get a second instrument in the way you feel most comfortable.

TYPES OF GUITARS

By this time, you will have decided which style of music you are beginning to gravitate toward. With that in mind, remember there are three types of guitar to consider: classical, acoustic (and acoustic-electric) steel string, or solid-body electric. What you buy largely depends on the kind of music you are listening to and learning to play.

Musical Notes

There are different size options for younger people, whose hands are still growing, and for adults with small hands. If you have smaller hands, you might be more comfortable playing a smaller instrument. Besides full size, guitars also come in half-size and three-quarter-size versions with shorter necks (which means less finger stretching) and smaller bodies, which are easier to reach around. Both steel-string and nylon-string guitars come in these sizes.

If you've decided you want to learn to play a number of styles, you should always have either a classical or folk (acoustic) guitar in your guitar arsenal. A classical guitar uses nylon strings, which are a little easier on your left-hand fingertips (assuming you're right-handed), though the neck is a little broader than a folk guitar. A folk guitar has steel strings, which are a little tougher on your fingertips at first, but it has a narrower neck. Most styles of music incorporate an acoustic guitar, so having an acoustic or classical guitar is always a good choice.

There are lots of different types of guitars built for the many different kinds of music you can play. If you go into a music store and say you're looking for a guitar to play Eric Clapton–like rock blues, the salesperson will show you a solid-bodied electric like the Fender Stratocaster or a Gibson Les Paul. Say that you want to play jazz guitar like Emily Remler or Johnny Smith, and the salesperson will bring you an F-hole, hollow-bodied guitar like the Gibson ES-175 or a lesser-name brand guitar of similar quality.

For blues and rhythm-and-blues, there are several axes that will do the job, such as the Gibson ES-335 or ES-355. If your second instrument is for acoustic music, go for a Takamine or a Walden guitar for the mid-priced quality purchase, and a Martin, Taylor, or an Ovation on the higher end. If you want to play classical or flamenco, start on a nylon-string guitar from the aforementioned acoustic manufacturers.

The kind of acoustic guitar you buy depends a lot on the kind of music you want to play. Here are some styles of playing and the best guitar(s) to play them on:

- Rock/alternative rock: Six-string steel, twelve-string steel
- Funk: Six-string steel
- Folk: Six-string steel, twelve-string steel, classical
- Fingerpicking style: Six-string steel, twelve-string steel, classical
- Blues: Six-string steel, twelve-string steel, resonator
- Jazz: Six-string steel, twelve-string steel, classical
- Brazilian: Classical
- Flamenco: Classical
- Bluegrass: Six-string steel, twelve-string steel, resonator
- Flatpicking style: Six-string steel
- Country: Six-string steel, twelve-string steel
- Classical: Classical
- Slide: Six-string steel, resonator

The truth is, though, that you can play anything on any kind of guitar. What counts is not the kind of guitar you have, but what's in your head. The best advice is to keep it simple. Remember, even rockers like Jimi Hendrix, Chuck Berry, and Steve Vai played acoustic guitar as well as they could play electric.

EXPENSE

First things first: money. Buying cheap is not necessarily the best idea, though you don't have to spend thousands of dollars on an instrument and equipment either. Don't put yourself into debt, but be aware that you should think in terms of spending at least $200 to $300. You could easily spend $1000 or more if you're not careful.

The more expensive the guitar is, the better (and more seductive) it seems to be. You need to try to balance the "new toy" syndrome with a realistic understanding of what you can afford, and what you need to learn to play well. Play a really expensive guitar and compare it to a much cheaper model. What differences do you notice?

Unless you are working as a musician and you're buying yourself a new tool of the trade, don't spend too much. It won't be worth it.

USED OR SECOND-HAND INSTRUMENTS

Musical Notes

Call a music store, or check out manufacturer catalogs, for models of instruments and prices. For example, a Gibson Les Paul sells for approximately $2,500. A Fender Stratocaster costs around $1,000, and a decent factory-made nylon-string classical guitar can be bought for as little as $300 or so.

Is it a good idea to buy a guitar used or second-hand? Certainly. While a new guitar has to be broken in and can take up to six months to "wake up," a used guitar in good condition is "alive" and could be a bargain. You can expect to pay as much as 40 percent less than list price for a used guitar (unless it's a classic of some sort), depending on where you get it. Compare the prices in music stores, pawnshops, and newspaper ads, and gather as much knowledge and information as you can.

AESTHETICS/APPEARANCE

A blue guitar does not inherently play better than a red or blonde one. Of course, what your new "partner" looks like is important in terms of your desire to spend a lot of time with it. Still, never buy a guitar on looks alone. There may be a lot of guitars from the 1980s with really fancy graphics on them. This was a direct result of the dawning of the MTV era. These particular instruments may be more fun to look at than they are to play.

LISTENING FOR A NEW SOUND

Remember to gently tap the top and back of the instrument to make sure nothing rattles. (You're listening for loose bracing struts inside.) Look inside the sound hole for glue spills and other signs of sloppy workmanship. Check that all the pieces of wood join together smoothly and that there are no gaps between pieces.

An acoustic guitar's sound is principally made by the top—the back and sides reflect and amplify the sound. So a solid-wood acoustic guitar is preferable to a laminated-wood guitar (where the manufacturer presses together layers of inexpensive wood and covers the top layer with veneer). However, solid-wood guitars can be very expensive, and laminated-wood guitars can be pretty good. They are sometimes stronger than solid-wood guitars; the lamination process results in a stronger (though less acoustically responsive) wood.

With electric guitars, make sure that knobs, wires, and other metal parts are secure and rattle-free. Strum the open strings strongly and listen for rattles. A solid-body guitar is basically an electric instrument with no real loud acoustic sound. Some people will try and tell you that the wood an electric guitar is made from is irrelevant, and that it is all in the electronics. Not true! You should also make sure the pickups and wiring are in good working order. There should be no hum or shorts, and the volume and tone controls should all work without crackles and other noises.

As when you checked out your first guitar, listen to how long the note will sustain. Fret a note and play it. Don't use an open string and don't move the string, just keep fretting the note until it fades away. Why bother with this? Well, a good sustain period is four seconds or more, which means the guitar will be good for playing fusion and rock. It also means the guitar is in good order. If the sustain is less than four seconds, then it's a questionable instrument and you should think twice about buying it.

Bear in mind, however, that this doesn't necessarily make it a bad instrument. There could be a number of reasons that the sustain is not longer. If the guitar is otherwise a bargain, a guitar repairman might be able to easily fix this problem. Have a professional check out the instrument before you make a final decision. The lack of sustain could be something as simple as a bridge that is out of alignment, a nut that needs to be filed properly, or old or low-quality strings.

Neck

Pick up the guitar by the head and peer down the neck to make sure it's not warped. Does the guitar have a truss rod? Most guitars now come with them, but make sure. Does the neck bolt on? You can usually see where the neck is attached at the heel with a heel plate, under which are four or five bolts. Fender-style guitars have bolt-on necks. Is

---

Musical Notes

An extremely important subject to discuss with your salesperson is the store's return policy. You should have the right to return your instrument for any reason, no questions asked, for at least a week after your purchase date, for a full refund (possibly less the ubiquitous "restocking fee") or an exchange. Make sure you clearly understand the return policy that will apply to your purchase.

the neck glued on? Classical guitars and the Gibson Les Paul have glued necks. It looks as though the neck and the body are made from one piece of wood.

Run your fingers along the edge of the neck to make sure the fret wire doesn't need filing or reseating. The fret wire should be seated well on the fingerboard, and the ends should not be loose or feel jagged. Do you prefer a neck made from ebony, rosewood, or maple? Cheaper guitars use mahogany or plywood stained black or rust red. The more expensive guitars with the better fingerboards are worth the money. Are the notes at the bottom of the neck in tune? Are they as easy to play as the notes at the top of the fingerboard? Do any of the notes have a buzzing sound even though you're stopping them properly? Is the intonation accurate? Do the notes on the twelfth fret correspond to the harmonics at the same place? The notes may have different tonal qualities, but they should have the pitch. Pay attention to the third and sixth strings in particular. On a guitar that's not set up well, or has a problem, these strings may be hard to keep in tune.

If you don't trust your own knowledge or ears, enlist the help of an experienced guitarist. It's vital that you don't buy something that's going to be really hard to play.

Action

The instrument's action, or playability, is determined by the setting of the string over and between the nut (at the bottom of the guitar) and the bridge (just before the tuning heads). Setting and adjusting these two things is a real art. The strings shouldn't be so low that the notes buzz when they are played, nor so high that the notes need a lot of physical strength to hold down. Since you are purchasing your second guitar, make sure you understand that this new instrument will feel different. Acoustic guitar action is always higher than a solid-body guitar action. If the notes are hard to play or out of tune, get someone in the store to adjust the instrument. If they can't—or won't—fix the instrument, don't buy it.

THE IMPORTANCE OF A GOOD CASE

Now that you have decided on your new second guitar, please make sure it has a good strong case. The temptation is to always buy a soft gig bag. Going back and forth from gig to gig or rehearsal may be practical with a gig bag, but a hard-shell case is always a better way to go when it comes to storing the instrument when you're not playing it. This is especially true for acoustic guitars. Hard-shell acoustic guitar cases are made out of plywood. Their strength comes in three-ply and the stronger (and heavier) five-ply cases. The five-ply cases usually have an arched top lid for added strength. There are also cases manufactured using an injection-molding process and special fiberglass polymers. These cases are usually black and light in weight, but very sturdy. They may sometime be less expensive than the wood cases because they can be churned out more quickly in the manufacturing process.

All hard-shell cases have a liner inside of them called high pile and low pile. This is the fuzzy velvet-feeling material that protects the surface of the instrument. Under the pile is foam that helps protect the instrument from shock. A good case should have at least four latches to lock the case lid securely with the body. The handle on the case should be strong as well. If you purchase a five-ply case, make sure the handle is not a soft one. It should be strong enough to keep the guitar balanced.

CLOSING THE DEAL

You've picked your instrument. Now your mission is to bring that guitar home for the lowest possible price! Note that this changes your relationship with your salesperson from teammate to adversary because his mission is to sell it to you for as much money as possible. Your mantra will be "Never pay list price." Many people assume that if the price tag on the guitar says $599, that's the price they'll be expected to pay. This is not true—music stores expect to sell you the guitar for less than list price. Many stores show both the list price and their own price on the tag in an effort to impress you in advance with the discount you'll be getting. Whatever the price tag says, remember that your salesperson has the power to significantly reduce the price of your guitar from the list price. The trick is to get him to do that for you. To make that happen, remember these tips:

- Keep your salesperson on a need-to-know basis. If you tell him that you're in love with this guitar and have to have it right now, you've tipped your hand, and your discount will be smaller as a result.
- Keep it casual. Mention to your salesperson that you've seen a lot of nice guitars in other stores around town. Also, try out a few other guitars besides the one you've got your eye on, including some that are cheaper so your salesperson will be happy when you "gravitate" toward your beloved selection. And don't appear to be in any hurry to buy a guitar today.

- Know if the price you're being quoted includes a case. If so, ask if the case is a hard-shell case or a soft gig bag. This is a significant difference because a hard-shell case sells for around $100, and a gig bag sells for around $40, on average.
- Never, ever pay list price for a guitar! No music store today could stay in business if it sold its instruments for list price when 30-percent discounts are commonplace.

QUICK TIPS FOR BUYING A SECOND GUITAR

You're about to walk into a guitar store and haven't done much research (though this is not recommended!). You wonder what points are crucial when it comes to buying a good-quality instrument. The following list summarizes the main features you will need to know when shopping. Bring this page with you, and make sure you have covered all the points listed before you invest your hard-earned money in a new guitar:

- Step up the instrument quality when possible, but don't overspend.
- Enjoy your instrument. Learn how to play it. It will feel different in your hands than your current instrument.
- Have an experienced guitar tech check the fingerboard for potential warping. The intonation and electronics should also be looked at.
- Make sure the action is set the way you like it. Look at the distance between the nut and the bridge. A low action means the strings are closer to the frets, so your fingers don't have to work as hard to press the strings to the fingerboard. Listen for buzzes and rattles. Once again, a guitar tech is best suited for these procedures.
- Check the tuning heads. If they turn too easily, the strings may slip, making the guitar difficult to keep in tune.
- Check for noise. With the guitar plugged in, stand it close to an amplifier and listen. Whistling or feedback might suggest the pickups aren't well isolated, and it could be a problem playing the guitar at high volume. Make sure the amplifier in the store is not masking faults with the guitar you're playing.

21

Home Recording 101

The technology for recording sound has been around for just a little more than a hundred years. But it has come a long way since it began. This chapter covers recording history and the development of an industry that was once exclusive and expensive and is now an affordable and practical alternative for home and semiprofessional musicians.

HOW IT ALL BEGAN

From cave paintings to the Dead Sea Scrolls, information has been written down and preserved for all to see for centuries. But recording sound has been around only since the late 1800s. Sadly, much of the history of sound itself has been lost because it occurred before it was possible to record it. Imagine being able to hear Mozart play his own piano pieces, or to hear Abraham Lincoln speak. These memories survive only through written words and recollections of the events. Recording sound has served not only as an important historical tool, but also as a way for music to be preserved and enjoyed.

RECORDING DEFINED

What exactly is recording? Recording is the transmittal of sound waves onto a device capable of preserving and reproducing that sound. Several components are necessary to make a music recording today. First, a sound source is needed—this can be an acoustic instrument, an electronic one, or, in the case of a computer-based synthesizer, a virtual one. Then, the sound needs to be transferred into the recording device. For acoustic instruments, a microphone is needed to convert the acoustic information into electrical signals.

Musical Notes

The first microphone was invented in 1876 for Alexander Graham Bell's telephone system, which received a patent that same year. Bell's microphone picked up sound and converted it to electricity that could be transmitted and reproduced. Chronologically, the microphone predates all recording by one year!

Electronic instruments, such as keyboards, interface directly with the recorder, bypassing the need for a microphone, although it's also possible to use an amplifier and then record the sound conventionally. Because all electronic keyboards output their sound as an electrical signal, recording directly this way and bypassing the amplifier ensures the purest signal.

Now that we have generated and captured the sound, we need somewhere to store it.

Today, sound is stored in either of two ways: as an analog signal (a continuous periodic signal) or as a digital representation of an analog signal. A continuous periodic signal is like a wave in its periodic nature. Like waves breaking on the beach, first comes the crest of a wave followed by a trough, then another crest, then another trough, and so on. Analog media stores the waves themselves as a continuous electrical charge. Magnetic tape is the most common analog medium.

Digital media store a numerical representation of the wave using a code consisting of only zeroes and ones, called binary code. In the early days of digital recording, the common way to store this binary information was on magnetic tape. Digital audiotape, unlike traditional analog media, recorded only digital information—there was no sound on digital audiotape. Today, an audio interface converts analog signals to a digital representation, called encoding, on the way into the computer and converts the digital representation to analog signals, called decoding, on the way out. These two processes are commonly called A/D and D/A conversions. A/D is read as "A to D" or "analog to digital;" D/A means digital to analog.

Musical Notes

Analog tape recording has been around since the 1950s and is still favored by many artists and producers for its warm, rich sound. A reel of two-inch tape retails for nearly $300. The same amount of information can be recorded to a computer hard drive or CD for a fraction of the cost.

Traditional analog tape is very expensive and hard to get, more so now than ever. Because of the tremendous size of modern hard drives and their low cost, they are a great choice for storing music. The format you ultimately use is unimportant; every recording format does the same basic job of recording sounds.

The final step in recording is playing back the recorded sound. Both analog and digital media must convert information to electrical signals, which are rendered as audible sound waves by speakers, called monitors, or through headphones.

ELEMENTS OF A PROFESSIONAL RECORDING

As a home studio owner, you should be aware of how the professional studios operate and what techniques they employ. In the end, we are all trying to do the same thing: get sound onto a recording device, spice it up, and mix it to a final product. We all want to get the best sound possible. The differences in techniques directly affect the quality of the final product.

Why Your Favorite Recordings Sound So Good

Cue up your favorite recording, one that you think is recorded well. Sit back and listen closely. Notice how all the instruments blend together, how no instrument sticks out of the mix more than it should. All the instruments sound present, the drums don't sound far away, and the overall effect puts you in the same room as the band. Notice the lack of background noise. The recording has a smooth and polished sound to it, without harshness. These are all qualities of good engineering, good mixing, and good mastering.

When you listen to a professional recording, realize that you are listening to months, if not years, of hard work recording and mixing the music. Big studios also have access to the finest equipment, the best microphones, acoustically perfect rooms, and most important of all, experienced engineers to run the sessions. Does this mean your home studio masterpiece will sound bad? No, not at all! With some basic equipment, a little knowledge, and your inspired music, you can make professional-sounding recordings.

Recording sessions are broken up into three main components: preproduction, production and engineering, and postproduction. Each component plays an important part in the quality of the finished product.

Preproduction

Preproduction involves everything that happens before the actual recording session. This can include selecting the right material to record, rehearsing the band, and getting ready for the recording sessions. For the home studio owner, it involves working out your material so that you can record it. It also might include purchasing gear to

Musical Notes

Professional recording studios can charge up to several thousand dollars an hour for recording services! For the cost of one session in a professional studio, you could take that money and invest it in your own studio and work whenever you want to.

facilitate a particular project, such as a second vocal microphone to record a vocal duet for a new song. Basically, preproduction is anything you can do in advance to make your recordings go more smoothly.

Production and Engineering

Production involves the actual recording sessions. At the sessions, the engineer runs the recording show. It's up to the engineer and any assistants she might have to set up and place the microphones for optimum sound, get proper recording levels, run the mixing board, operate the recording device, and make sure everything sounds good. The engineer is the most important link in the chain (besides the musicians themselves) in getting a great-sounding recording. Engineering, like any other skill, requires a certain level of artistry and practice. An experienced engineer will be able to identify problems and quickly find solutions.

Editing and overdubbing might take place in subsequent sessions, but it's still considered production. In your studio, you will most likely be wearing all of the various hats needed to make a recording. It will be up to you to properly set up your equipment and the microphones, run the recording device, and engineer the recording. This can be a tall order to do all at once, but this book will show you how to get started easily. With a little practice, you'll be off and running!

Postproduction

Postproduction includes anything that happens after the recording sessions. Most often, postproduction involves mixing the tracks to a polished, uniform sound. Mixing involves several key elements:

- **Track levels:** Loudness of each track
- **Panning:** Side-to-side placement of instruments and voices in the mix
- **Equalization:** Boosting or cutting certain frequencies in the mix
- **Effects:** Adding signal processing such as reverb, delay, and compression in order to achieve a polished sound
- **Mix down:** Mixing all the tracks into a single stereo pair suitable for distribution or mastering

Even the most basic studio has the capability to do all these things. Remember that the basic sequence of events is always the same: sound capture, recording, and playback. Now that we explained a little about the history of the recording process and got you thinking about some concepts, it's time to shift gears and move into your home studio to find out what you need to get started.

BRINGING IT HOME

You're ready to make the leap from weekend warrior to home recording studio owner—but how do you do it? What do you need? It's easy to become overwhelmed with all the choices when you're getting started.

So just what *can* you do in a home studio? What is it, exactly, that you will be able to do once you have your studio set up? Even if you have no recording experience, you'll find that your natural talent and years of listening to well-produced music have given you more tools than you thought you had. It's all about listening.

Recording

The most obvious thing you can do in a home studio is to record sound into your computer. Whether you are learning to use microphones effectively or just plugging in a keyboard, recording covers the whole spectrum of capturing sound. For those who have never recorded before, the process can be very rewarding. Having the ability to come home from work and spend a few hours in your studio creating music is very freeing, and the icing on the cake is that you have total control. Whether you are making an elaborate multitrack masterpiece or simply singing and playing guitar, you need to know how to get a good sound. This is where you learn the basics of engineering: setting levels, choosing and placing the correct microphones for the best sound, and mixing tracks. For the keyboard players out there, using MIDI, an electronic standard used for the transmission of digital music, is an important part of the recording process. All these elements fall under the umbrella of recording.

Mixing

Mixing is generally done after the initial recording sessions. Mixing is the art of setting the loudness and sound color of each instrument that you record. Mixing is a learned art, and like any other skill, it takes practice. Using faders to control the volume of tracks helps the instruments sound more cohesive and balanced. Equalization (EQ) is the process of boosting or lowering certain frequencies. Using EQ you can clarify the sound of a muddy bass, or create a round, warm sound from a thin, lifeless guitar.

Effects are also a major component of mixing; they can help you achieve a more polished final sound. For instance, you can add reverb to give the illusion of having recorded in a large space or use compression to even out sudden changes in volume.

Editing

Look at music editing as the ability to cut, copy, paste, and whiteout your sound. In the world of editing, you can cut a section and rerecord it, or you can go back and fix a note that sounds bad.

Imagine you are recording a song with the structure: chorus, solo, chorus. Suppose the choruses are exactly the same, and when you recorded the piece, the second chorus sounds better. Computer software gives you the ability to cut the first chorus and copy the second in its place. You don't even have to play repeat sections twice; you can just loop together small repeating bars of music. You can even click and drag sections of music around with your mouse. Did you decide after the fact that you want to record an introduction to your masterpiece? Just drag the original audio to the right, make room for the new, and paste it all together. This is just the tip of a very large iceberg—so how do you get started? First, you've got to determine what your needs are.

ASSESSING YOUR NEEDS

You've scoured the Internet. You get every music gear catalog known to mankind. You've been to the local music store countless times. You know it's time to start doing some home recording, but the myriad choices and lack of concrete how-to instructions is getting to you. Have no fear! You're in the right place now.

"Home recording" is a broad term—musicians have different needs and ideas about what the studio is going to provide. For some, home recording is a sketchpad for small ideas that might be taken to a professional studio later. For others, their home studios are used to flesh out ideas so they can present them to members of their bands. Still others use home recording as a way to save money. Because professional recording studios can be very costly, they invest in a home studio and can make demo recordings as frequently as they want. And finally, some musicians use their home studio as a creative tool to write, produce, and ultimately sell their own music. Some home studio owners enjoy the process so much that they eventually upgrade their equipment and open their studios to the public. What you do with your studio is as personal as the music you create. The sky is the limit and, with modern technology at your side, you will be armed with all the tools to make recordings that sound great.

Start Simple

It's very easy to go overboard in this field. There is plenty of equipment out there, and you could spend lots of money on it. Everyone fantasizes about the professional studio with a ten-foot-wide mixing board and floor-to-ceiling rack equipment. Some musicians do need all that stuff, but what do *you* need? The first step is assessing your needs. Ask yourself these questions before you start buying gear:

- How many instruments do I need to record at the same time?
- Are the instruments electric or acoustic?
- Will I use MIDI or sequenced instruments?
- Do I need portability?
- Do I plan to distribute or sell the music recordings I make?

Keep the answers to these questions in the back of your mind as you read this chapter. The theme you'll see repeated throughout is: make the most of what you have. Expensive gear won't necessarily make anything better. What really matters is what you do with what you have. Too many studio owners get caught in the trap of having the nicest toys without understanding or utilizing their gear to the fullest. Imagine Grandma driving a Ferrari to church once a week. Bit of a waste, eh?

Musical Notes

The recordings of the 1950s and 1960s were recorded with equipment that would be considered limiting nowadays. You'd be amazed at how many major recordings that you know and love were done by a highly skilled recording engineer on very basic equipment. Rudy Van Gelder's 1950s and 1960s Blue Note jazz sessions come to mind, as do George Martin and the Beatles.

Have a Goal

Having a goal seems like a simple idea. However, many people jump on the home studio bandwagon without even considering a goal. Ask yourself, "What do I want to do with a home studio?" The result you're looking for—be it demo tapes to send to local clubs, or recordings to sell after a show—will help you determine what you need in a home studio. More often than not, at first you'll want to start small. You can always upgrade as you become more skilled at the process. Remember, home recording is a skill like any other, and it takes a while to get really good at it.

Seek Advice from Others

More than likely, you know other musicians. It's safe to assume that a percentage of them will also own home studios, in one form or another. Spend some time talking with them and, if possible, get hands-on demonstrations of the equipment they use. Find out how they use it and listen to how their final product sounds.

Another invaluable resource is your local music store. Many of these stores are staffed with very talented musicians. Many of them, in addition to knowing a great deal about the equipment they sell, have home studios of their own. Ask them what they use, and what they use it for.

SHOPPING FOR GEAR

Okay. Now you're really excited. You're ready to start. You've thought through the whole process. You've talked to other studio owners. You've looked around on the web.

Start Shopping

Depending on where you live, you might have access to music stores that carry a lot of recording equipment. Your best bet is to buy from a store, instead of online. There are a bunch of good reasons you should buy from a store. For starters, you'll get to see, touch, and even use some of the gear you are planning to purchase before you spend your money. You'll also be able to get advice from the salesperson on what might suit you best. Developing rapport with an individual salesperson is important because, as you keep going back to the same person for all your gear, not only do you develop a nice business relationship (which might result in discounts), you might also get honest, real-world advice.

But there's nothing wrong with buying gear online, either. If you live in a remote area, this might be your only option. If you purchase online, returning gear you don't like is a pain. But then again, there are some great deals online. If you shop around, you can get a great price. Many stores also price-match, so even if you've found a better deal somewhere else, bring the information to the attention of your salesperson. Many stores will accommodate you in an effort to keep you as a loyal customer. You can also find some great deals in the used-gear market; check out eBay.

Musical Notes

Don't feel pressured into buying more than you need at first. You can always upgrade as you go. Certain components, such as cables and microphone stands, don't change from setup to setup, so you won't waste money upgrading those items.

CREATING A BUDGET

Here comes everyone's least favorite subject—spending money. You work hard for it, and the last thing you want to do is squander it on equipment that isn't suitable for you or doesn't get the job done. The good news is that there is a studio to be had at almost every price level, and you can get started with a basic studio for around $250—maybe even less, depending on your configuration and what you already own. The bad news is that there's a lot of equipment available, and you can easily get carried away and spend many thousands of dollars on all the various gear out there. Figure out exactly what you can spend at first. Your budget should take into consideration the following:

- What is the maximum you can spend?
- Do you want the ability to record more than one track at a time?
- How many microphones do you need?
- How many interconnecting cables does your setup require?
- Do you need computer recording software?
- Do you need a computer recording interface?
- Does your computer need to be upgraded to handle the demands of working with large music files?
- What signal effects do you need?
- Do you need a separate mixer? (This is becoming less necessary these days.)
- How do you plan on listening to your work—headphones or speakers?

As you can see, these are important issues. You must take all these points into consideration when planning your budget. Since every studio is different, this book talks about general setups, and you can modify the setup that is closest to your needs.

THE THREE MAIN RECORDING ELEMENTS

You've already learned the three elements necessary for recording sound: something to capture the sound, something to store it and play it back, and something to enable you to hear it played back. First, you need a sound and a device capable of capturing that sound, usually a microphone. Some instruments interface directly via cables; keyboards and amplifier line-out jacks are examples of direct instruments. Next, you need a recorder capable of recording the sound and playing it back later. Last, you need something to hear the recording with—either speakers or headphones. These elements are commonly found in all studios, regardless of price or quality.

Capturing Sound

Microphones are typically used for sound input. Prices of microphones range widely; you can pay around $60 for a starter variety, $200 for a good one, and $500 and above for a top-of-the-line model. Figure out how many you'll need. You will probably need one microphone for each acoustic instrument or vocalist, and two to four for a drum kit, depending on how you set up the kit. If you are recording one instrument at a time, you can get away with fewer microphones. You might pool the money you save by doing this and buy one or two higher quality microphones.

Instruments such as keyboards, drum machines, and guitar effects processors plug directly into an audio interface. Also, many amplifiers feature direct outputs and bypass the need for a microphone; all you need is a cable. Cables are cheap, thank goodness! You might also need a direct box to change the impedance of certain instruments to match the input of the recorder.

Finding a Recorder

For quick and simple recording, there are many portable digital recorders on the market. Some of these offer features like built-in stereo microphones, onboard digital effects, and overdubbing capabilities. Many are small enough to fit in your hand. Portable digital recorders can run as little as $150 to as much as $900.

You can also record with a computer, though you'll need software, which ranges from free to $1,000. You'll also need a computer interface that accepts audio and possibly MIDI if you plan to use that. Depending on how many sources you need to record at once, computer audio interfaces can range from $100 to more than $1,000. MIDI interfaces are less expensive, and you pay more depending on how many MIDI inputs, or separate instruments, you need to use at the same time. Expect to spend between $30 for a simple one-input/one-output MIDI interface and up to $550 for eight MIDI devices.

Musical Notes

Since the majority of recording systems are based around computers, why would you consider a dedicated hardware recording system? Dedicated hardware recording systems can be perfect for those who need a simple setup and who rely on portability. Computers are expensive, and only laptops are easily portable. Computers can also be susceptible to viruses and crashes. You won't encounter those issues with a dedicated hardware recording system.

Playing the Music Back

In order to play back the recorded sound, most home studio owners start with a pair of decent headphones. Headphones range from $30 to $200. If you choose to use professional speakers, called monitor speakers, you can expect to pay anywhere from $100 to $800 or more for a set. Some monitors are self-powered and don't require additional amplifiers to run; others need an amplifier, which will cost you money as well! Your best bet is to go for self-powered monitors. There are some great ones in the $200–$300 range. A low-tech solution is to monitor through your home stereo. It's not the optimal way to go, but it might tide you over until you can afford dedicated monitors.

Don't Get Carried Away

It's so easy to get carried away in a music store. You go in for one thing and walk out with five things you didn't need. This is known as Gear Acquisition Syndrome (GAS). This ailment affects many musicians who fall victim to the grandeur of a music store that has "everything." Out of the three elements of your studio, it's important to balance the quality of each part. The result is only as good as all the equipment you use. Add one weak link and the chain will break. For example, if you blow all your cash on a top-of-the-line audio interface and you plug a cheap, noisy microphone into it, your computer will play back a noisy signal, in perfect digital quality. See the problem? Go into this process with a clear understanding of your needs and your means. Try your best to choose components that work together to deliver a quality result.

TYPICAL SETUPS

Let's take a look at some typical setups for various types of recording systems so you can get an idea of what equipment is commonly used.

For Working Alone

Many "solo" engineers and players own just a few microphones, usually one all-purpose and one specialized microphone. They focus on quality purchases over quantity. For example, it wouldn't make sense to have eight average-sounding channels in an audio interface when two great ones cost about the same and will be enough for your needs. A lot depends on what instruments you plan to record. Many studios involve MIDI to control drum machines and keyboards. While standalone sequencers and standalone recorders do exist, they are rarely used anymore as computers have all but replaced their functionality at a lower cost with added flexibility. The solo home studio owner doesn't require huge amounts of space, and usually a corner of a room or a desk area is enough to get anyone started. Since the computer is the modern recording standard, many home studios are built around computer workstations and desks.

For Working in Groups

If you're in a group or you plan to record a lot at one time, you have some choices on how to proceed. For live groups, multitrack recording isn't a necessity, although it's nice to have. A good-quality portable digital recorder can do a great job. If the recorder includes a stereo microphone, you can place the unit in the center of the group and get above-average results. If the portable digital recorder doesn't include a stereo microphone, you'll need a mixer.

A mixer allows several sources of sound to be mixed together into one stereo output. You can connect eight or more microphones to the mixer, which will output one stereo sound to your recorder. The nice part about this system is that it's not all that expensive; however, there are some serious drawbacks to it.

First, the balance of the group has to be set in the mixer before the recording takes place. Since you're not multitrack recording, you can only record the single output of the mixer. Also, you have very little opportunity to add individual effects, except again through the mixer at the time of recording. If you set up the microphones, digital interfaces, and effects carefully, you can get a good sound, but it's very difficult. If, after you're done, you realize the snare drum is too loud, for example, there's little you can do. Even so, you'd be surprised to know how many albums—especially jazz records—have been recorded this way.

Those who step up to multitrack recording do so in much the same way the solo artist does. However, there are specific concerns that need to be addressed, such as the number of instruments that are going to be recorded at once. Having the right number of simultaneous inputs is crucial to be able to mix the sounds after the fact. By placing individual instruments on individual tracks, you have greater control over their relative timbre and volume levels. When you are limited to a few inputs, you have no choice but to place multiple instruments on the same track, thereby losing the ability to balance them after you record. Typically these setups use a lot of microphones. You'll need one input for every microphone you use. Your needs as a multitracker really depend on what you're recording and how much control you want.

Portable Setups

If you are doing a lot of your recording at gigs, you'll need a setup that is portable and easy to move. Portable stereo recorders are great for this. If your live gig has a soundperson, you can benefit from her gear as well. You can get a stereo mix from the soundperson and plug into your portable stereo recorder and you are good to go. (That is, of course, assuming that the mix off the board sounds good.)

If you have a laptop and an audio interface, you can take this setup with you to record gigs. With this kind of setup, you could record the stereo mix from the soundperson, or set up your own microphones and direct boxes and multitrack record the gig; if you have enough inputs on your audio interface, you can do both.

What's been missing in all this discussion about gear, options, and budgets is the creative spark. That is the spark that only you can provide. Recordings can't make things magically appear. No matter what kind of gear you have, if you don't bring your creativity into play, nothing happens. We've all heard good players playing cheap instruments who still sound great. We've also experienced amateurs playing expensive gear and sounding terrible. *You* make it happen.

SETTING UP A SPACE

Having a comfortable work space is critical to working efficiently. If your gear isn't readily available, you aren't going to be as likely to use it, so don't cram yourself into a corner someplace or exile yourself to a basement.

Being comfortable is vital to working efficiently. You can either make do with the tables and chairs you already own or invest in studio furniture. Yes, they make furniture just for this kind of thing! But before you furnish your studio, establish your main focus. For most people, easy access to their primary instrument is their greatest concern. Then comes placement of the recording device or mixer. If you use a computer, do yourself a favor and put the computer on the floor if you can. This will free up much-needed desk space. Figure 21-1 shows a well-organized recording space.

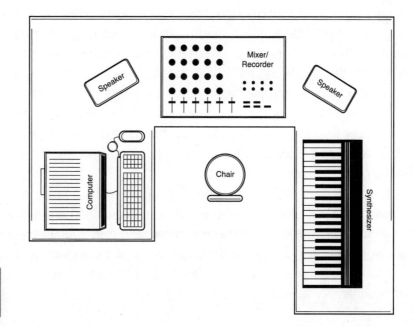

FIGURE 21-1:
Setting up a good space

You need a place where you can get work done. Your music requires concentration. Selecting a spot for your studio might not always be in your complete control, but you should take a few things into account when setting up your space. To record with microphones you will need a quiet place. Microphones have this pesky little way of hearing things you don't want them to hear: dogs barking, doors shutting, and phones ringing, just to name a few. If you plan to work late at night, you'll want to be someplace out of the way so you don't disturb anyone.

INSTRUMENTS

The discussion so far has emphasized equipment, but you can't forget about the instruments you're going to play. They're pretty important to this process because, no matter how good your recording gear is, your instruments need to sound good. It stands to reason that any problems you have with your instruments are going to get worse when you record them. There's a widely used phrase in the recording world: Garbage In, Garbage Out. Make sure you have decent-sounding equipment. It's a myth that "you can fix it in the mix."

Experiment

Adding new sounds to your music is one of the fun parts about home recording. Even if you only play guitar, adding several different-sounding guitars on different tracks can widen the scope of your music. Experimentation is the name of the game here; you'd be amazed at what sounds good together. Keyboard players can really go to town with different sounds, layers of instruments, and even drum kits from the keyboard.

Drum machines have always been useful to nondrummers and home studio musicians alike. Acoustic drums can be difficult to record well and can be too loud for many apartments and houses. Sample-based drum programs such as Battery from Native Instruments and EZdrummer from Toontrack sound so realistic it's uncanny. Their quality is so high because samples are actual recordings of drums, not synthetic versions. That's right, someone recorded each drum one by one at different volume levels and the sampler plays them back for you!

Another option, if you're not going to play individual drums, is premade drum loops. These loops are professionally recorded in studios and are every bit as real as having the drummer with you. They're well mixed, and they sound very cool, so they're definitely worth checking into. To utilize loops, you use a computer and recording software. Loops come as premixed audio files; you simply add them into your recording program on an empty track and voilà, instant drums!

All recording software works with loops. From Apple's highly intuitive GarageBand to the über-powerful Pro Tools 8 software from Digidesign, loops are a common way for musicians to work.

Collaborate

Just because you can lay down eight or more tracks of yourself playing each instrument one pass at a time doesn't mean that you should. Why use a sampled drum when a real drummer is close by? By getting to know other musicians and home studio owners, you can collaborate with each other and utilize the combined power of all your talents. Maybe you'll even make a record together. Who knows what could happen. The possibilities are endless.

Guitar Tricks

Guitar players have invented many clever ways to play the instrument to take advantage of its unique characteristics. Some tricks are merely modifications of your current technique, while others involve gadgets. This chapter explores the unique ways to play the guitar, and the fun noises and sounds you can create with it.

PICK A SPOT

Everyone looks for ways to change his or her tone. Whether they're trying to emulate the sound of a great player or they're looking for new sounds, most players look to different guitars and amps for tone changes. In reality, guitars and amps have little to do with your tone; it originates from your hands.

Have you ever noticed that, while Eddie Van Halen has changed guitars and amps over the course of his life, he still sounds the same? Although string gauge, string height, and pick can make some difference, the sound of his guitar has more to do with the way he approaches the instrument than the equipment he uses.

The most immediate tone change you can get comes from moving the location of your pick. The guitar, especially the acoustic guitar, has a remarkable range of colors that you can create just by changing where you pick. Most players tend to pick halfway between the end of the neck and the bridge. This is a nice place to pick because it gives you an excellent round sound for most playing situations. But move away from this central spot and you alter your tone dramatically.

Musical Notes

On an electric guitar, you'll get some changes in tone by changing where you pick, but the effect will be much more pronounced on an acoustic guitar.

Experiment with pick placement for some dramatic tone changes. If you pick closer to the bridge, you'll get a more metallic sound; as you approach the fingerboard, you'll get a very sweet, syrupy sound. Playing closer to the neck can help an appealing chordal passage sound more delicate. Playing up near the bridge can help to emphasize a lead part or an important melody that needs to stand out.

CONTROLLING SOUNDS ON AN ELECTRIC GUITAR

Are you puzzled by all of the control knobs and switches on your electric guitar? Many guitar students, especially beginners, have little idea what the controls on an electric guitar do. Most electric guitars have of three main control knobs—the volume knob(s), tone knob(s), and the pickup selector, which is what transfers the sound of the guitar to the amplifier.

Volume

Volume knobs may seem fairly self-explanatory, but there are some things you may not know about them. When your guitar is going through a clean amplifier with no distortion, a volume knob acts just as you think it should: It controls the volume of the instrument. However, when you apply distortion to your sound you'll notice that the volume knob no longer controls the overall volume. When distortion is turned on, the volume knob acts as a distortion filter, essentially turning up and down the level of distortion. You can change your guitar from a semiclean sound by turning the volume knob down (but not off) while distortion is on. As you turn the volume knob up, your guitar sound becomes more distorted. This is a handy way to make adjustments without bending down to change your effect pedal or amp distortion settings mid-song.

Tone

The tone knob adjusts the frequencies that go through the guitar and into the amplifier. By changing the position of the tone knob, you can adjust the sound from treble to bass (just as you do with the tone knob on stereo equipment). When the tone knob is all the way up (10), the guitar acts normally—the tone knob is not doing anything but letting the natural sound of the pickups pass through to the speakers. Rolling the knob down limits the amount of high frequencies the guitar emits, so the sound gets muddier and more bass heavy. This has long been a secret of jazz and blues players who want to warm up their clean sound. The tone knob can dramatically alter your sound, so experiment with it!

Pickup Selector

Pickup switches typically come in two varieties: Stratocaster 5 position and Les Paul 3 position. Each serves the same purpose. Did you ever wonder why you have pickups at different spots on the guitar? The location of the pickup affects the sound, just as the location of the pick affects the sound on an acoustic guitar.

The pickup closer to the bridge has a more treble-like sound; the pickup closer to the neck sounds sweeter and has more bass. The pickup selector chooses between the different pickup locations and thus acts as the sound selector—when the pickup selector is in the forward position (toward the neck) the sound is softer; when the pickup selector is in the back position (the bridge) the sound is heavier.

ADD-ONS

Now we get to the fun stuff. There are things that you can add to the guitar to change the sound. The place to start is the last place you might think to look: the pick. The pick is the direct connection between you and the guitar and has the greatest effect on your tone. Many players just pick with whatever is convenient, while others realize that variety is the spice of life (and sound).

The Twenty-Five-Cent Tone Shift

The number of picks on the market is staggering. The variety of different materials, colors, shapes, and thicknesses make for much variation. Some players are content to stick with the normal Fender-type heavy pick, while others prefer small teardrop-shaped picks. If you've been using the same pick for a long time, buy some new picks. Most picks are about twenty-five cents each, so buy several. Experiment with shape, hardness, and material—each pick will give you a different sound. You can even buy picks made out of steel and copper (heavy metal?). You may be shocked at how much a new pick can affect your sound.

Certain picks are better suited to certain types of playing. Rhythm players tend to like light picks that have a fair amount of flex. The flex helps facilitate strumming without getting in the way. Players who enjoy playing fast tend to like small, hard picks. The size lets them move around the guitar with more efficiency, and the hardness translates directly to speed: the harder the pick, the faster it moves through the strings.

Musical Notes

Don't think that you have to hold the pick point down all the time. Try turning your pick every which way for different sounds, especially upside down. You don't even have to use a pick at all. Many players successfully use their fingers to play. Mark Knopfler of Dire Straits uses his fingers all the time. Some acoustic players grow out their fingernails to imitate the sounds of a pick, while others use the fleshy pads of their fingers.

Strings

Strings are another crucial factor that influences your sound. The type of metal they're made of and the gauge of string can change your sound dramatically. Bigger is better. The heavier gauge you can use, the better and fatter your tone will be. Light strings can sound anemic and weak. If you play on 9-gauge strings, try going to 10, and you'll notice a nice change, especially in the low end. Stevie Ray Vaughan is legendary for using 13-gauge strings on his guitar. These huge strings contributed to his huge tone.

If you play acoustic guitar, experiment with gauge and metal types. You can commonly find strings of bronze, phosphor bronze, and other metals. These different metal wraps have an effect on your sound. For you speed freaks, lighter is better (usually). Many shredders like Yngwie Malmsteen use 8-gauge strings because the lightened string gauge helps increase overall facility. Heavy strings can make bending very difficult, so if you plan to increase your string gauge, do it slowly in steps so you can get used to the new tension.

Every time you change your string gauge, you should have your guitar set up by a qualified repairman. The new string tension may affect the neck angle and intonation.

Capos

A capo is a small device that attaches to the neck of the guitar. It changes the location of the nut so that the open position can be replicated in other places on the neck. Usually, capos are an elastic wraparound or spring-loaded clamp. The spring-loaded clamp is often easier to take off and on. Capos can cost between $10 and $15.

In first position, you get certain chords that are easy to play. For the most part, the pitches of the open strings dictate these chords. Because these chords contain open strings, they're easier to play than barre chords. A capo allows you to play the easy shapes from the first position, yet have different chords come out. It's very useful for transposing chords to other keys. For instance, many singers/songwriters use capos to match the natural keys of their voice while keeping the chord shapes simple. Try placing a capo across the third fret. No matter what capo you use, it's important to get the capo right next to the third fret, but not on it! Once you're set, go ahead and play what you know as an open C chord. With the capo, all your open strings are three frets higher so you're not playing the C chord anymore. You're playing the C chord shape, but it is now an E♭ because the capo has changed the open strings. Before, the E♭ chord involved an uncomfortable barre.

- C becomes E♭.
- G becomes B♭.
- A becomes C.
- D becomes F.

The capo can be placed anywhere on the neck you want. The third fret is a handy spot because it gives you chords that are very difficult to achieve in the first position. Using the capo effectively will allow you to play parts that are otherwise impossible.

If you play a song with a lot of barre chords, the capo makes your life easier. Try it on different frets to see how the simple chord shapes change.

PHYSICS 101 AND NATURAL HARMONICS

Harmonics are the tones made by vibrating strings to produce overtones. When you pluck a string, the string vibrates in waves. However, there are points along the string where there is no motion; this point is called a node. (If you remember a sine wave from math class, it crosses the zero point, and that's called a node.) A guitar string has many nodes, which always cut the string in half. For an open string, cutting the string into two equal parts takes you to the twelfth fret, which is the first node.

So what does this have to do with harmonics? At these node points, you can play a harmonic. Harmonics are played with a very different technique than other notes on the guitar. To play a harmonic, you don't push the string down; instead you lightly place your finger directly over the twelfth fret and just barely touch it. As long as you're directly over the twelfth fret, and you haven't pushed down too hard, you will get a note. This note is the same note that you would have gotten had you played the twelfth fret normally. But because the note is a harmonic, it has a unique sound.

One of the neat things about harmonics is that after you play the harmonic, the string will continue to ring out; you don't have to leave your finger over the twelfth fret. Leaving your finger over the fret may mute the note, so after you play it, get out of the way and let it ring. Harmonics like this exist all over the guitar because you can keep dividing the string in half forever! The most popular harmonics are the twelfth fret, the seventh fret, and the fifth fret. Playing harmonics from open strings is called natural harmonics. They occur on every string and on almost every fret. Some frets have harmonics that are so high that you can barely hear them—that's why they don't always sound great.

Musical Notes

If you want to play harmonics, go to the pickup closest to the bridge. If you're on an acoustic guitar, pick closer to bridge. Playing in that area will help the harmonics ring out clearly. Distortion will also help.

Artificial Harmonics

Artificial harmonics are those amazing-sounding notes that seem to scream out from a lead guitar solo. Artificial harmonics are relatively easy to play, but are very hard to explain. You may get a little frustrated while trying to get these to work. Keep trying and you will be able to do it in no time!

Artificial harmonics have little to do with natural harmonics. While they're both called harmonics and both use nodes of a vibrating string, the technique behind them is quite different. Artificial harmonics are done from your picking hand; your fretting hand plays normally as it always does. Now, here's the hard part—to play an artificial harmonic you need to choke up on the pick and let only a bit of it show. There should be only a nub sticking out. When you go to pick a note, instead of picking and then getting out of the way as you normally do, pick with a slight downward angle, forcing a small part of your thumb to hit the string. If you choked up enough, the fat part of your thumb should be right there. You'll need to do a lot of experimenting to find the sweet spot!

There are several sweet spots, and most exist right over the sound hole, or between the pickups. Since you are very high up on the string, you get a very high harmonic. But there's a catch: The location of the harmonics changes every time you fret a different note. So don't think that because you've found the location for one note it will work every note. The good news is that the nodes are very close together, so you're bound to hit one of them. The secret to this technique is getting your thumb to hit the string at the same time that the pick does. If you're early or late, you'll hear a thud. If you hit it right, you'll get a high note that seems to come from nowhere.

Harmonics like this require some form of distortion to come out well. You can play them clean, but they sound much better with distortion on. Until you get the feel of this, you may be frustrated, but keep trying. Artificial harmonics are a staple of rock guitar playing. Once you figure out the technique, you never forget it.

Hammer-On

This is used a lot in rock, blues, and folk playing. Fret a note with your first finger, say D at the fifth fret, String 5. Now, while the note is still ringing, "hammer down" your finger on E at the seventh fret, String 5, and keep it there.

Pull-Off

This is really a hammer-on in reverse. You need to have both fingers on the fret. Play the note E, as before, then pull off your finger so the D will sound clearly.

Trill

If you rapidly combine both techniques above, you get a trick often used in rock-and-roll that may sound familiar, called a trill.

String Bends

A lot of rock guitarists and blues guitarists use a string bend. If you pull or push the string, once you've fretted the note, you can actually bend it almost to the note on the next fret. It's the same sort of technique as using a mechanical tremolo arm. It generally works best if you use thin-gauge strings.

Double-String Bends

A rock and blues cliché, but effective on occasion if the spirit moves you. The trick is to have both fingers in place ahead of time. Here, you play the D, on the seventh fret of String 3, bending it until you've reached the pitch of E, and—while still sounding the bent note—play E on an adjacent string (fifth fret, String 2), letting the two notes ring together.

Another trick is to play the D and E together (major second), fingering them as above, and then bend the D into an E, letting the two Es sound together.

Vibrato

This just means deliberately invoking a "wow-wow" kind of effect. All you do is rock your finger back and forth on the note as you fret it. The more exaggerated the movement of your hand, the broader will be the "vib."

The EBow

The EBow is a small hand-held device that uses a magnetic force field to make a guitar string vibrate forever (or until the battery runs out). Unfortunately acoustic players are left out of this party, because it works only in combination with a magnetic pickup and an amplifier. It sets up a loop between the pickup and the string, causing the string to vibrate seemingly forever. Because you use the EBow in lieu of a pick, there's no pick attack, and the sound is very smooth. The EBow can generate some wild effects on the guitar, and in the right hands, can be a wonderfully creative tool.

Many players have used the EBow on recordings. The performance that stands out is REM's Peter Buck and his EBow playing on "What's the Frequency, Kenneth?" John Petrucci of Dream Theater also uses an EBow on the album *Six Degrees of Inner Turbulence,* and Metallica uses one on "The Unforgiven." You will find the EBow listed in everyone's trick bag and gear list. It's relatively inexpensive (between $80 and $100) and can lead to some very original results.

SLIDES

A slide is a finger device that temporarily takes the place of a fret; unlike a fret, a slide can be moved around freely. The use of slides could take the rest of this book to discuss completely, but this section will at least get you started. Playing with slides began with the blues. Early slides were bottle necks from beer bottles and small medicine bottles. Modern slides are made of glass or metal and are molded to perfectly match your finger; they come in different shapes and sizes to match every player. They run from around $5 to $10.

Slide Mechanics

Because slides can move around "in between" the frets, they're great for imitating the voice, which naturally scoops and slides between the notes. The slide rests gently on top of the string, and like a harmonic, doesn't push down, but floats along the length of the string.

When playing slides, you have to determine what finger you want to place the slide on—middle, ring, or pinky finger. Most players use their middle or ring finger. You can't use the index finger because an essential part of slide playing is muting behind the slide to keep the strings quiet. If you put the slide on your index finger, you won't have a finger to mute with. Pick the finger that can reach all the strings comfortably.

In Tune

Playing a slide can be great fun, but if it's not played in tune, no one will want to

Musical Notes

Some great slide players include Jeff Beck, Duane Allman, Eric Johnson, Muddy Waters, Bonnie Raitt, and Ry Cooder.

hear it. The fret takes care of the tuning for you, but when you play with a slide, the slide takes over for the fret. You have to control where the slide is on the string in order to tune the note. To get the slide in tune, you must be directly over the fret. Because this can be difficult, many slide players use back-and-forth vibrato motion to hide their tuning problems—which is fine and sounds vocal-like (shhh . . . that's why singers use vibrato, too).

Application

The slide mimics your fretting hand, so you can use it on scales, single notes, and some chords, but because the slide is a straight line, it works only on a few chords. The slide is used for the blues scale almost exclusively. You can trace the scale shape with the slide in the same way that you play it with your fingers. Because the slide is straight across, you can jump to adjacent frets much easier than normal. When you use a slide, try to use it differently. Don't just recreate your old licks with a slide—try to create new ones that are not possible without the slide.

Alternate Tuning

Alternate tuning implies that you are retuning the strings to anything other than standard E-A-D-G-B-E tuning. Alternate tunings are great for finding new chord shapes and unusual sounds that aren't possible on a standard tuned guitar. You will need a good chromatic tuner to help retune your strings. Here are three examples of some common alternate tunings:

- Drop-D tuning: Drop your lowest E string down one whole step to D. The strings are then D, A, D, G, B, E. Drop D is useful for heavy music because it gives you some lower power chords. Power chords can be played with one finger.
- "DADGAD" tuning: Tune your sixth string down to D, second string down to A, and first string down to D. Leave others unchanged. This is a common tuning that can give you some unexpected results. Jimmy Page used this on "Black Mountain Side."
- Open-E tuning: Tune fifth string up to B, fourth string up to E, and third string up to G♯. Leave the others unchanged. Open-E tuning is a great slide tuning because you can play major chords with a straight slide played across one fret. It's also a nice tuning because your open strings make a nice-sounding E chord.

There are millions of other tunings, and you should try to invent new ones. Typically, alternate tunings are great for one song here and there, not for exclusive use. (But don't tell that to Joni Mitchell, who plays exclusively in open alternate tunings.)

Songwriting Basics

Many people think that songwriters just sit down and *voilà!*—a beautiful, perfect song magically starts pouring out within seconds. While this does happen sometimes, it's the exception and not the rule. It takes hard work and some preparation, and there are lots of tricks and tools used by professionals that can help get you off on the right track.

THE MOST IMPORTANT POINTS

What do you need to know in order to write a song? Many people, including professional musicians and singers, feel that there are a number of important things they absolutely *must* know even before they can begin. The problem is, they have no idea what these things *are* or where they can be learned. But in reality, the only crucial element you absolutely must know before you can write your first song is, simply, that you can do it.

So the good news is, you don't need any special knowledge to write a song. You can go and write one now. But it doesn't mean it's going to be a *great* song. With a few extremely rare exceptions, songwriters usually spend several years learning how to make a good song great.

The First Rule of Songwriting

The one unchangeable rule of songwriting is this: All rules are subject to change. If you walk into a publisher's office with a song that's a surefire hit for 1987, you will probably walk out with a disappointed look on your face three and a half minutes later. But that could change next year: Eighties revival music could be the next big thing. Of course, it could be Bolivian folk music or polka—you just never know. A few years ago, salsa and Christian contemporary formats weren't even listed on major music charts. These days, you can make serious money writing for these genres.

Most rules of songwriting have changed at one time or another. Think lyrics are a must for a pop hit? Look up Floyd Cramer's "Last Date" or Vangelis's "Chariots of Fire"—the melody may be the most crucial element. On the other hand, most rap songs replace melodies (as they are recognizable to people brought up listening to the twelve-note scale, used in most popular music) with music samples. The point is this: Pay attention to what's going on *right now* and try to figure out what will happen next. Trends in popular music can change quickly and dramatically. It's not unheard of for a publisher to fire half of the songwriting staff after a market change. The rules change from time to time. If you know them, you'll be prepared for the changes and able to deal with them.

THE SONGWRITER'S TOOLBOX

The first order of business for a beginning songwriter is to assemble the tools needed for the job. Which tools you need is your decision. The important thing is to assemble them in one place and keep them there when not in use. Otherwise, you may find that your significant other has written a grocery list on your new song or your dog has made a chew toy of your "lucky lyric" pen. A desk drawer makes a good songwriter's toolbox. Backpacks, briefcases, tackle boxes, and book bags have the advantage of being portable. Some writers even pack the bare essentials into their guitar cases. Things you might want in your toolbox are simple—something with which to write (like a pen), something on which to write (like paper), some reference books, and a small, portable recording device.

Pens, Pencils, Chalkboards, and Word Processors

Some songwriters can write on anything or with anything. As rumor has it, a popular Rolling Stones song was written with an eyeliner pencil on the back of a hotel room ironing board. Other songwriters are particular, even superstitious, about what they use. The most popular combination is probably a #2 pencil and a yellow legal pad. Some songwriters prefer ballpoint pens and unlined paper. Others prefer a mechanical pencil, a gum eraser, and "eleven-line" paper (which allows for the melody to be written above the chords in standard notation and the bottom line for lyrics). Some even use large chalkboards. Many songwriters find that a computer gives them the option of creating multiple versions of a song, cutting and pasting words or lines to different places, and having "ready to print" lyric sheets when finished. Try all of these options and find the one that works best for you.

Whatever you use, make at least two copies as soon as the song is finished. Put one in your toolbox and put one in a safe place other than your home. Why? If your computer crashes, your house burns down, or your significant other goes insane and starts merrily feeding your songs into the shredder, you'll be very glad that you have extra copies stashed away.

You'll also want a recording device to capture the melody and groove of your song. Portable recorders with built-in microphones are available in a number of recording formats and are perfect for your toolbox. Make sure the recorder you buy has either removable media (something you can take out of the machine and copy, like a cassette) or a "line out" so you can transfer the recording to another medium.

Reference Books Every Songwriter Should Own

Somewhere, you'll want to keep a stash of books to be used as part of the songwriting process, and you may want paperback versions if you travel frequently. Here's a list to get you started:

- A new dictionary that includes slang terms
- A rhyming dictionary
- A thesaurus and/or synonym finder
- At least one book of popular quotations
- A set of encyclopedias
- Recent newspapers or periodicals (for song ideas)

Also consider reference books that list homonyms, homophones, antonyms, phrases, sayings, quotes, puns, and so forth—anything that helps you think about words. Many of these reference materials can be found in software or online versions.

WHERE DO I BEGIN?

For many songwriters, getting started is the absolute hardest part of writing a song. Some write down the first thing they think of, knowing that they can rewrite or make changes later. Others use techniques like brainstorming or word palettes to get the creative juices flowing. Many start with music and worry about lyrics once a "mood" has been established through composing. In short, there are many ways to begin a song. It doesn't matter where you start. What matters is that you *do*.

Starting with an Idea

Starting with an idea is good if there's something going on that inspires or moves you. Current news, neighborhood gossip, books, movies, and relationships provide a never-ending source of new ideas for songs. Learn to look and listen with a writer's eyes and ears; you'll be amazed how much there is to write about.

Starting with Words

The different meanings of a word, the rhythm of a particular phrase, the sound of a rhyme, or the flow of a sentence can all be good jumping-off points to a writing session. Don't be afraid to "doodle" or play with words as if they are building blocks or puzzle pieces. If you find a word or phrase you like, look for other words and phrases that go with it and find rhymes for all of them. Try twisting or reversing the meanings of things.

Countless songs have been written with a common phrase as the starting point. Even if you start with an idea, you may want to look for a short phrase that sums it up nicely. A short phrase used as a central theme is called a "hook." Many professionals prefer to start with a hook and build a song around it.

Starting with Music

A bit of melody, a chord sequence, or an instrumental lick have inspired countless songs. Some writers prefer to create within the confines of the imagination, whereas others may hum, whistle, or plink around on the guitar or piano, looking for the little something special that gets things moving.

Many songs use identical chord patterns but, if the words and melodies are different, people don't usually notice. A good exercise is to take the chords from a favorite song and write your own song over them. Try putting familiar chord patterns to a different groove or arranging the chords in a different order.

Starting with a Beat or Groove

Starting with a beat or groove is a great way to write a specific kind of song. Left to their own devices, most songwriters write ballads (slow songs) nine out of ten times. Publishers and recording artists, however, are usually looking for fast songs (up-tempos). See a problem? A good way to overcome the natural inclination toward ballads is to write to a beat or groove from a drum machine.

WHEN IS A SONG FINISHED?

That's your decision to make, and of course you may change your mind later. Market changes and artistic growth can lead you to change a song that was finished years ago. A better question may be, "Is it complete?" Or, "Is it done, for now?" Here's a handy checklist to help you determine if a song is complete:

- Does it say everything it needs to say?
- Is everything said in the best possible way?

- Does each line say something?
- Is there any unnecessary information that doesn't add to the song?
- Are the tenses and viewpoints consistent and easy to follow?
- Are the parts of the story in the best possible order?
- Do the words of one section connect well to the next?
- Do the melodic elements flow and connect from section to section?
- Is the song's length approximately where you want it to be?
- Does it *feel* done?

Editing and Rewrites

A change often made in completed songs is "editing down" for time. Radio stations want songs in the two-and-a-half to four-minute range. While it's true that many songs outside these parameters have become hits, it's much easier to get airplay for a three-minute song than for a five-minute song. Solutions may be as simple as speeding up the song a little (be careful not to push the tempo to a pace that rushes the singer or ruins the feel of the song) or removing or shortening intro sections and instrumental passages that aren't adding anything important to the song. Cutting out entire verses is an option; advanced options include condensing two verses into one, cutting a verse in half, or using an implied chorus—a severely shortened chorus (usually just the first line) that leads directly to the bridge or to a fadeout.

You may also find it prudent, from time to time, to edit for content and market. Certain words, topics, situations, or portrayals of racial or ethnic stereotypes may hinder a song's chances of being recorded or played. It's not only what you say, but how you say it: A rap song can get plenty of airplay with a line like, "Keep gettin' hassled by the cops. Fo' a playa, the heat never stops." But a line that goes: "Metro cop Nazis got me in stitches. Get me an Uzi they'll be dead sons of . . ." probably won't get played. Neither of these examples would be appropriate language for a country song—they just aren't consistent with this particular genre. Keep in mind the intended audience for a song and adjust the language to get the story or message across to that group.

As you become a better writer, go back over your catalog of songs every so often to fix problems that you couldn't solve (or didn't see) back in your newbie days. You may also want to regularly check the language, situations, and musical content of your songs to see if they are relevant in the current market.

THINKING LIKE A SONGWRITER

Language and music skills play key roles in songwriting success, but the most important, overlooked, and easily learned talent is the ability to think like a writer. Ideas are the most valuable commodity in any form of art. If you learn how to originate and develop ideas, the battle is half won.

Where do songwriters get their ideas? The answer is simple; hit songwriters get ideas from their own lives and the world around them. Perhaps the most important thing you can do in the idea department is to simply be aware of the world around and within you from a writer's perspective. At first, this will be a very self-conscious process. Listening to your own conversations and examining your life for ideas will make the world seem a little unreal until you get used to it.

Always have a recording device, pen, and paper within easy reach to save a catchy phrase, a situation, or a concept. Taken to excess, this can drive your friends and family nuts, so try not to be too obvious. With practice, this process becomes second nature and you'll no longer be conscious of it—your writer's alarm will simply alert you when a song idea presents itself.

Priming the Pump

Ideas may come to you in the strangest settings or in the most mundane of circumstances. Some writers have special places or activities that seem to get them going. For Tony Lane, Neil Young, and many others, driving around does the trick. Van Dyke Parks and Carlos Santana get ideas in the shower. Among the places, situations, and activities that have proved fertile ground for songwriters are vacuuming, golfing, "doodling" on an instrument, walking, contact juggling, sitting in a Laundromat, and grocery shopping. On the opposite end of the spectrum, some writers require quiet or solitude to get the ideas flowing. For them, sitting in the woods, engaging in prayer or meditation, watching the ocean, and lying in bed before falling asleep are the situations that work best.

WRITE WHAT YOU KNOW

When you write a song, you create a world for the listener. To draw someone into that world, it must be convincing enough to make him or her want to believe that it's real. This is why many writers peak in their forties and fifties; people who have lived more can convincingly portray more situations.

This doesn't mean that young writers can't write great songs. If a young writer is careful to write from an authentic perspective, he or she may have advantages in some areas. A song about first love from a fifty-year-old writer will tend to be a fond remembrance, while a song on the same topic from a fifteen-year-old may more accurately capture the urgency, magic, and uncertainty of the situation.

Writing what you know can mean different things, depending on your level of songwriting experience. For the beginner, it means sticking with places, situations, and emotions you have actually encountered. As your writing progresses, you'll be more able to extrapolate and project your own feelings and experiences into semi fictional or even totally made-up situations.

Brainstorming

Brainstorming is the act of defining what you will write. This includes idea and hook generation, picking topics, experimenting with melodies and grooves, playing with rhyme schemes and meter configurations, and anything else that gets you going. Brainstorming should be part of your scheduled activities. If something clicks, stop brainstorming and start songwriting.

Some suggestions to get your brainstorming session started:

- Make a list of your favorite songs. Look at each song and ask yourself where the idea might have originated.
- Think about current events in your life and in the world. Is there anything you feel moved to write about today?
- Are there any new musical trends with which you've had the desire to experiment?
- Watch and listen to the world around you. A song idea could come from something as simple as watching pigeons in the park or seeing two people on a first date. Don't spy or pry, just be alert and let your imagination provide the rest.
- Be aware of your own thoughts and feelings, too. Most things we feel are similar to feelings that all people have had at one time or another. Finding a way to relate these common feelings is one of the most important parts of a songwriter's work.

Ideas from Literature, Movies, and TV

Characters, places, and situations from history, myth, and mass media can provide an almost limitless source of song ideas. Here are some examples:

- Plays: *Romeo and Juliet* resulted in "Fire" by Bruce Springsteen
- Books: *Tom Sawyer* inspired Rush's "Tom Sawyer"
- Movies: *Key Largo* led to "Key Largo" by Bertie Higgins
- Cartoons: Road Runner served as inspiration to "Wile E. Coyote" by Great Divide
- TV: Late-night Westerns inspired "Roy Rogers" by Sir Elton John
- Mythology: "God of Thunder" by KISS is a song about Zeus
- Historic places: "Waterloo" by Abba refers to the scene of the Battle of Waterloo

Sometimes these characters or places will provide the hook or central idea; other times, they can help set a scene or provide a rich metaphor to spice up your song. Mentioning a well-known character or place can often conjure up whole volumes in the listener's imagination.

Relationship Mining

When writing about a relationship or emotional situation, reflect on similar experiences you've had from several different perspectives: Compare how you feel about the situation now and how you felt at the time. Imagine how the other people involved might have felt. This will give you a choice of viewpoints and degrees of objectivity or subjectivity, and also the benefit of being able to write a heartbreak song without having to get your heart broken all over again.

The next best thing to writing from personal experience is writing from situations you have seen or heard about. In some cases, writing from direct observation may have a small advantage over writing from personal experience: You may see some situations more objectively. Writing from observation can also give you the opportunity to better understand situations, places, and feelings you might not be personally familiar with, like giving birth or fighting in a war. This is where friends and family come in. Be a good listener when Uncle Ralph wants to tell war stories. Ask questions, too: How did it feel? What did you eat? Who were your friends? Turn on your "write brain" and see through someone else's eyes.

A Few Words of Warning

You must be very careful about how you use the information gained by observing and talking to others. Uncle Ralph may not want the world to know he got a tattoo of a hyena on his left calf while on shore leave in Singapore. Likewise, your best buddy, Sue, might not want her secret childhood crush on your brother made public knowledge. One option is to change things around a bit: "My cousin (uncle) Charlie (Ralph) got a tattoo of a dingo (hyena) while on vacation (shore leave) in Sydney (Singapore)." Another way is to simply ask permission. It might make Uncle Ralph's day to be in a song. Either way, from a legal standpoint, it's better to change the names of anyone involved.

DEVELOPING YOUR IDEA

Let's say you've got a great new hook idea, "Love in the Jungle." You're not sure if the song is about love in an actual jungle or if the jungle is a metaphor for the city or the modern world. In fact, other than the hook and a vague idea of the groove, you have no idea what the song is about. What do you do now? Define the set of possibilities at your command and pick the ones that you think will work best for the song. Don't worry, you can always change your mind later and go back as many steps as you want.

Word Palettes

Making a word palette can help get the ideas flowing. Look at the idea: What's happening? Love! Where? The jungle! Hmmm . . . What are some words that would paint a picture of where the song (at least metaphorically) takes place?

- Make a list of words that mean jungle: Congo, Amazon, veldt, forest.
- Make a list of things and creatures you might find in the jungle: vine, tiger, lion, gazelle, trees, monkeys, parrots, toucans, waterfall, blue lagoon.
- Make a list of sensations and conditions in the jungle: hot, humid, steamy, dark, the smell of tropical flowers, the sound of drums in the distance.
- List words that describe feelings about the jungle: scary, wild, savage, primitive, dangerous, sexy.
- List the characters, real or fictional, you might encounter in the jungle: witch doctor, Tarzan and Jane, native tribes, headhunters, Amazons, Dr. Livingstone.

For more options, get a thesaurus or synonym finder and look up the words you have written down.

Now you have a list of images, feelings, sensations, and characters to add life and dimension to your song. Even if the jungle in the song ends up being a metaphor, these things, properly applied, can help to connect the rest of the song to the central idea. Look for phrases based on the words in your palette: monkey around, king of the jungle, swingin' through the trees. Find wordplays based on your palette selections: only toucan (two can) play, I'm not lion (lying). You can worry about what's too silly or too obscure when you actually start putting the song together. For now, just let your mind roam freely and see what happens.

Rhyme Palettes

Instead of having a primary focus on meaning or context, the rhyme palette's main purpose is to find words that rhyme with the song's hook or with things on the word palette. You can search for rhymes in one of three ways:

1. With the aid of a rhyming dictionary or similar software application.
2. By mentally running through the alphabet (at, bat, cat, fat, gat, hat, and so forth).
3. By trying really hard to think of rhymes.

Options one and two may yield more rhymes. Option three is better for finding near rhymes that are a bit more interesting and also helps warm up the creative part of the brain.

GETTING THE STORY ACROSS

Remember that the listeners only know what you tell them. You can do this through direct information: "I was a poor kid from a small town in Louisiana." Or you can provide information to be inferred: "I grew up on the wrong side of the tracks in a one-horse Bayou town." Melody, groove, and chord structure can also convey emotional information (minor keys tend to sound sad) or help set the scene (a chord pattern of C/Am/F/G over a medium cha-cha groove conjures up the 1950s).

Continuity

Make sure that your storyline is clear and easy to follow. If you lose a listener's attention, you probably won't get it back. The events in your song should all connect to the hook in some way. Verses don't have to relate to each other, but elements within a verse should all work together and support the central theme. The event flow of your songs doesn't have to be linear. Flashbacks and foreshadowing can be useful, but make sure the storyline can be followed and to develop the idea or plot at a pace that doesn't bore the listener.

It's easy to fool yourself into thinking your storyline is clear. After all, *you* know the whole story. Test your story's clarity by getting outside feedback. Remember not to tell your test audience what the song is about before you play it. Instead, ask questions about the story after you play the song for someone.

Songs in the Moment

Tense, to put it simply, is when the action in your song takes place. Tense can be a tricky business, especially when changing tense within a song. This must be done carefully, so as not to confuse the listener. Be careful and consistent.

Present tense is often best for love songs, statement-of-self songs, heartbreak songs, or any song in which you want to express vivid emotions. The power of these songs is in helping the listener become the singer in his or her imagination. Since the listener is hearing the song now, putting the song's action in the present can help someone connect more directly to your song.

If you need to give past information in a present tense song, do it from a viewpoint that sets up a contrast to the present: If you say, "I was lonely," you are frontloading to be able to say, "Now, I'm not." If you say, "I've been working up my nerve," it's easy to move ahead to, "Now the moment is here." To flash back from a present moment, a phrase like, "I remember the time" gives a connection from the *now* to the *then*.

Telling a Story

For story songs, past tense usually works well. As long as the story events are told in the order in which they happened, it's relatively easy to jump forward along a timeline to different story scenes without confusing the listener. Usually, a story song will use the first verse to set the time and the scene, the second verse to give more specific or more personal information, and the chorus to reinforce the central theme or idea. The bridge or third verse may give the climax of the story or detail present situations or emotions that were affected by the events in the story. "Strawberry Wine" is a beautiful example of this form.

"The Devil Went Down to Georgia" is a story song in past tense. The story takes place in the past. However, the song makes good use of present-tense quotes from the two characters in the story. In Anthony Smith's "Impossible to Do," the verses list a series of seemingly impossible things the singer plans to do in the future and contrasts them against a chorus focusing on past events that, while easily accomplished, can't be undone.

Choosing the Tense

There are usually several possible ways to set the tense of a song or song section. You'll have to decide what's best on a case-by-case basis. During the writing of your first few hundred songs, you'll develop an instinct for dealing with tense.

Meanwhile, the best way to learn tense sense is by doing. Try the following exercises:

- Write a story song in past tense. Use the first half of the first verse to connect present to past. Stay in past tense through the rest of the verses and the chorus. Use a bridge after the second chorus to connect the past back to the present.
- Write a "wish list" song. Use present tense in the verses to talk about things you already have. Use future tense in the chorus for your wish list.
- Write a story song about a historical event. Create two characters, one who lived at the time and the other a present-day descendant who finds a letter from the ancestor detailing a story, real or made up, relating to the historical event. Write the whole song in past tense. The challenge is to make the jumps from "long ago" past tense to recent past tense in a clear and easy-to-follow manner.

- Write a "life cycle" song with a verse-chorus-verse-chorus-bridge-chorus structure. Use past tense in the first verse, present tense in the second verse, and future tense in the bridge. Write one chorus that works without changing it.
- Write a song in present tense with no reference to things in the past or future. Apply this to other tenses, too. If you try it, you'll see that this may seem simple, but it's really tough.

The Art of Saying Without Saying

Simplicity and directness are some of the prime virtues of songwriting, but sometimes just saying something outright sounds drab. What to do? A simple but indirect description can liven up an otherwise boring lyric. Instead of saying: "She was happily married but life was tough / She worked too much but at least she had love . . . " try something more like: "Days at the fact'ry were hard and too long / But the ring on her finger helped her keep keepin' on."

Instead of narrating your song like a wildlife documentary or a tennis match, use objects, places, actions, and expressions to color your story. This involves the minds of listeners in two ways; it makes them visualize the object, place, action, or expression, and it also gets the deductive part of the brain working. ("Watson, by the ring on her finger, I deduce that she is *married!*" "Amazing, Holmes, how *do* you do it?")

Don't make the listener work *too* hard to figure things out. Pointing out that a character walks with a limp will not tell everyone that he was shot in the leg during an argument over a poker game in pre–Civil War New Orleans. When the song is complete, check through and make sure that the average person will be able to figure out your story.

DEALING WITH WRITER'S BLOCK

Sometimes no matter what you do, nothing comes—at least nothing that's any good. You can't get warmed up at the start of a session, you're in the middle of a new song and your brain locks up, or everything's great right up to the last line of the song and, all of a sudden, the muse has left the building. You keep trying, but nothing happens. You start to panic. "What if this feeling never goes away?"

Welcome to the club. Writer's block has been around as long as writing, and it happens to the best writers in the world. It's not fatal or permanent, though it usually feels that way. No need to panic, it usually passes quickly on its own.

Breaking the Block

If you don't feel like waiting, there are several time-tested cures. Here are a few favorites for jump-starting a stalled song:

- **Take a break.** Sometimes your brain overloads and needs to cool down. Go get something to drink, have a snack, take a walk. Don't even think about the song while you're taking a break. That's why it's called a break!
- **Look for corners.** Have you painted yourself into a corner? Killing off your hero halfway through can make things anticlimactic. Maybe he should die in the last verse. This cure works especially well after taking a break first.
- **Switch gears.** Stuck on lyrics? Work on the melody. Can't get the beat right? Get back to the lyrics.
- **Make a move.** Work on a different part of the song. Chorus trouble? Skip down to the bridge. Can't get the second line of the verse quite right? Write the third line, then come back. If you have several trouble spots, try working on each one for ten minutes and then switching to a different part when time's up.
- **Mix it up.** Rearrange the words in the line you're trying to write or rearrange the lines in that particular section of the song. You may even want to try switching the order of the verses, starting with the chorus or moving the bridge to a different spot. If it doesn't work out, you can always put things back where they were.

Whatever approach you take, keep in mind that the writer's block will pass, and you are just going to have to keep going until you get back into the flow of things.

Index

About the Experts

Advice on scales, chords, rock and blues guitar, home recording, and music theory
Marc Schonbrun is an educator, writer, and performer in the San Francisco Bay Area. Marc's musical resume ranges from classical guitar concertos to jazz trios and rock concerts. He is an active lecturer on guitar and music technology, and he frequently tours the country educating musicians and teachers. He is the author of several books on music, including *The Everything® Rock & Blues Guitar Book*, *The Everything® Guide to Digital Home Recording*, and *The Everything® Guitar Chords Book*. He lives in San Jose, CA.

Advice on general guitar instruction
Ernie Jackson is a classical guitarist, musicology scholar, and trainer for Sibelius, the world market leader in software for writing, teaching, and publishing music. With more than thirty-two years of guitar experience, Mr. Jackson is a full-time lecturer at Queensborough Community College and an adjunct lecturer at Wagner College. He is the author of *The Music of Justin Holland*, *The Everything® Guitar Book*, and *The Guitar Chord Composer*. He lives on Staten Island, NY.